The Supreme Court and
the Decline of
Constitutional Aspiration

THE SUPREME COURT AND THE DECLINE OF CONSTITUTIONAL ASPIRATION

Gary J. Jacobsohn

WILLIAMS COLLEGE

DAR 10/16

Rowman & Littlefield
PUBLISHERS

ROWMAN & LITTLEFIELD

Published in the United States of America in 1986
by Rowman & Littlefield, Publishers
(a division of Littlefield, Adams & Company)
81 Adams Drive, Totowa, New Jersey 07512

Library of Congress Cataloging-in-Publication Data

Jacobsohn, Gary J., 1946-
    The Supreme Court and the decline of constitutional
aspiration.

    Bibliography: p. 169
    Includes index.
    1. United States—Constitutional law—Interpretation
and construction.   2. Political questions and judicial
power—United States.   3. United States. Supreme Court.
I. Title.
KF4550.J33   1986   342.73′023   86-6489
ISBN 0-8476-7465-7   347.30223

88 87 86
10 9 8 7 6 5 4 3 2 1

Printed in the United States of America

For Beth and Vanessa

Contents

Acknowledgments

I WISH TO THANK John Agresto of the National Endowment for the Humanities, John Burke of the University of Vermont, Leslie Friedman Goldstein of the University of Delaware, and Richard E. Morgan of Bowdoin College for their critical readings of the manuscript. Their advice has made this a better book, and while each will see ways in which the final product could have been improved still more, they will at least know that they bear no responsibility for its shortcomings.

For their assistance in manuscript preparation, I am also grateful for the excellent work of Judy Raab, Gary Selinger, and Michael Weber.

Revised versions of some of the material in Chapter 2 to 6 have appeared in *The Journal of Politics* (vol. 47, no. 2, 1985), *Polity* (vol. 14, no. 1, 1981), *The Western Political Quarterly* (vol. 36, no. 1, 1983), *Constitutional Commentary* (vol. 1, no. 1, 1984), and in *The Constitutional Polity: Essays on the Founding of Principles of American Politics* (Washington, D.C., 1983). Permission to incorporate this material is gratefully acknowledged.

CHAPTER 1

Introduction

ROCHESTER, NEW YORK, July 5, 1852. The speaker, an ex-slave, is blunt: "This Fourth of July is *yours*, not *mine*. *You* may rejoice, *I* must mourn."[1] And with the eloquence and dignity that made him perhaps the greatest orator of his time, Frederick Douglass then explained to his northern audience what was difficult for them to hear but necessary for them to contemplate: "The existence of slavery in this country brands your republicanism as a sham, your humanity as a base pretence, and your christianity as a lie."[2] And he asked: "What have I, or those I represent, to do with your national independence? Are the great principles of political freedom and of natural justice. embodied in the Declaration of Independence, extended to us?"[3]

It is not surprising that Douglass responds to his own question in the negative. Yet in his assessment of the aspirational content of the Declaration, and its correlative lessons for constitutional interpretation, Douglass differed from many who would have joined him in his answer, people as diverse in their views as Roger Taney and William Lloyd Garrison. "There is consolation in the thought," he pointed out, "that America is young."[4] Douglass's oration anticipated Abraham Lincoln's position in the debates with Stephen A. Douglas that the Declaration and the Constitution were intended, in part, as statements of ideals or fundamental principles, to be achieved as part of a process of progressive realization. For the founders, according to Douglass, "nothing was 'settled' that was not right. With them, justice, liberty and humanity were 'final'; not slavery and oppression."[5] This sentiment was later to find expression in Lincoln's most critical reflections on constitutional obligation, when in response to the *Dred Scott* ruling, he argued against the finality of any Supreme Court decision that was not "fully settled," that is, not directed toward fulfillment of goals ordained by the Declaration.[6]

One hundred and one years after Douglass's oration, standing in the shadow of the Lincoln Memorial, Martin Luther King, Jr., spoke in similarly aspirational terms:

> When the architects of our Republic wrote the magnificent words of the Constitution and the Declaration of Independence, they were signing a promissory note to which every American was to fall heir. This note was

1

a promise that all men—yes, black men as well as white men—would be guaranteed the unalienable rights of life, liberty and the pursuit of happiness.[7]

Noble rhetoric and—judging by what eventually followed—effective rhetoric. But what, in 1963, was the intellectual status of the sentiments expressed by King? For example, did the notion of a "promissory note" command much authority in the arena of constitutional interpretation? If it did, would this particular "note" be commonly seen as incorporating the substance attributed to it by King? And if so, what relevance was any longer to be found in the eighteenth century idea of "unalienable rights?" Following Lincoln, would serious consideration be accorded anyone employing these sentiments as the basis for a refusal to accede to the finality of a Supreme Court ruling?

Douglass had spoken of a Constitution, which, if "interpreted as it *ought* to be interpreted," would enforce the "eternal principles" mandated by the regime's founders.[8] His claim was that there are "certain rules of interpretation, for the proper understanding of all legal instruments."[9] In the pages to follow we will examine several modern approaches to constitutional interpretation that were developed during a time distinguished by its rejection of eternal principles of natural justice. While each approach is distinctive, these approaches reflect a common jurisprudential perspective at variance with the philosophy underlying the interpretive framework of eighteenth-century constitutional theory (as well as the understandings of Douglass and Lincoln). This book takes a measure of the theoretical span separating recent constitutional jurisprudence from antecedents of the founding period. Although not pretending to be a comprehensive comparative analysis, it explores alternative intellectual structures in the belief that an appreciation of the distance we have traveled will illuminate our current constitutional predicament. In this sense the effort will be animated by the Tocquevillian example, in which radically different alternatives are contrasted against a backdrop of historical inevitability. Thus, for Tocqueville, democratic inevitability negated any effective choice between aristocracy and democracy, but did not prevent us from using our understanding of the old regime to inform our efforts to enhance the quality of the new.

It is still useful to appeal to the language of natural rights. The Declaration of Independence has not noticeably withered as a source for public debate, but its appeal now occurs on the level of rhetoric, not, as it once did, as a commitment to absolute principles of justice. The decline of natural rights doctrine, which is the setting for this study, is manifest, among other places, in jurisprudence. As one leading commentator has observed: "To reject natural right is tanta-mount to saying that all right is . . . determined exclusively by the legislators and the courts of the various countries."[10] While the recent past has experienced a proliferation of rights, the philosophical justification accompanying this expansion bears only slight resem-blance to that which provided legitimacy for the constitutionally grounded rights of the more distant past. Furthermore, the role of the courts in facilitating this creation of constitutional rights forms the basis for most contemporary argument over judicial activism. If the Constitution, as Chief Justice Hughes once suggested, is what the Supreme Court says it is, then this proliferation of rights is largely attributable to the Court's having assumed the responsibility of adapt-ing the Constitution to accommodate the moral and political environ-ment of our time. This accommodation may succeed in fulfilling the particular contemporary moral aspirations of a highly articulate segment of American society, while abandoning the particular consti-tutional aspirations of the founders.

Although accommodation is arguably a feature that has never been absent throughout our history, a critical juncture occurred at the turn of the century with the emergence of the pragmatic movement in American jurisprudence, a movement devoted to achieving congru-ence between law and rapid societal transformation. The instrumen-tal orientation underlying sociological jurisprudence and legal real-ism was unable to coexist with a constitutional model based upon what were perceived as growth-retarding epistemological assumptions of the eighteenth century. It was taken for granted, for example, that immutable standards of justice necessarily impeded the course of societal adaptation to a changing environment. Even when the vocab-ulary of natural rights survived, as, for example, in Cardozo, it was the language of interests, mores, social wants and claims that really counted.

The significance of this movement—for present purposes—lies not in its direct influence on the development of our constitutional law, but rather in the fact that it represents a turning point in American legal philosophy. Henceforth advocates of distinct and often contra-dictory views on the role of the Supreme Court came to share important theoretical assumptions that have collectively set them apart from predecessors in the pre-modern era. Now "interpretivists" and "noninterpretivists," activists and self-restrainters, interest-based theorists and rights-based theorists contest within a common intellec-tual paradigm. The noninterpretivist berates the interpretivist for slavish devotion to the written word, but does not condemn him for abandoning principles of natural right. The activist is critical of the judicial timidity of the proponent of self-restraint, but does not find fault in the latter's avoidance of theoretical constructs popularized in the eighteenth century. The rights-oriented legal philosopher is alarmed at the consequentialist implications of interest-based adjudication, but is not disturbed at this theory's less than reverential attitude toward the self-evident principles of the founders.

Rarely, however, have the shared theoretical assumptions of modern constitutional thought been given scholarly consideration. There is no need to focus on their common ground, some would say, when there are still so many important areas of disagreement. While there is considerable truth in this, the issue is more complicated. To the extent that the common ground is defined in relation to views and expectations of the founders, then the fact that most of the differing approaches to constitutional jurisprudence claim essential continuity with these older perspectives indicates a lack of common agreement over the existence of common ground. It is the atypical study that does not seek to legitimate its claim upon our consideration by establishing the consistency of its commitments with those of the founders.

What we will see, though, is that in all the examples to be discussed, little warrant exists for the claim of essential continuity. In each instance we will compare the work of an important contemporary (or in the case of Roscoe Pound, near contemporary) constitutional theorist with the writings of influential architects of our constitutional system from the founding period, with the exception of Lincoln. While he was not from the generation of the founders, he was a legitimate heir to their jurisprudential legacy. Indeed, Lincoln's position is particularly important, since he formulated many of his ideas on the Constitution and the role of the courts in response to what he felt to be a dangerous political assault upon the understandings of the founders.

The unifying thread weaving through the various comparisons is that the Constitution is a written document within which are embodied principles of natural justice intended by its framers to be relevant to constitutional interpretation. Implicit in our approach is a dual challenge: first to the positivists, who dismiss natural rights as irrelevent to the Constitution, and second to the "higher lawyers," who claim the appropriateness of going outside the Constitution for determining adjudicative outcomes. Of course, even if the argument is correct, its translation into specific standards of interpretation for resolving today's tough questions of constitutional law is, in an age lacking anything like a consensus capable of sustaining a natural rights approach, highly improbable at best. Narrow interpretivism and freewheeling noninterpretivism, while popular for many reasons, may be understood as responses to modernity in jurisprudence; that is, to the inability to agree upon constitutional substance at a level more general than what is clearly indicated by textual and historical analysis. The dilemma of contemporary jurisprudence is bound up in the choice between, on the one hand, a constitutional theory that reflects the intentions of the founders but no longer lends itself to full implementation, and on the other, theories that depart, in varying degrees, from the animating principles of original intent but are easily adaptable to the spirit of the times.

Chapters 2 through 6 explore principal themes in contemporary "classics" of constitutional jurisprudence. These works are juxtaposed with earlier writings on similar matters of legal philosophy. The first encounter, in Chapter 2, is with the work of Roscoe Pound, whose views are distinguishable from the other theorists to be discussed in that they are intended explicitly to replace the natural rights orientation of the formative period in American constitutional law. He is also the theorist most directly influenced by the profound changes occurring in modern science. The development of natural rights theory to a position of constitutional irrelevance is not simply a function of judicial decision, but is bound up in much larger forces beyond judicial control, not the least of which is the scientific revolution of the twentieth century. Pound is a critical figure in what has become a familiar insistence in the study and practice of public law in this century: that science play a larger role in constitutional adjudication. Of course, similar pleadings were heard in the eighteenth century regarding the salutóry effects of the law-science nexus; but, as we shall see, both law and science have come to mean different things.

Pound agreed with John Marshall that "[a] Constitution [is] intended to endure for ages to come, and, consequently, to be adapted to the various *crises* of human affairs."[11] But Pound's pragmatism provided a significantly different gloss to Marshall's observation. The process of adaptation, according to Pound, required that the Constitution be seen as possessing a variable content. "We do not base institutions upon deduction from assumed principles of human nature; we require them to exhibit practical utility, and we rest them upon a foundation of policy and established adaptation to human needs."[12] It is in fact the needs, claims, interests, and wants of groups within society that ultimately establish the course of constitutional modernization. In this regard, Pound's political jurisprudence can easily be confused with the interest orientation of Madisonian political science. Whereas Madisonian liberalism was more bounded in the sense that the pursuit of interest was supposed to lead to the attainment of specific substantive goals—the securing of particular natural rights—Pound's rejection of natural rights leads the later interest-oriented jurisprudence to legitimize the relativistic goal of autonomy as the end of the liberal state.

How far liberalism has evolved from its Federalist design may be glimpsed through the prism of Ronald Dworkin's writings. Unlike Pound, Dworkin believes the work of the courts is not to be evaluated against a standard of "practical utility" or based upon a "foundation of policy." Yet as we shall see in Chapter 3, the logic of his constitutional and moral theories leads to a liberalism similar to Pound's. Even so, Dworkin does not acknowledge the liberal constitutionalism of the present to be a departure from the liberal constitutionalism of the founding period. The Constitution in effect becomes an object of transvaluation that involves an important reordering of its underlying philosophical assumptions and commitment. The considerable infusion of Rawlsian moral theory into constitutional theory has influenced both the substance of constitutional scholarship and the perception of the role of the judiciary in American politics. The implications of this infusion for the enforcement of individual rights are explored in Chapter 3 through a contrast of Dworkin's ideas with Madison's *Federalist* contributions. The counter-majoritarian impulses common to both theories turn out to have quite different lessons for students of judicial authority.

Dworkin, however, does not see this approach as diverging significantly from founding intent. This, for Dworkin, is clear once one has grasped the simple, but important, distinction between constitutional concepts and conceptions. Thus, the formulation of a specific conception on a constitutional question that differs in substance from that of the framers may be required if one adheres to their general principles, or concepts. This suggests an aspirational dimension to the interpretive assignment, although, as we shall see, what really is highlighted is the distinction between judicial aspirations and constitutional aspirations. Indeed, the decline of constitutional aspiration is the flip side of the ascendance of judicial aspiration.

No such distinction appears in, or is suggested by, the work of Raoul Berger. To be sure, the predominant theme of his scholarly output is that the Constitution possesses meaning independent of judicial interpretation (and is more often than not disserved through interpretation); yet the meaning of the constitutional text is not a matter of aspiration but contextually defined histories. There is no provision in the theory for constitutional growth through judicial adaptation of the document to conform to changing agendas of social needs. Nor is there provision for judicial elaboration of constitutional principles containing a logic of expansion immanent to the principles themselves. In terms of the Constitution, what you see is what you get, or at least ought to get.

Chapter 4 argues that Berger's effort to establish limits to judicial discretion through an appeal to founding intentions, particularly those of Alexander Hamilton, does not succeed. Of course, intentions on that subject are not absent from the historical record, but Berger fails to draw the correct conclusions from the fact of the founders' commitment to a written constitution. That commitment set limits upon judicial discretion and created a basis for determining when legitimate exercise of discretion—judgment informed by constitutional principles expressive of the spirit of the polity—lapses into the abuse of discretion. Hamilton's compelling case for a written constitution was not a forerunner of the modern positivist's denial of the binding character of principles that claimed authority for reasons transcending the fact of their creation by a duly recognized lawmaking authority. Willful constitutional adjudication, then, cannot be established by citing judicial reliance upon principles of natural right.

Inevitably this creates complications of the kind that heighten the appeal of Berger's approach. For if reliance upon natural rights principles is permissible, then wherein does the advantage of a written constitution lie? Berger, in fact, reserves some of his harshest criticism for Thomas C. Grey, who argues that judges appealing to the "unwritten constitution" are acting in conformity with the intentions of the framers of the constitutional system. Berger's attention to Grey's claim is not misplaced; if correct, the practical implications of the latter's conclusions are significant. Supreme Court decisions considered questionable because of their lack of grounding in constitutional text might have their legitimacy enhanced if respected scholarly authority placed its imprimatur upon an extra-textual or "noninterpretive jurisprudence." Moreover, judges with an eye toward posterity might feel less inhibited about broad-ranging adjudication if it were understood that an unwritten constitution rendered much of this adjudication consistent with original intent.

Grey, like Berger, begins from an initial premise that comports with constitutional assumptions prevailing during the founding generation. Thus, Berger rightly emphasizes the importance attributed by the founders to a written constitution; and Grey is correct to insist upon the relevance of a natural rights tradition for constitutional interpretation. Chapter 5 shows that for each of these premises to culminate in an accurate depiction of founding purpose, each requires the other as a complement. The focus of this chapter is Grey's work, which, in effect, licenses judicial appeal to a variety of extra-constitutional sources, the particular selection of which depends upon the socially desirable goal to be achieved. What we discover, however, is that the early sources from which this expansive rendering of judicial review is deduced do not support the latitudinous interpretation fashioned by Grey. The written Constitution does serve to restrict judges in important ways, limiting them to natural rights principles that are embodied in the text, even while the principles are ultimately derivative from sources external to it.

It was Lincoln who perhaps best understood this. His political opponents in the North included radical abolitionists as well as those prepared to accept slavery, if the practice had popular support. The first group was known for going beyond the Constitution, a document they regarded contemptuously for its obliviousness to substantive moral principles that might serve to nullify the results of popular decision-making. Lincoln's position was to steer a middle course between the transcendentalism of the former and the positivism of the latter, by elaborating a constitutional alternative which, he contended, expressed the expectations guiding the achievement of the founders. Thus we find in Lincoln's opposition to the *Dred Scott* decision a *constitutional* argument rooted in natural rights principles, specifically those of the Declaration of Independence. The judges were tragically mistaken in that case precisely because they did not take the Constitution seriously; that is, they failed to acknowledge the moral dimensions of American constitutionalism.

For some scholars constitutional morality is a matter of procedure, not substance. John Hart Ely, whose process oriented approach is contrasted with Lincoln's in Chapter 6, believes that the democratic commitment of our political system is irreconcilable with a judicial role that includes enforcement of specific substantive values. Written to some extent as a rejoinder to fundamental values-oriented theorists such as Dworkin and Grey, his work fits comfortably within the same contemporary jurisprudential context as the efforts of those he criticizes. Thus, in the course of his articulation of a constitutional order characterized by openness and accessibility, Ely marches to familiar egalitarian rhythms, which culminate in an embrace of conventionally progressive ideals. He is as outspoken in his repudiation of natural rights sources as Berger. For Ely, the Declaration of Independence, for example, emerges as a document of only antiquarian interest. Our juxtaposition of Ely with Lincoln highlights the radical departure of recent strands of jurisprudential thought from the premises of an earlier mode of constitutional understanding.

On a formal level, however, there is this similarity: aspirational principles play an important role in the theories of both Ely and Lincoln. In each case we are presented with a constitutional polity striving to realize more fully its essential character. For Ely aspiration leads ultimately to a polity of, by, and for the people; for Lincoln a polity of this kind needs, in addition, dedication to a certain proposition. It is this last object of constitutional aspiration that finally serves to establish the theoretical boundaries that demarcate the old and the new in constitutional jurisprudence. Pound's social interests, Dworkin's moral theory, Berger's narrow interpretivism, Grey's unwritten constitution, and Ely's proceduralism all affirm something other than a proposition recognized by the founders as intrinsic to the natural order of things, to be central to the work of constitutional interpretation.

The issue that perhaps best reveals this line of demarcation is the finality of judicial decisions in matters of constitutional interpretation. Although debates over the legitimacy of judicial review can still be heard, they mainly have the ring of academic exercises about a question that is no longer in dispute. They are, nevertheless, worth engaging in, because inevitably they raise provocative and important issues of democratic theory that may provide insight into the nature of our constitutional system. One also confronts these issues in debates over judicial finality, but here the question is very much alive in political as well as academic circles. Whether or not the Supreme Court can lay claim to exclusive title over determinations of constitutionality is frequently, and with increasing regularity, argued in Congress. Sometimes the argument focuses upon the jurisdiction of the federal courts, sometimes upon the authority of Congress to reverse a particular judgment of the Supreme Court.

The issue of finality is not simply a matter of who has the last word. It also poses the question, who may legitimately participate in the decision-making process leading to a final determination? The argument of Chapter 7 is that the particular aspirational dimension of the older constitutional jurisprudence—that which sets it apart from contemporary constitutional theory—also distinguishes the two theories with respect to the binding character of judicial decisions. Specifically, we will look at the role of Congress in assigning constitutional meanings, the inquiry to be aided by an examination of the recent legislative attempt to nullify the Court's abortion ruling in *Roe* v. *Wade*. What we will discover is that the logic of the various theoretical orientations previously analyzed leads, despite their often contrary prescriptions, to a convergence of view on the issue of judicial finality. The jurisprudential assumptions supportive of modern contemporary constitutional adjudication fail to support a coherent, principled argument for qualifying the finality of judicial decisions through an exercise of congressional power not designed to amend the Constitution. This failure may serve the ends of justice in a given case. It suggests, however, a weakness in much of recent constitutional theory—the difficulty it has in relating the exercise of judicial power to the broader purposes and aspirations of the polity.

The ability to establish this connection was what distinguished the constitutional theory of the founding period, and later of Lincoln. These efforts were aided by the presence of wider agreement over the substance of the aspirations that defined the polity. Judges were advantageously situated to give expression to these aspirations, the realization of which could never be achieved unilaterally. Recognizing the special assets of the judiciary, they nevertheless understood that the fulfillment of ideals embodied in constitutional principles necessitated a collective enterprise involving the inputs of more than one institution. The exercise of judicial power—its scope, magnitude, and limits—was ultimately traceable to this fundamental task. The language and rhetoric of activism and self-restraint, so prominent lately, appear misplaced in the context of this older understanding; for the aspirational goals established by permanent constitutional principles give a formalistic ring to a debate in which the role of the Court needs to be determined in advance of actual cases and controversies. What, the founders might have said, is gained by prescribing an activist role for the Court when the realization of their aspirations may require passivity, or a deferential role when situations might arise where this same consideration demands assertive intervention?

But as we shall see, founding aims and principles no longer display a decisive (as in deciding cases) presence in contemporary American constitutional theory. When not dismissed as a figment of some overactive jurisprudential imagination, their irrelevance to modern constitutional adjudication renders them nugatory. Sometimes it is deemed efficacious to retain the idea of aspiration, but only to the extent that it serves to legitimate the judicial realization of certain contemporary conceptions of natural fairness and justice. Of course, the fact that the framers' convictions were informed and animated by natural rights commitments means that theorists who argue that the Supreme Court should play a leading role in facilitating our collective moral evolution as a people can, without too much difficulty, align their objectives with those of the founders. More revealing than this, however, is that other theorists, with similar objectives, no longer perceive a need to establish such an alignment. Their position is encouraging for the intellectual honesty it displays, while discouraging for the troubling jurisprudential trend it reveals.

This, then, is not a book about the decline of aspiration in constitutional theory, but rather of the decline of *constitutional* aspiration. The distinction is important. The Constitution embodies a theory of aspiration reflective of its underlying spirit, a spirit subsumed in the natural rights commitments of its framers. To aspire, of course, is to strive toward an end, which, as Lincoln and Douglass understood, in the case of the Constitution meant ensuring that no person living under the authority of the document stood exposed to the imposition of arbitrary power upon his person. It is at once a narrow and broad theory of constitutional aspiration: narrow in the sense that it does not address itself directly to the way people see fit to conduct their lives, and broad in the sense that it provides a constitutional foundation for a people to define and pursue their particular aspirations.

What we will see in the chapters to follow are movements within contemporary constitutional theory to depart from the original idea of aspiration. On the one hand are those who cannot abide the limited nature of the ends generated by eighteenth-century natural rights theory, and seek to engage constitutional interpretation in a more ambitious agenda of aspirational striving. On the other hand are those who, partly in reaction to the perceived excesses of the first group, have abandoned entirely the notion of aspiration, retreating instead to the seemingly safe haven of narrow interpretivism. Their differences are many but should not be allowed to conceal a common thread: the decline of constitutional aspiration.

CHAPTER 2

Legal Science Revisited and Reinterpreted: Roscoe Pound and the Jurisprudence of the Founders

LET US CONSIDER Oliver Wendell Holmes and Earl Warren. On one level, two more different men can scarcely be imagined. Holmes's philosophical bent, aloofness, political passivity, and biting cynicism present a marked contrast to Warren's nontheoretical temperament, gregariousness, political activism, and plainspoken ingenuousness. Yet on a more critical level there is a continuity between these very different personalities and judges—a continuity, moreover, that represents a basic commitment of twentieth-century legal thought. Holmes, in a slightly exaggerated version of this commitment, articulated it in this way: "I have in mind an ultimate dependence [of law] upon science because it is finally for science to determine, so far as it can, the relative worth of our different social ends."[1]

Holmes was not alone in the call for this dependence but, as the most illustrious of the founding fathers of sociological jurisprudence, his voice was particularly influential. His goal may never be fully realized, although developments in constitutional law since Holmes have seen an increasing reliance upon scientific evidence and method. It is here that Holmes connects with Earl Warren, for it was during the latter's tenure as chief justice that science gained a renewed respectability in the principal forum of constitutional adjudication. It was, of course, Warren's opinion in *Brown* v. *Board of Education* that highlighted the Holmesian ideal; but off the Court, too, Warren was heard to echo the earlier justice's sentiments. In unmistakable tones of regret, he observed that "The simple fact is that law has not kept abreast of science."[2] "Scientists," he opined, "are not the ogres of society. They are more concerned with laws than the rest of us."[3]

That judges committed to the precepts of sociological jurisprudence should be attracted to science is not surprising. Modern science is contemporary in a way that law can only hope to be. A discipline that thinks it *should* keep up to date could do worse than to become dependent upon a discipline that *must* keep up to date. If, as Holmes and Warren (and many others) believed, the Constitution should be

12

interpreted to facilitate change, then (though logically it does not directly follow) legal rules and principles should be viewed as working hypotheses, and law, like science, should be a process continually redefining itself as it develops—never fixed, always changing. Indeed, the principal article of faith underlying the modern commitment to science in constitutional jurisprudence is that the Constitution ought continually to be brought up to date to render it responsive to the needs of a society in transition.

Perhaps the central figure in the American school of sociological jurisprudence, a school whose members insist on applying a rigorous empiricism to the analysis of law, was Roscoe Pound. Pound's early career as a scientist—he had a doctorate in botany—may be viewed, in hindsight, as the formative stage of his legal training. This background was most welcome at a time when it was widely felt that American law suffered from a growth-retarding deductive abstractionism. Pound challenged the orthodoxy of his day and had the satisfaction of witnessing the ascension of his own ideas to a place of prominence. Alexander Bickel, for example, depicted the justices of the Warren Court as "children of the Progressive realists." Among this latter group none was more important than Roscoe Pound.

This chapter will examine Pound's science of law and contrast it with the science of law of the founding period. Both Pound and the founders viewed their respective philosophies as scientific, but at this point the similarity ends. Pound's work constitutes an explicit rejection of the prevailing jurisprudence of the founding period, a fact sometimes unappreciated or overlooked by some theorists operating within the Poundian tradition so characteristic of the modern era. This rejection went to the very core of the founders' constitutional philosophy—their definition of rights and the relation of government thereto. His writings enable us to distinguish between the principal jurisprudential commitments of the two periods and to consider what we have gained and lost in the movement from one to the other. Among his numerous writings we focus here upon *The Spirit of the Common Law*, written originally as a series of lectures delivered at Dartmouth College and published at a time of profound reexamination of the scientific view of the universe. An important work, it effectively summarizes the major ideas of Pound's earlier writings and anticipates many of those that followed.

Finally, Pound's examination of American law is quite important for our discussion of contemporary constitutional jurisprudence. The story of the decline of constitutional aspiration is also a story of the decline of natural rights; which in turn is part of a much larger story involving paradigmatic changes in scientific understanding. The insistence upon a greater judicial reliance upon science in constitutional adjudication is not new; in the eighteenth century similar pleadings were heard regarding the salutory effects of the law-science nexus. The difference lies in the way one understands law and science, so that, in itself, a simple evocation of science provides little insight into the constitutional implications of the relationship. In Pound these implications become clearer.

I. Law, Politics, and the Scientific Age

As Garry Wills has argued in his study of the Declaration of Independence, the Newtonian opening "When in the course of human events it becomes necessary" puts "us firmly in the age of the scientific revolution."[4] Jefferson, who revered Newton and his science, speaks of the Revolution as a matter of necessity, much as the great scientist did in describing the movement of the heavenly bodies. It was common in the eighteenth century for intellectuals to employ concepts of Newtonian mechanics—prominent among which was necessity—in their analyses and understandings of human affairs. J. H. Randall observed: "Never in human history, perhaps, have scientific conceptions had such a powerful reaction upon the actual life and ideals of men."[5]

Indeed, when we look at the political and legal ideas of the founding period, the common denominator, though not always the most direct influence, is Newton. Scholars will agree on the differences between Jefferson and Adams, or Hamilton and Wilson, and disagree intensely over the connection and relative importance of Locke and Hutcheson to these colonial thinkers. But the one common thread is Newton. So, for example, James Wilson is commonly identified as belonging to the "moral sense" school of philosophy associated with the Scottish Enlightenment and personified by Francis Hutcheson. This school in turn is contrasted with the philosophical system of John Locke, principally regarding the role of reason in moral choice. Locke, of course, was the great champion of Newtonian thought in philosophy, and during the Enlightenment the two were perceived as coordinate authorities in questions of mind and matter.[6] Indeed, Locke's science of human nature was modeled after Newton's mechanics. But Wilson's political, moral, and legal beliefs were also modeled after the man he refers to as "the immortal Newton."[7] "Order, proportion, and fitness pervade the universe. Around us, we see; within us, we feel; above us, we admire a rule, from which a deviation cannot, or should not, or will not be made."[8] This thought supported all Wilson's legal principles and placed him, along with the rest of the framers, unambiguously within the ambit of the prevailing Newtonian consensus.

Cotton Mather's *Christian Philosopher* was the first Newtonian approach to physical science published by an American.[9] Mather, of course, was as dogmatic in outlook as he was scientific; his was a quest for certainty. Although science and dogmatism may seem an odd pairing initially, the Newtonian depiction of order, harmony, and predictability provided confirmation for Mather's ethical and religious teachings. A God, who is author of the universe, was seen as governing his creation through the issuance of moral directives respecting proper opinions and right conduct.

Two centuries later John Dewey entered a vehement assault against this "quest for certainty," and it is not surprising that Newton emerges as the principal villain of his piece. Dewey speaks of a "now discredited Newtonian natural philosophy."[10] His principal objection is that Newton's science paralyzes human action, and correspondingly, that infallible knowledge endorses the immutable as the only true reality. In Newton he sees metaphysical theories parading in the garb of the physical sciences. This not only obstructs the course of scientific progress and understanding; it stands in the way of social change as well. The influence of science extends well beyond the laboratory; it becomes a vital force in shaping the world view of important actors, affecting their ideas in nonscientific fields of endeavor. Thus, Dewey recounts and regrets the eighteenth-century intellectual-political development that saw the natural laws of science support the adoption of natural laws applicable to human and social affairs. Dewey's goal was to replace the antiquated scientific world view with its modern equivalent and then apply *it* to the problems of humanity.[11]

This call for a new science of society resonated widely within intellectual circles during the first decades of the twentieth century. Similar pleadings were heard in all the social sciences. The president of the American Political Science Association reproached his discipline for being "still in bondage to eighteenth century" ideas, and suggested it was "time for political science to step up into line with the new physics."[12] To the extent that such a bondage existed in the twenties, it would surely be broken by a commitment to the new physics, for it was the old Newtonian science that figured so prominently in the formulation of eighteenth-century ideas about law and politics. Important jurisprudential figures of the period made frequent references to Einstein, the theory of relativity, and the new quantum mechanics.[13] In the accounts of the legal realists, where the enthusiasm for the new science was most pronounced, there seemed to be an implicit assumption that progress in the sciences would be matched by progress in legal science if the latter followed in the path of the natural sciences.

This in itself—that is, the belief in progress—did not distinguish the twentieth-century legal philosophers from their eighteenth-century precursors. But unlike the later group, the earlier thinkers saw progress inhering in the application of principles believed to be universal and complete. As James Wilson wrote, "The law of nature, though immutable in its principles, will be progressive in its operations and effects."[14] Wilson and other American legal philosophers of the eighteenth century would have noted with interest, and perhaps concern, Roscoe Pound's reference to a "practical natural law, . . . a natural law with a changing or a growing content."[15] They would have been perplexed by Charles Beard's proclamation of the end of determinism in the social sciences, an ending signaled by the dropping of assumptions once considered appropriate in the natural sciences. In short, they would have pondered the profound changes in the scientific assumptions that had been so vital in supporting their political and constitutional commitments.

II. A Feudal Challenge: Beyond the Pursuit of Happiness

Roscoe Pound's analysis of American law in the late eighteenth century is best appreciated if viewed in the context of his reaction to the legal condition of his own time, the early twentieth century. "The present crisis" of American law thus serves to inform and illuminate his reflections on the past.[16] The crisis referred to by Pound resulted from the judiciary's inability or unwillingness to adapt the techniques and sources of their adjudication to the demands of a rapidly evolving industrial society. The realities of the social situation required a new definition of justice, one more consonant with "the world-wide movement for socialization of the law,"[17] that acknowledged the ineluctable trend toward interdependence that characterizes the human situation. But the sad fact, as Pound saw it, was that judges were, on the whole, wedded to the ideas of the past, incapable of transcending their commitment to abstract individualism in favor of a judicial empiricism responsive to actual needs and wants. Thus, for example, the Supreme Court could cavalierly assert and defend the primacy of liberty of contract in the face of accumulating evidence that the contractual parties to whom this liberty applies were obligated to accept any agreement dictated by the superior economic position of the industrial elite.[18]

Pound, we should note, was a critic of the economic interpretation of legal history; thus, his understanding of the judiciary did not require it to be viewed as a co-conspirator in a cabal of the economic elite or as a part of the superstructure of the society's mode of production.[19] This view had its positive and negative implications. One did not have to wait for further evolution of the economic order to alter the behavior of judges. On the other hand, the extraordinary attraction of outmoded ideas on the part of jurists (and scholars as well), who should have known better, testified to the formidable impediments standing in the way of any fundamental reorientation in judicial attitudes and performance. "Tenacity of a taught legal tradition is much more significant in our legal history than the economic conditions of time and place."[20]

Pound's objectives were thus formidable. Challenging a tenaciously held tradition is difficult enough; challenging one that had been sanctified by the founding fathers is even more so. The legal tradition that engaged Pound in intellectual combat was a legacy of the generation of Hamilton, Jefferson, Adams, and Wilson. That tradition was not always faithful to the commitments of these men, but it never wavered from the basic assumption underlying their considerable achievement. For Pound, this assumption was individualism, or more to the point, "ultraindividualism."

As far as the law is concerned, this ultraindividualism is defined as "an uncompromising insistence upon individual interests and individual property as the focal point of jurisprudence."[21] It is uncompromising in that it makes no concession to "social righteousness." "It is so zealous to secure fair play to the individual that often it secures very little fair play to the public."[22] This is not meant to deny the importance of protecting individuals in their personal rights, and in this regard Pound more than once expresses his appreciation of the founders' achievement. But he does dichotomize private right and public welfare, seeing them, in an age of interdependence, in fundamental tension and contradiction. Inadequate, in Pound's view, is Blackstone's assertion that "the public good is in nothing more essentially interested than in the protection of every individual's private rights."[23] Indeed, Blackstone's "complacent nothing-needs-to-be-done attitude" is in large measure attributable to this narrow focus on the individual abstracted from his social context.[24] That the English legal authority was so influential in colonial America is, for Pound, as noteworthy as it is regrettable.[25]

The causes of our ultraindividualistic jurisprudence, according to Pound's analysis of early American law, were plural, not singular. They ranged from the environmental (the conditions of a pioneer society) to the historical (the contrast between the courts and the crown in the seventeenth century) to the religious (the demands of

Puritan doctrine) to the intellectual (the attraction of the political, philosophical, and scientific ideas of the eighteenth century). His analysis, however, extends to the question of what might have been as well as what was. Pound introduces an historical model of legal interaction that, he feels, has important contemporary significance. This model is the common law as perceived in terms of its original spirit, feudalism.

Now it may appear strange for a social reformer like Pound to advocate a feudal model as appropriate for our circumstances. More-over, it is initially jarring to confront the observation that the Anglo-American common law of the founding period, in grounding itself in notions of contract and transaction, had departed from the true spirit of the common law, based upon the feudal idea of relationship. But it is obviously not the feudal social order to which Pound was attracted. To him the feudal ideal gave us "a fundamental mode of thought, a mode of dealing with legal situations and with legal problems which . . . has always tempered the individualism of our law."[26] Where the individualism of our law in its beginning "insisted that every man should stand upon his own feet and should play the game as a man, without squealing," the "feudal relation of lord and man regarded man in quite another way."[27] Obligations between men existed not so much as a matter of contract and rights but as incidents of a relation. These relations bound not only individuals but rulers and ruled. "In the feudal way of looking at it, the relations of King and subject involved duties of protection as well as rights to allegience. The King, then, was charged with the duty of protecting public and social interests, and he wielded something like our modern police power."[28] The feudal model, Pound believed, should thus be treasured in our present condition, where respect for the public interest is a matter of survival and where such an interest must be distinguished from the totality of private interests. Whereas we used to say by way of reproach that the common law was feudal, we should today be greatful for this heritage and the lessons to be learned from it.

Pound's history of the common law has a profound bearing upon his jurisprudence. It enabled him to claim that "the natural rights of man deduced from a social contract . . . is an alien conception in our law."[29] This observation is ultimately critical in understanding the difference between the founders' perspective on law and that of the sociological school of jurisprudence. Unlike those who erroneously deny the founders' jurisprudential commitment to eighteenth-century natural rights philosophy, Pound correctly acknowledged their fundamental attachment to these principles.[30] His purpose, however, was to juxtapose these principles with alternative principles of justice in order to demonstrate the superiority of the latter in securing the social good, and with it the happiness of the many. We will see later that this involves the application of the feudal legal model to a new egalitarian social context.

Stated differently, Pound's objective, like Dewey's, was to replace an old legal science with a new one. He was careful to avoid the common misconstruction of characterizing the eighteenth-century natural law school as pre-scientific.[31] Instead he understood the principles of law inherent in nature and derivative from nature as scientific within the Newtonian paradigm of the day. For Pound the key figure was Grotius, for it was he who "made reason the measure of all obligation."[32] Eventually, through the work of his philosophical successors—primarily Coke—the common law of England was transformed into a closed system of legal rules and principles derivative from an immutable and eternal natural law. The founders accepted this transformation and manifested their acceptance most clearly and emphatically, Pound claimed, in the various bills of rights that came to characterize their approach to law and obligation. In time a "stone wall of natural rights" that served as a "clog upon social legislation"[33] was constructed. Pound tends to view the later uses (or abuses) of natural rights doctrine by the Supreme Court of the late nineteenth and early twentieth centuries as more or less faithful adherence to the tradition of the founders. Thus, for example, Justice Field's enlistment of the language of the Declaration of Independence for the purpose of thwarting governmental regulation represents an appropriate application of Jeffersonian principles.[34] In both cases the appeal to eternal verities forecloses enquiry into underlying social realities.

Accordingly, the legal science of the eighteenth century (witness again our Bill of Rights) conceived of law as something that the individual invoked against society, with full anticipation that a rational dispensation would be forthcoming from the legal system.[35] For Pound, on the other hand, law was something created by society for the realization of social interests and the protection of social relations. The proper criterion to be applied in evaluating law is social utility, that is, the securing of as many interests as possible without sacrificing other interests. More will be said of this criterion in Chapter 3. For now it is sufficient to note that this utilitarian principle constitutes a major departure from the jurisprudence of the formative era.

The commitment of the founders to self-evident truths concerning man and nature, a commitment that extended to matters of law, precluded their adoption of a utilitarian jurisprudence. As Morton White astutely observed, "[T]he reason why the American revolutionaries were not utilitarians is that they thought that man had certain duties and rights by nature in the sense of 'essence.'"[36] They did not accept the utilitarian theory "according to which man's duties and rights were expressed in contingent principles."[37] Pound's rejection of the founders' self-evident propositions was a reaction to the fact that the rights deduced from these propositions were necessarily impervious to the results of computations about social felicity. Any law based upon propositions that are "self-evident" is not scientific, at least not in the sense of the modern paradigm accepted by Pound's sociological orientation. That paradigm acknowledged "the impotence of science to establish ultimate standards of justice."[38]

Alexander Hamilton, on the other hand, expressed the prevailing sentiments of the founders when in *Federalist* number 31 he analogized the "primary truths of first principles" of ethics and politics to maxims of geometry. Indeed, geometry, morals, and politics were all referred to as "sciences."[39] When, in an earlier writing, he quoted Blackstone's observation that "the first and primary end of human laws is to maintain and regulate [the] absolute rights of individuals,"[40] he was indulging not in idealistic rhetoric, but in scientific assertion. Moreover, the term "science" was not being employed loosely, for in the eighteenth century it was proper to speak of a science of morals and politics, because facts possessed a twofold significance—descriptive and normative. The "self-evident truth that all men are created equal" had a factual validity that defied empirical refutation, and certain moral and political implications that were similarly irreproachable. As Wilson put it, "in the sciences, truths, if self-evident, are instantly known."[41]

Of course, from the perspective of modern science, the truth of the Declaration is not an empirical verity in any scientifically meaningful sense.[42] From a founder's perspective, however, its sanctification is not contingent upon being empiricially demonstrable according to the fallibilistic assumptions of modern scientific method. Moreover, if, as Lincoln believed, the Constitution implicitly assumes the validity of the self-evident truth of the Declaration and seeks to consecrate the political principles extending from them, then those engaged in constitutional interpretation must steer a course between a narrow interpretivism that severs the text from any background of large moral principle, and an ambitious noninterpretivism that pursues justice with pointed disregard for objective constitutional meanings.

Pound and other legal philosophers in the realist movement quickly exploited the new non-Euclidean geometry to substantiate their denial of self-evident truths in jurisprudence. Even the maxims of geometry, analogized by Hamilton to moral and political principles, but considered by him to be more certain than these latter precepts because of their uncontroversial and passionless quality, have been undermined by the passage of time. The postulates of Euclidean geometry had been regarded as self-evident, lending support to the view that we can have an a priori knowledge of nature and, further, that we can, as Hamilton suggested, make consequent deductions that are as self-evident as the truths from which they are derived.

For Pound, however, maintenance and regulation of the absolute rights of individuals suggested a too passive and narrow role for law and government. "Suppose," he suggests, "we think of law not negatively as a system of hands off while individuals assert themselves freely, but positively as a social institution existing for social ends."[43] Law, we might say, should seek more than to guarantee the *pursuit* of happiness; it should also secure some measure of happiness. It is worth noting in this context that Jefferson's rough draft of the Declaration of Independence read: "That to secure these ends governments are instituted among men, deriving their just powers from the governed," whereas in the final version the word "ends" was replaced by "rights." The change, as White has demonstrated, is significant. In the first case the verb "secure" means "attain," whereas in the second case it must mean "make secure" or "guard," since, when speaking of rights, government need not "attain" what people already have.[44] White's point is that the substitution represents a change in the intended purpose of government from that of abettor of men in the attainment of specific ends to protector of their unalienable rights.[45] If in fact the revision has these substantive implications (rather than a mere stylistic significance), then we can say of Pound that his philosophy of law is much more in the spirit of the rough draft than of the actual Declaration. It suggests, as did Jefferson's original formulation, that those bearing the responsibility of the public trust have an affirmative duty to ensure the people's well-being, that this duty has both a moral and legal significance.[46]

Does it necessarily follow from the distinction between happiness and its pursuit, and from the distinction between social and individual interests, that law must either be a progressive or conservative force in society? Pound imagined natural rights as the bane of all social legislation, an observation historically accurate for the period during which he did most of his important work. It is therefore understandable when he says:

> When houses are scarce and landlords are grasping, Blackstone's proposition that the public good is nothing more essentially interested than in the protection of every individual's private rights is not the popular view. A crowded, urban, industrial community looks to society for protection against predatory individuals, natural or artificial, and resents doctrines that protect these individuals against society for fear society will oppress them.[47]

Thus, in the early years of the republic, when society was much less complex, the natural rights doctrine, in Pound's view, did not obstruct the way of social happiness. Implicit in his analysis is the notion that even before the law had reached its "state of maturity" in the nineteenth century, its underlying natural rights doctrine predictably inclined it against organized societal efforts at social improvement through law.

This analysis raises a number of problems. For example, Pound writes: "Under the influence of the theory of natural rights and of the actual equality in pioneer society, American common law assumed that there were no classes and that normally men dealt with one another on equal terms."[48] A classless society, however, was never an assumption of Lockean natural rights philosophy, as critics and defenders of Locke have long agreed. As Madison put it in *Federalist* number 10, the first object of government is the protection of the "different and unequal faculties of acquiring property."[49] This acquisition would surely not eventuate in equality, but it would, so the theory went, lead to general well-being (that is, the public interest). Moreover, it is easy to see how the protection of this right of acquisition might partake of positive as well as negative governmental action. If private factors are themselves responsible for the infringement upon the right of acquisition (for example, through the accumulation of monopoly power), then it becomes the obligation (moral if not legal) of government to intervene in behalf of those individuals whose exercise of a natural right is being effectively denied. This is in part the theory behind the "police power" of the state, a term first appearing in Chief Justice Marshall's opinion in *Brown* v. *Maryland*.[50] The unlimited acquisition of the few may have to be regulated to secure the basic right of acquisition of the many. Pound appeals to the feudal conception of law to legitimate the police power. But the defense of the police power, and also the case against the old "property Court," may be made in Lockean terms, which is to say in the founders' terms.

A second problem in Pound's consideration of natural rights is his failure to acknowledge the reasonable limits to the exercise of any absolute right that the leading exponents of the theory themselves insisted upon. In civil society the regulation of rights is necessary for the maintenance of rights. Thus, Pound's depiction of a radical separation between private rights and public good in the theories of Blackstone and his American followers is exaggerated. To be sure, Blackstone *did* say that the "first and primary end of human laws is to maintain and regulate [the] *absolute* rights of individuals." But on the next page he defined civil liberty (the end of *civil* society) as a "natural liberty so far restrained by human laws (and no further) as is necessary and expedient for the general advantage of the public."[51] This, of course, falls considerably short of Pound's own expectations for law, but it does indicate an important omission in his assertion that "eighteenth century justice meant the securing of absolute, eternal, universal natural rights of individuals."[52] This should be qualified to indicate that while the goal of justice in the abstract was absolute individual natural rights, the practical goal in civil society allowed for something less ambitious in scale. The use of natural rights became the abuse of natural rights when judges and others failed to appreciate the significance of this distinction. Jefferson, for example, defined justice in terms of natural rights ("Nothing . . . is unchangeable but the inherent and unalienable rights of man"),[53] but he was a social and institutional reformer all the same. He was indeed an individualist, but he was not (and this applies to someone like Hamilton as well), as Pound would have him, an ultraindividualist. His commitment to natural rights, the basis of constitutional aspiration, did not conflict with his particular aspirations for social justice.

III. "What Is God Doing Now?"

Pound's criticism of eighteenth-century natural rights philosophy has an important bearing upon the role of judges in a constitutional democracy. We hear a great deal today of judicial policy-making, not simply the kind that is an inevitable part of all judging, but the determined, active, discretionary exercises of judicial power to effect desirable social change. A debate rages between those seeking to justify the expanded judicial role and others questioning the capacity and legitimacy of the courts acting in this manner. It is a new debate about an old issue—the status of adjudication in a constitutional system of separated powers.

Pound goes to the core of this issue. "We have to combat the political theory and the dogma of separation of powers."[54] Of course, at the time of Pound's writing it was not unusual to see attacks on the separation of powers; progressives such as Herbert Croly, Woodrow Wilson, and Arthur Bentley were well known for their critiques. Like these thinkers, Pound was distressed by the seeming inability of government to act effectively in dealing with social and economic problems, and like them he felt that the doctrine of the separation of powers, with its unrealistic division of authority in terms of function, prevented concerted, purposeful government action. Unlike these others, however, Pound focused his attention upon the courts. The separation of powers stood in the way of judicial empiricism.

As in the discussion of natural rights, Pound seeks to make clear that our political theory of the judicial function, in which judges interpret and apply law but do not make it, is a departure from the true common law tradition. Rather, "in its origin it is a fiction, born in periods of absolute and unchangeable law."[55] The notion that certain immutable laws are merely discovered and then applied by judges (one of Blackstone's more familiar doctrines) means that whenever judges make law, as they must and have always done, they become vulnerable to the charge of exercising a usurped authority. "Today, when all recognize, nay insist, that legal systems do and must grow, that legal principles are not absolute, but are relative to time and place, and that judicial idealism may go no further than the ideals of an epoch, the fiction should be discarded."[56] Legal realists developed this point and carried its logic to an extreme from which Pound felt compelled to withhold his assent. Nevertheless, it illustrates, even in this moderate version of the argument, a decisive difference in the two approaches to jurisprudence under consideration. Compare, for example, John Adams, who declared in 1786, in reference to the separation of powers, that "It was not so much from attachment by habit to such a plan of power, as from conviction that it was founded in nature and reason, that it was continued."[57] Hamilton echoed these sentiments, describing the doctrine in *The Federalist* as a "celebrated maxim" and affirming that "there is no liberty if the power of judging be not separated from the legislative and executive powers."[58]

Hamilton's famous statement that the judiciary "may truly be said to have neither FORCE nor WILL, but merely judgment"[59] has been generally taken to mean that the power of judicial review does not confer upon judges discretion in matters of policy-making. The opponents of the Constitution had attacked the document in part for what they perceived to be potential abuses in the grant of judicial authority. Hamilton was defending against these charges by asserting that the rule of law, the very essence of constitutional government, precluded broad judicial discretion. As Marshall said some years later, the "Courts are mere instruments of the law and can will nothing."[60] In large measure, according to the founders, the rule of law means that government officials must stay within the prescribed limits established by the Constitution for the institutions of which they are a part. Applied to the courts this implies that judges transgress the rule of law whenever they set out to determine policy instead of adhering strictly to their assigned tasks—the policing of constitutional boundaries, the enforcing of constitutional rights, and the application of statutory law. As we will see in Chapter 4, these tasks did not preclude an appeal to natural rights even while seeking to limit judicial discretion.

Pound was correct in linking this separation of powers argument to natural rights commitments. If we turn to common law adjudication, Pound's principal concern, we note that the idea that judges could make law as an instrument of social change was alien to the thinking of the constitutional period. The reason for this is discussed in an important essay by Morton J. Horwitz. Judges were not to exercise discretion in the application of common law rules because those rules were perceived as derivative from natural law principles of justice.[61] They were, therefore, to be discovered, not made, in contrast to statutes, which were acts of will and hence suitable instruments of innovation. Horwitz argues that the eventual change that saw common law judges assuming some importance in directing the course of social change came about only because the prevailing attitude of the common law as embodiment of permanent and immutable principles lost its hold upon the legal and popular imagination.

It is thus clear why Pound, believing that "legal principles are not absolute, but are relative to time and place," should find disagreeable a doctrine that constrains judges in adapting these principles to changing values and conditions. A story told to Pound by William James expresses very nicely what is at issue.

> A small boy asked his mother if it were really true that God had made the whole world in six days. "Oh yes," she answered, "it was quite true." "Did he make it *all* in six days?" asked the boy. "Oh yes," she said, "it's all done." "Well then," said he, "Mamma, what is God doing now?"[62]

From Pound's perspective, the Hamiltonian view of the judicial power left the judges with nothing to do. It sapped them of their creative potential, making of them automatons engaged in a sterile, mechanical jurisprudence. But in doing nothing they were, of course, doing something. They were, Pound felt, playing into the hands of those whose interests lay in the perpetuation of an unjust status quo.

IV. From Rights to Interests

What, then, is the Poundian solution? It is not surprising that it emerges out of the true "spirit of the common law." "It assumes that experience will afford the most satisfactory foundation for standards of action and principles of decision."[63] It is, in short, a pragmatic solution, in which principled judgments are not derived from a fixed code of ethics, but from an objective, problematic situation that indicates an objective need to the observer (for example, a judge)—the particular "good" that is to be the goal of his actions.[64] Pound presents his alternative in terms of a novel jurisprudential example.

> Let us put the new point of view in terms of engineering; let us speak of a change from a political or ethical idealistic interpretation to an engineering interpretation. Let us think of the problem of the end of law in terms of a great task or great series of tasks of social engineering.[65]

Social engineering is now a familiar term, although in some circles it has acquired a pejorative connotation over the years. When used today it is frequently intended to convey a sense of disenchantment with governmental efforts to restructure a social situation in conformity with some theoretician's vision of the good life. Judges are accused of being "social engineers" by those dissatisfied with judicial policy-making efforts. Indeed, the frequency of the allegation has varied in proportion with the increasing boldness of the courts in attempting to resolve social policy questions. The Warren Court has, rightly or wrongly, come to symbolize the engineer in judicial garb.[66]

If we examine Pound's concept of social engineering we may discern the jurisprudential foundation for much of the work of the modern Court. Pound was himself rather prophetic on this point. In speaking of the need for working over the jural materials of the past, he said:

> We shall be warranted in prophesying that this working over will be effected by means of a philosophical theory of right and justice and conscious attempt to make the law conform to ideals. Such a period will be a period of scientific law, made, if not by judges, then by lawyers trained in the universalities.[67]

In this he was influenced by Justice Holmes, who, we recall, had advocated an ultimate dependence of law upon science. Once again, it is important to note that the normative implications of the old science do not apply to this new dependency. The modern scientific approach provides the engineer with his methodology, not his ends.

Social engineering does not require a new vocabulary, only new meanings. Thus, it is not even necessary to discard the term "natural rights" as long as we abandon its eighteenth century definition. Instead we shall take it to mean "interests which we think ought to be satisfied."[68] Our focus, according to Pound, should henceforth be on the demands, claims, desires, and wants involved in social life rather than upon the rights of abstract man. Pound acknowledges, in this context, a considerable debt to William James's ethical philosophy, a cardinal principle of which was that "the essence of good is simply to satisfy demand." "Since everything which is demanded is by that fact a good, must not the guiding principle for ethical philosophy (since all demands conjointly cannot be satisfied in this poor world) be simply to satisfy at all times *as many demands as we can?*"[69] Pound applies this Jamesian formulation to the law in a statement repeated in a number of his writings. "For the purpose of understanding the law of today I am content with a picture of satisfying as much of the whole body of human wants as we may with the least sacrifice."[70] The task of the legal order is one of precluding friction and eliminating waste, of "seeking to secure as much of human claims and desires" as possible.[71] This Pound calls the "engineering interpretation."

Throughout his writings Pound, like James, insisted that the law is not equipped to make distinctions between competing demands according to their intrinsic worth. Skepticism best describes his attitude toward the possibility of developing any absolute standard by which the law can determine the relative weight of the various claims that cry out for recognition. At one point, for example, he suggests that while lawyers as a rule still believe in absolute, eternal legal principles of universal validity, the people know better.[72] They understand that law is the reflection of their desires. The appeal of this orientation in a populistic era is unmistakable, as is its attraction to a Supreme Court whose judges, as Alexander Bickel put it, marched to the tune of egalitarianism.[73]

Pound, to be sure, was determined to limit the satisfaction of wants to those that would not disrupt the pattern of civilized society. His formula for addressing this problem, "the theory of social interests," does not, in the end, serve as a significant limiting factor over demand.[74] There is a sense in which his Jamesian ideal is consistent with the intentions of the founders, although they would have vigorously dissented from this ideal's formulation of the political good. The founders, particularly Madison, also viewed the political community in terms of "various and interfering interests," each of which would be asserting want-regarding claims in the public arena. And since, as Martin Diamond has argued, their new political science "gave a primacy to the efficacy of means rather than to the nobility of ends,"[75] the new regime did not seek to elevate these wants in the direction of virtue and the good life. Their ethical aims were much less lofty than those of the ancients, and their politics—the unspectacular goals of which were comfort, security, and liberty—reflected these lowered expectations. With this much, Pound's pluralism was in essential agreement.

But ultimately, the purpose of the founders' reliance upon a multiplicity of competing interests was the advancement of the public good defined in terms of individual liberty. Maximum aggregate want satisfaction, the hallmark of Pound's social utilitarianism, was not the purpose of the political order. In fact, given their overriding concern with majority faction, a system of this kind was part of the problem, not the solution. The founders sought the satisfaction of wants only within the framework of a just distribution of rights. Madison's famous definition of faction is suggestive of the difference:

a number of citizens, whether amounting to a majority or minority of the whole, who are united and actuated by some common impulse of passion, or of interest, adverse to the rights of other citizens, or to the permanent and aggregate interests of the community.[76]

Unlike the ethical philosophy of James, relied upon by Pound, Madison does not view "anything which is demanded (as) by that fact a good." To the contrary, he assumes that many claims of groups and interests are adverse to the rights of others and the interests of the whole. Moreover, the community is said to have *permanent* interests separate from the totality of group interests. In the end it is the commitment to this idea of permanence (as opposed to Pound's "ideals of the epoch") that served to limit demand and circumscribe the satisfaction of wants.

The contrast between these two want-regarding approaches sharpens further if we turn once again from the subject of Madison's essay to the subject of Hamilton's. In *Federalist* number 10 the permanent interest is to be protected by indirection, through the multiple interactions occurring within the political economy. In number 78 it is the role of spokesman for a body of permanent political principles that legitimized the judiciary's power in a constitutional democracy. It is in the judicial context, in the treatment of individual cases, that the critical evaluation of claims and desires can be accomplished with special regard given to the primacy of fundamental rights. In a certain sense, then, Pound was correct in saying that "a body of law which will satisfy the demands of the society of today cannot by made of the ultraindividualist materials of eighteenth-century jurisprudence."[77]

It is, finally, Pound's image of the social engineer that perhaps best suggests the distance we have traveled in American jurisprudence. An engineer, be he of the social or electrical variety, has an obligation to the present. His is an applied science, the task of which is to make useful to man the multiple sources of the physical (or legal) world. He is to accomplish this, in Pound's words, with a minimum of friction and waste; that is, the satisfaction of the desires of those to whom he is responding must seek to maximize efficiency. While the founders surely did not countenance inefficiency, their view of the judicial role ensured some sacrifice in that direction. Thus, in number 78, Hamilton views as "indispensable in the courts of justice" the "inflexible and uniform adherence to the rights of the constitution and the individuals."[78] This necessarily invites a certain measure of friction and waste, for uniformity and inflexibility are rarely the basis of engineering efficiency. The system, however, will tolerate the judiciary's sacrifice inasmuch as its overriding commitment is not to the gratification of immediate desire. Rather, it is to the timeless principles of morals and politics which, according to Hamilton in number 31, only the "passions and prejudices" of men can subvert. Thus it is that in number 78 he sees as the unique function of the judges the guarding of the Constitution and the rights of individuals "from the effects of those ill humours" associated with "the arts of designing men."[79] The judge as guardian is to be replaced by Pound's engineer. Guardianship and engineering are, of course, not mutually exclusive activities, but the terms do convey a sense of the difference between the old and the new legal science. Guardians can be innovative and creative—indeed they may have to be to fulfill their raison d'être, resistance to threats against a set of permanent legal-political principles. Engineers, in turn, cannot ignore the essential judicial function of protecting rights; but their abandonment of the natural rights perspective that informed the work of the founders means that the rights to be guarded vary with the adaptation of law to changing mores and values—vary, in other words, with what is perceived by the new legal science as the central task of adjudication.

V. Of Juries and Jurisprudence

To appreciate in a more concrete way what followed from this reworking of legal science, it is helpful to take a glance at the evolution of a particular legal institution, the criminal trial jury, which in salient respects parallels the transformation of jurisprudential theory. Pound had a good deal to say about the role of the jury; his comments illustrate the larger themes of his work and their relationship to the science of law of the early period.

According to Pound, "Jury lawlessness is the great corrective of law in its actual administration."[80] He did not, however, favor an unchecked discretion of juries, believing that a "crude individualization" was as unjust as a mechanical application of law by juries.[81] But under certain circumstances jury lawlessness—the refusal of juries to follow a court's instruction—was necessary to achieve justice. In this he appealed to Aristotle, who had related justice to equity, recognizing that legal rules require continual modification and adaptation to changing circumstances.[82] The jury was to be the institution through which equitable principles would function to mitigate the rigor, severity, and universality of the statutory law.

Pound's views were much cited by advocates of the doctrine of jury nullification, the right of jurors to ignore a court's instructions in order to reach a verdict based upon their own consciences or their own interpretations of the law.[83] Jurors, of course, through the verdict of acquittal, have always had the power to nullify law. The question raised by these advocates is whether juries may exercise that power as a matter of *right*, and be so informed by the presiding judge. But the proponents of this view did not only cite Pound. They also relied heavily upon the early American trial court experience.

Indeed, this reliance is not entirely misplaced, for in fact our early juries were given the authority to rule on questions of law in criminal cases. The history of the American petit jury involves a progression from a sharing of responsibilities between judge and jury to a division of responsibilities. In a landmark decision of the Supreme Court, the first Justice Harlan wrote in his opinion for the Court that "In [the] separation of the functions of court and jury is found the chief value, as well as safety, of the jury system."[84] Juries should be the triers of fact; judges the judges of law. Although a long common law tradition supported Harlan's claim, an examination of early American judicial experience suggests that it was the *fusion* of the functions of court and jury that was originally thought to be a principal structural asset of the jury system. Statesmen as diverse in their political views as Jefferson and Hamilton were in agreement that the jury should not be excluded from playing a role in the interpretation of law and the resolution of legal issues.[85] The prevailing practice in colonial times and well into the nineteenth century was to allow, and often to encourage, the jury to consider the law as well as the facts in the exercise of its responsibilities.[86] The jury was expected to be an active participant in the trial process, not the passive and compliant recipient of judicial instructions that later become the norm.

There is, of course, a structural, or functional, explanation for the changes in jury role. The increasing complexity in the substantive law during the nineteenth century accompanied a steady accretion in judicial expertise and professionalism. Whereas in colonial times a large percentage of judges were laymen, the drift of developments within the legal profession ultimately led to a general expectation that judges be learned in the law. Concurrent with this growth in specialization was a tightening in the definition of the role of judge and jury. This development is somewhat analogous to the process of institutionalization that occurred in the House of Representatives during the same period.[87] The structural distribution of power within the House evolved from a situation of very little or no internal differentiation to one of well-defined specialization.

From our perspective, however, a jurisprudential explanation (which need not be seen as mutually exclusive of the other) is more interesting. Thus, the alignment of Hamilton, Jefferson, and Pound on the same side of the nullification controversy prompts us to examine the theoretical background to what might initially appear to be an unlikely association. When this is done, the conflicting assumptions of the two traditions become at least as obvious as the apparently similar conclusions to which, in the case of the jury, they lead.

In a discussion of Thomas Hobbes, Carl J. Friedrich observed:

> It is not surprising . . . that Hobbes would claim laymen to be capable of being judges. He refers to the Parliament as the highest judge, as well as to juries, and observes that finding the law and the decision concerning it does not depend upon a knowledge of the entire law such as is possessed by jurists.[88]

Why is such knowledge not required? Because "[t]he law of nature addresses itself in its rules directly to the reasonable insight and understanding of every man [and] does not require proclamation."[89]

In colonial America and during the first part of the nineteenth century, this view of the natural law and its relationship to the civil law, as we have seen, was a widely held article of political belief. As a result, the legitimation of the jury's right to decide questions of law did not trouble such stalwart defenders of the rule of law as John Adams.[90] The accessibility of ordinary individuals to a shared natural rights tradition meant that the law of the juries would be both stable and just. A "widely shared consensus about free men's immutable rights" served to legitimate an active jury role. As John Adams wrote, "The great Principles of the Constitution, are intimately known, they are sensibly felt by every Briton—it is scarcely extravagant to say, they are drawn in and imbibed with the nurses milk and first air."[91]

It was an age when, as Pound wrote, conventional wisdom held that "each individual was competent to exercise his own reason with respect to legal institutions and legal precepts."[92] Carried to its extreme by the abolitionist Lysander Spooner, this argument led to a theory of plebiscitary democracy, which held that "any government, that can, *for a day*, enforce its own laws without appealing to the people (or to a tribunal fairly representing the people) for their consent, is, in theory, an absolute government."[93] Trial by jury, according to Spooner, was based upon a recognition of this principle. Natural law is "the *science of justice*, and almost all men have the same perception of what constitutes justice."[94] While most people were not prepared to accept the implications of Spooner's theory, his view that natural law was at once stable and the source of stability in the statutory and constitutional law was by no means uncommon. Indeed, those far less enthusiastic in their support of participatory democracy could nevertheless agree with Spooner that, because of this "science of justice," the jury could safely be entrusted with the authority to resolve questions of law.

It was not long, however, before this science found itself under vigorous attack, which was in part attributable to the ascendancy in England, and later in the United States, of the positivistic insistence upon a strict separation of law from morality or ethics.[95] This separation coincided with the articulation of a command theory of law, in which the law of any given society is defined and limited by its formal sources. Such a theory was consonant with a steady trend in American law in the nineteenth century, a trend away from the concept of the common-law crime toward codification of the penal law in clear, prospective statutory rules.[96] As noted by Pound, "Legislation has always brought with it an imperative theory of law, a theory that law was the command of the sovereign."[97]

The logic of the imperative theory required that law not only had to be told to the jurors, it had to be accepted by them. The idea that individual juries could interpret the law for themselves and, in effect, create new law was destructive of a well-ordered legal system that valued predictable results. The jury's function was to apply the law of the state to a given set of facts, and thereby to augment the authority of that law. The statutory law, as interpreted by the courts, was the sovereign law of the land. There could be no place for the substitution of jurors' conceptions of what the law of the land ought to be for what was in fact the positive law.

This was a point that Pound understood very well. He suggested that a consensus on the substantive content of natural law was necessary if that law was to be relied upon in such settings as jury decision-making.[98] "In a diversified industrial society there is and can be no general agreement as to the details of natural rights."[99] Pound referred to the period in which the jury had a more active role as a "homogeneous pioneer society," characterized by infrequent clashes of interest.[100] Although this characterization might strike historians as somewhat simplistic, it is doubtless the case that as industry and science advance, traditional codes of morality and ethical conduct become less secure and generally persuasive. In terms of the jury system, structural differentiation and legal positivism converge at the point where it becomes apparent that only a well-defined division of functions will maintain the authority of law. Thus, the binding character of the court's instructions fulfills the function of imposing a uniformity and order (that might otherwise not exist) upon a diverse group of citizens lacking common agreement concerning fundamental precepts of right conduct.

As we have seen, Pound's sociological jurisprudence developed in reaction to what he saw as the inflexible, doctrinaire application of law in the preceding period. It therefore called for the individualization of justice, a process that would recognize the group reality of social experience and accommodate change within a framework of legal stability. Thus, Pound argued, the appropriate response to a diversity induced by industrialization was not an artificial imposition of conformity to a legislative will, but a judicial accommodation of the various interests, claims, demands, and expectations that competed for public attention. Hence the appeal to "jury lawlessness" and the principles of equity.

But these principles of equity were quite different from traditional principles, and in particular from those relied upon in the early American jury experience. Public opinion (relative to groups and communities) rather than natural right (assumed to be objective and universal) was the source for equitable consideration. Thus Holmes, who influenced and was influenced by Pound, said of the jury that it "will [and should] introduce into their verdict a certain amount—a very large amount, so far as I have observed—of popular prejudice, and thus keep the administration of the law in accord with the wishes and feelings of the community."[101] This is consistent with Holmes's oft-quoted view from *The Common Law* that "The first requirement of a sound body of law is, that it should correspond with the actual feelings and demands of the community, whether right or wrong."[102] Thus, the analytical positivism of the previous era was to be replaced by a kind of sociological positivism, in which law was to be defined, as it were, from the bottom up rather than from the top down.[103] Pound's appeal to Aristotle, then, did not eventuate in an Aristotelian solution. For in Aristotle "equity embodies a moral ideal and is constant and immutable."[104] Whereas for the Greeks the end of law was perceived in terms of the unity of the whole, for the new school of sociological jurisprudence the goal was the protection of group diversity and integrity.

The contrasting sources for jury law-making (and equity-dispensing) that distinguish the two jury models have significantly different functional implications. Under the old model the jury performed a function analogous to judicial review, measuring the positive law against natural rights that were accessible to most people. Under the Poundian model the jury is to function as a community agent of nullification, reflecting the prevailing sentiments of the community with regard to the positive law and its proper application.

VI. Conclusion

The prevailing sentiments of the community may be seen to embrace community aspirations as well as opinion on particular topics of public interest. These aspirations often reflect the temper of the times, as when we say, for example, that a post-Watergate mentality led a jury to insist, through its verdict, that government officials comply with popular expectations regarding the ethical conduct of those holding public trust; or that a jury, reflecting the community's acceptance of a "sixties" approach to human relationships, exonerated a violator of the selective service law because his act advanced their aspirations toward peace and brotherhood. One may be the victim, or the beneficiary, of community aspirations.

Judicial interpretation of the Constitution differs from jury application of the criminal law in at least one important respect: the jury is responsible only for the present. Its transient character and the anonymity of its members contrast sharply with the rootedness of the Court. Unlike the jury, the Court is expected to explain its decisions with reference to the past and in anticipation of the future, suggesting an orientation toward aspiration of a fundamentally different sort. Imagining the Court in the role of articulating community aspirations conjures up an infelicitous relationship between institution and function. Sociological jurisprudence makes no provision for aspirations embodied in the language of the Constitution, which was intended to serve as a set of permanent principles to guide constitutional adjudication. For example, the most thoughtful theoretician of sociological jurisprudence, Benjamin Cardozo, wrote: "My duty as a judge may be to objectify in law . . . the aspirations and convictions and philosophies of the men and women of my time. Hardly shall I do this well if my own sympathies and beliefs and passionate devotions are with a time that is past."[105] To the extent that the securing of rights is a major concern of the Court, and to the extent that rights are entwined in constitutional principle, a jurisprudence that has difficulty distinguishing aspirations from immediate wants and preferences will fail to satisfy those whose object it is to take rights seriously. In the next chapter we examine the constitutional theory of perhaps the most prominent of the rights-oriented approaches. Before turning to that theory, and its call for a partnership between constitutional law and contemporary moral theory, let us take an additional glance at the older science of morals that no longer dominates jurisprudential discourse.

James Wilson is again quite helpful.

> When we view the inanimate and irrational creation around and above us, and contemplate the beautiful order observed in all its motions and appearances, is not the supposition unnatural and improbable—that the rational and moral world should be abandoned to the frolicks of chance, or to the ravage of disorder?[106]

James Wilson's rhetorical question should be juxtaposed with a later comment of his upon the role of the courts. "The judicial authority consists in applying, according to the principles of right and justice, the constitution and laws to facts and transactions in cases."[107] Taken together these comments explain the mission and task of constitutional adjudication in a way that makes clear the influence of the scientific world view on the governance of men. The harmony, law, and order that pervade the physical world make it "improbable," indeed "unnatural," to assume that something less describes the moral world, a world governed by principles of right and justice. The application of these principles in legal cases means that judges serve, in effect, as intermediaries between the universe and the polity, seeking to structure the civic realm in accordance with the regularity and symmetry of nature. When such application occurs it can further be said that the resulting law or decision will not be compromised by uncertainties related to the "frolicks of chance."

This image of the judicial function conveys a sense of power, perhaps inordinate power. But from an eighteenth-century perspective little is to be feared. The judges will be limited in their discretion by the consensus issuing from the science of morality and politics. Theirs will be a role analogous to the geometer who reasons mechanically from axiom to conclusion. More metaphorically, they will attend to the proper functioning of the machinery of political justice.

The state (represented by the judges) as machine is thus a microcosm of the universe and a macrocosm of man. One is obliged here to call attention to Hobbes and the origins of the modern liberal state.

> Nature, the art whereby God has made and governs the world, is by the *art* of man, as in many other things, so in this also imitated—that it can make an artificial animal. For seeing life is but a motion of limbs, the beginning whereof is in some principal part within, why may we not say that all *automata* (engines that move themselves by springs and wheels as does a watch) have an artificial life? For what is the *heart* but a *spring*, and the *nerves* but so many *strings*, and the *joints* but so many *wheels* giving motion to the whole body such as was intended by the artificer?[108]

Hobbes adopted the concepts of space, mass, and motion used in seventeenth-century mechanics as the basis of his theory of the state. His claim was to have developed the first science of politics, and it is significant, recalling Hamilton's scientific explication of the Constitution, that Hobbes says of geometry that it is "the only Science that it hath pleased God hitherto to bestow on mankind."[109] Hamilton was, of course, Hobbesian in more ways than one, but in his commitment to Euclidean methodology, in particular, we see the scientific basis of our early constitutional jurisprudence.

Indeed, the constitutional system itself is structured around the mechanistic system of checks and balances, described by Hamilton in the following way:

> The science of politics . . . like most other sciences has received great improvement. The efficacy of various principles is now well understood,

which were either not known at all, or imperfectly known to the ancients. The regular distribution of power into distinct departments—the introduction of legislative balances and checks—the institution of courts composed of judges . . . these are either wholly new discoveries or have made their principal progress towards perfection in modern times. They are means, and powerful means, by which the excellence of republican government may be reformed and its imperfections lessened or avoided.[110]

The judiciary, in short, is part of the system of checks and balances introduced by a science of politics in order to preserve republican government. Balance, equilibrium, order, creative tension—these are the Newtonian features of this scientific solution. But it is the goal of the enterprise—republican government (one that embodies principles of right and justice)—that is to be the quintessential scientific achievement. For the founders, most notably Hamilton and Wilson, judges are at their best when they participate in the realization of this ideal through objective, impersonal, commonsensical application of the fundamental law.

CHAPTER 3

Modern Jurisprudence and the Transvaluation of Liberal Constitutionalism

TO ENHANCE THE QUALITY of constitutional decision-making, Ronald Dworkin has urged a "fusion of constitutional law and moral theory," one that "incredibly, has yet to take place."[1] His call is directed, in the first instance, to the academy and only indirectly to the Court; and, if we are to judge by the amount of scholarly activity in recent years, it has been taken seriously. Constitutional theory has received a massive infusion of moral philosophy—largely from the Rawlsian school— directed toward the construction of a coherent jurisprudence of rights that addresses the concerns of modern constitutional adjudication. This chapter will explore some of the implications of this evolving jurisprudence, focusing in particular on the work of Dworkin and its relation to the prevailing constitutional theory of the founding period.

The argument to be developed is that this contemporary jurisprudence, which Dworkin describes as a "liberal theory of law,"[2] represents an important departure from the earlier constitutional theory, a theory for which historical accuracy also requires a liberal designation. Indeed, this shift in jurisprudential perspective is reflective of the significant innovations on the liberal philosophy of the seventeenth and eighteenth centuries that have emerged in this era. Theorists writing from the modern liberal point of view vary in the extent to which they acknowledge departures from the older tradition. Among this group there is broad recognition of the legitimacy inhering in fidelity to the principles of the framers; however, their efforts in affirming continuity with the founding period show considerable diversity. But even those, such as Dworkin, who occasionally render explicit their differences with the founding philosophy do not fully articulate the extent to which their views constitute a profoundly divergent jurisprudential alternative. To the degree that we still have a choice in these matters it is important that we understand what precisely there is to choose from. To this end, the chapter will discuss the principal constitutional assumptions of the liberal theory of law against the backdrop of the earlier liberal constitutionalism.

37

The argument will proceed in two stages. First we will distinguish between two alternative models of individual rights enforcement grounded in the differing constitutional premises of these two liberalisms. The similarity of concerns and language expressed in the two approaches can easily allow the relevant theoretical innovations to pass unnoticed. Thus, it will be necessary to show that despite surface similarities, the counter-majoritarian constitutional premise present in both theories does not lead to similar conclusions regarding judicial authority and the protection of individual rights. Second, the modern jurisprudential effort through which rights are derived will be scrutinized. It will be shown that this process has enabled Dworkin and others to effect a reordering of priorities in the underlying assumptions of liberal constitutionalism, in effect making the Constitution an object of transvaluation through a substitution of one set of philosophical principles for another. The issue here is not the strength or weakness of these principles; it is whether they support constitutional conclusions that can claim legitimacy from their presumed adherence to broad founding intentions.

I. Constitutional Theory and the Counter-Majoritarian Premise

For all the attention it has received, Madison's number 10 *Federalist* has not figured prominently in discussions of constitutional theory and the role of the Supreme Court. Hamilton, after all, dealt explicitly with this subject in later essays, providing ample material for scholars of the Court. Nevertheless, the current liberal theory of law provokes one to reconsider number 10 for its jurisprudential implications. Its subject, the problem of faction—especially majority faction—speaks directly to the concerns of contemporary legal philosophers, who see the task of jurisprudence as that of accounting for the counter-majoritarian character of individual moral rights.

> The constitutional theory on which our government rests is not a simple majoritarian theory. The Constitution, and particularly the Bill of Rights, is designed to protect individual citizens and groups against certain decisions that a majority of citizens might want to make, even when that majority acts in what it takes to be the general or common interest.[3]

This is the major premise underlying Dworkin's "rights thesis"; and although its meaning is rather straightforward, notice should be made of which part of the Constitution is mentioned as critical in the defense of individual rights against the majority. The anti-Federalists come readily to mind here, for it was they who argued that the Constitution without a Bill of Rights would prove an inadequate guarantee of personal freedom. The authors of *The Federalist*, on the other hand, believed, in Hamilton's words, that "the original Constitution is itself, in every rational sense, and to every useful purpose, A BILL OF RIGHTS."[4] Madison's argument in number 10 assumes that rights will be upheld in the pursuit of interest, which, as we shall see, differs from the contemporary notion of rights upheld against aggregate interest through the agency of judicial review. His quarrel with Dworkin would not be with the latter's definition of constitutionalism—"The theory that the majority must be restrained to protect individual rights"[5]—but with the institutional implications that follow from the requirements of restraint. To see why this is so, we should begin with a brief outline of Dworkin's rights argument.

Dworkin attempts in his theory of rights to resolve a critical tension in American constitutionalism, what Michael Walzer has referred to as the pluralism of the constitutional tradition and the universalism of philosophy.[6] Thus, the draftsmen of the Constitution are understood by Dworkin as endorsing subsequent appeals of philosophically derived moral rights that became the function of the Court to defend against popular majorities.[7] "[I]n the United States citizens are supposed to have certain fundamental rights against their Government, certain moral rights made into legal rights by the Constitution."[8] This in effect means that the Court has the responsibility of ensuring that specific constitutional guarantees (which may involve quite general language) are interpreted to institutionalize the moral rights that define a just society. Dworkin rejects Chief Justice Hughes's familiar aphorism that the Constitution is what the Supreme Court says it is. The contention of this chapter is that the ultimate logic of the rights thesis gives a hollow, or at best formalistic, look to this rejection.

No doubt this is an observation Dworkin would strongly contest, for it is the burden of his well-known case against legal positivism that "judicial decisions enforce existing political rights."[9] Our legal system, for example, contains principles analytically distinguishable from rules, providing judges with the constitutional wherewithal to resolve hard cases, and to resolve them with *the* right answers. No judicial discretion, Dworkin maintains, is involved here, even though the determination of what the law is is inseparable from considerations of political morality.[10] Hughes's cynicism would suggest that judges create legal rights, whereas the truth of the matter is that judges are, or should be, engaged (creatively perhaps) in the enforcement of preexisting rights—in short, a process of discovery, not invention. This all sounds quite Blackstonian and rather old-fashioned; yet Dworkin reminds us on more than one occasion that his theory is very different from the older theories of rights that rely on the supposition that some peculiar metaphysical character defines the substance of rights.[11]

It is, indeed, in the novelty of Dworkin's rights thesis that one begins to suspect the commitment in his denial of Hughes's aphorism. The thesis "encourages a connection between law and political and moral philosophy that must be for the benefit of both."[12] Dworkin insists that judicial fidelity to the constitutional text requires a choice between competing conceptions of morality,[13] but it is a choice not limited by the understanding of rights embodied in the framers' vision. Unless, then, the incorporation of the latter-day moral philosophy within the ambit of legal protection provided by the Constitution is consistent with constitutional intent—an understanding held by most proponents of the liberal theory of law—it is difficult to see how a judge can avoid validating Hughes's observation.

In Dworkin's work the concept of rights contains an important distinction between principle and policy that suggests a contrast with Madison's solution to the problem posed by the majority. The reason individual rights are understood in the liberal theory of law as political trumps held by individuals[14] is that they are grounded in principle. A principle is a "standard that is to be observed, not because it will advance or secure an economic, political, or social situation deemed desirable, but because it is a requirement of justice or fairness or some other dimension of morality."[15] Rawls's formulation is evident in Dworkin's account. "[A] conception of right," according to Rawls, "is a set of principles, general in form and universal in application, that is to be publicly recognized as a final court of appeal for ordering the conflicting claims of moral persons."[16] For Dworkin, the final court of appeal is, of course, the Supreme Court, which, insulated from the demands of the political majority, is ideally suited to evaluate the argument of principle.[17]

Once again there is a familiar ring to these thoughts, and so it is not surprising that the liberal theory of law occasionally takes for its own the eighteenth-century language of natural rights. For Dworkin, principles of justice vindicate individual rights when, as inevitably happens, they compete with public policies seeking to advance some goal of the community as a whole. Policies are conceptualized as utilitarian goals that, unconstrained by principle, render as vulnerable rights that emerge from moral considerations, rather than from calculations of aggregate good.[18] It is from this distinction that the notion of a political trump appears; so that "[i]f someone has a right to something, then it is wrong for the government to deny it to him even though it would be in the general interest to do so."[19]

The distinction between principles and policies thus illuminates the counter-majoritarian nature of the Constitution as well as the responsibilities of its official interpreters. This point is well formulated by David A.J. Richards, who, despite his reservations about the analytical rigor of Dworkin's key distinctions, is in essential agreement with its judicial implications.

> The moral legitimacy of constitutionalism is most felicitously explained in terms of the idea of human rights, for the normative structure of arguments of Moral Rights as trumps over countervailing utilitarian calculations, has in the American legal system an institutional correlate in terms of judicial supremacy which enforces a catalogue of human rights against majoritarian institutions which tend to be utilitarian.[20]

Policy, that which emerges from the political process, is fundamentally utilitarian and therefore potentially threatening to the rights of the minority. Principle, on the other hand, is protective of the rights of the minority, in that its validation depends not on popular approval but in its consistency with a coherent theory of political justice.

Seen in this way, however, the subtle intricacy of the Constitution's counter-majoritarianism is obfuscated. It is a commonplace among political scientists that policies in Western democracies, and especially in the United States, are typically products of incremental adjustments at the margin.[21] Thus, to characterize policy as utilitarian, with all of the rational-comprehensive connotations that the term implies, distorts the fundamental nature of the political process, including that of the Supreme Court. Richards's rationale for judicial supremacy is that the Court stands as the chief defender of rights *against* those institutions that reflect the will of the majority. But the will of the majority has not been left unattended by the framers of the Constitution to be juxtaposed in adversarial tension with the counter-majoritarian judiciary. That this occurs on occasion does not justify extravagant claims for judicial review in a constitutional democracy.

John Marshall himself declared at the Virginia Ratifying Convention of 1788 that a bill of rights "is merely recommendatory. Were it otherwise, the consequence would be that many laws which are found convenient would be unconstitutional."[22] Marshall was not exalting policy over principle, or expediency over right; rather he was reflecting the Federalist understanding of how a new experiment in popular government would uphold the regime's principles of justice. This, then, brings us back to number 10 and its famous cure of "the diseases most incident to republican government," a cure particularly relevant to the following observation of Dworkin's. "It has been typical of these disputes [over individual constitutional rights] that the interests of those in political control of the various institutions of the government have been both homogeneous and hostile."[23] His description parallels closely Madison's definition of a faction:

> a number of citizens, whether amounting to a majority or minority of the whole, who are united and actuated by some common impulse of passion, or of interest, adverse to the rights of other citizens, or the permanent and aggregate interests of the community.[24]

Both Dworkin and Madison have identified the same problem, but whereas this leads the former to assess the Constitution as counter-majoritarian and to demand an activist, rights-oriented Court, it leads the latter to mitigate the unjust effects of majoritarianism without undermining the essentially majoritarian thrust of the Constitution.

> To secure the public good and private rights against the danger of such a faction [one that constitutes a majority and is, in Dworkin's words, homogeneous and hostile], and at the same time to preserve the spirit and the form of popular government, is then the great object to which our inquiries are directed.[25]

Madison is, in brief, much more subtle and much more comprehensive than Dworkin. For Madison, only rarely will it be necessary to go beyond the ordinary democratic process to secure rights. For Dworkin, we must regularly look outside that process—to the courts in particular—to receive our rights. Dworkin is wrong. He is wrong for the simple reason that Madison knew and made real the distinction between a pure democracy and a republic. This second variation renders majority rule compatible with individual rights by broadening the scope of the governing coalition.

> Extend the sphere and you take in a greater variety of parties and interests; you make it less probable that a majority of the whole will have a common motive to invade the rights of other citizens; or if such a common motive exists, it will be more difficult for all who feel it to discover their own strength and to act in unison with each other.[26]

In short, the extended republic of a multiplicity of interests is designed to dilute the hostility of the majority by introducing heterogeneity into the policy-making process. Or in terms that directly address Dworkin's concerns, the protection of rights is implicit in the *pursuit* of policy.

Dependent as he is upon the notion of a hostile and homogeneous majority, Dworkin quite naturally rejects the argument for judicial self-restraint that stems from a deferential respect for democratic process. This claim "asks that those in political power be invited to be the sole judge of their own decisions, to see whether they have the right to do what they have decided they want to do."[27] Again, this reminds one of Madison, who emphasizes that "no man is allowed to be a judge in his own cause, because his interest would certainly bias his judgment and, not improbably, corrupt his integrity."[28] Madison goes on to say:

> With equal, nay, with greater reason, a body of men are unfit to be both judges and parties at the same time; yet what are many of the most important acts of legislation but so many judicial determinations, not indeed concerning the rights of single persons, but concerning the rights of large bodies of citizens? And what are the different classes of legislators but advocates and parties to the causes which they determine? Is a law proposed concerning private debts? It is a question to which the creditors are parties on one side and the debtors on the other. Justice ought to hold the balance between them. Yet the parties are, and must be, themselves the judges; and the most numerous party, or in other words, the most powerful faction must be expected to prevail.[29]

Accustomed as we are to discussions of judges performing as legislators, Madison's reflections on legislators in judicial role are refreshingly illuminating. Justice, he appears to be saying (in agreement with Dworkin's point) is impossible when the bias of law-makers is unchecked, allowing them untrammelled freedom to determine the rights of citizens. This leads Dworkin explicitly to reject judicial self-restraint, but what inferences on this matter can we derive from Madison's observation?

That this sentiment is expressed in the context of his analysis of the dangerous majoritarianism of traditional democracy has bearing on the issue of judicial activism. One might say, for example, that under the conditions of a popular regime of that variety, a Supreme Court with the power of judicial review might naturally—assuming that protection of individual rights was deemed important—entertain a presumption of unconstitutionality attaching to all legislation that might conceivably threaten the rights of a clearly recognizable minority. Since the time of Chief Justice Stone's famous footnote, this presumption has represented the aggressive judicial orientation on rights issues that Dworkin and others eloquently defend.[30] In Madison's political science, however, the bias associated with faction or interest is not permitted to govern untrammelled, and thus it is possible for "justice . . . to hold the balance" between the various contending interests. While individual interest still corrupts judgment, the outcome of the political process (at least on the federal level) has a strong presumption of being just. Or to use the language of Stone's footnote, the Madisonian system goes a long way to protect discrete and insular minorities without the active intervention and assistance of the Supreme Court.[31] This hardly means that the system is foolproof or that the judiciary is superfluous as a guardian of rights; it does suggest that Federalist theory would likely not share the activist presumption of the liberal theories of law on the subject of judicial review.

As a matter of fact, the Court has arguably *not* played a prominent rights-enforcing role vis-à-vis the actions of the federal government.[32] Indeed, it is ironic, but also perhaps instructive, that the most odious action ever taken by a branch of the federal government was the *Dred Scott* decision of the Supreme Court. Lincoln's controversial argument for congressional repudiation of this judicial monstrosity assumes, in the modern jurisprudential vernacular, the trumping power of moral rights. It does not, however, as we will see in Chapter 6, imply an institutional correlate of judicial supremacy. To be sure, in relation to the states, particularly in recent decades, the Court has provided a significant counter-majoritarian balance to legislative infringement of rights. Three things, however, need be said of this. First, it is consistent with Madisonian theory. One should expect more threats to individual rights where the political sphere is contracted, where, that is, factionalism is less splintered. Second, to the extent that our interest lies in discerning a founding intention regarding the Court's role in rights enforcement, we cannot ignore the fact that the states were exempted from the requirements imposed by the guarantees of the Bill of Rights.[33] And third, judicial review was explicitly mandated over state laws by the Supremacy Clause. Thus, its hands constitutionally tied with regard to most rights-threatening actions of the states, and its oversight of federal activity relaxed through ingenious innovations in political theory, the Court can only with exaggeration be described (according to original design) as the principal defender of our moral and human rights.

II. Moral Theory and the Constitutional Determination of Rights

The Concept of Property

There will always be occasions when the Court will have to assume major responsibility for protecting rights. In addition, the Court is uniquely constituted to perform a potentially vital educative role, including the illumination of the underlying principles of the political system. The historical record is clear that from the outset the justices regarded this function as a significant part of their constitutional assignment.[34] What is less clear is whether this assignment obliged them to convey faithfully the framers' intentions in constitutional interpretation or be permitted some measure of judicial innovation in the application of the fundamental law.

Dworkin and most advocates of the liberal theory of law would object to this choice—so formulated—as presenting a false dichotomy. Thus, the notion that judges must either be creative *or* faithful displays a gross misunderstanding of the necessary and proper dialectic between Court and Constitution.

> Our constitutional system rests on a particular moral theory, namely, that men have moral rights against the state. The difficult clauses of the Bill of Rights, like the due process and equal protection clauses, must be understood as appealing to moral concepts rather than laying down particular conceptions; therefore a court that undertakes the burden of applying these clauses fully as law must be an activist court, in the sense that it must be prepared to frame and answer questions of political morality.[35]

Thus, the Constitution, in the equal protection clause, for example, announces a standard of equality, but does not stipulate any particular conception of that concept. The distinction enables one to preserve the essential meaning of the Constitution without binding judges to the constitutional applications that would likely have occurred when the document was written. On the subject of rights, Richards's view that the "moral theory underlying the Constitution should not be limited to the kinds of moral rights that the country's founders regarded as fundamental"[36] is a fair representation of this general position.

This is an appealing, if not altogether novel, formulation that relies upon certain givens in our constitutional tradition, most notably the assumption that the Constitution was intended to endure for the ages. Often, as in the case of Marshall's comment that "it is a *constitution* we are expounding,"[37] sentiments about the resilience of the document are wrenched out of context in order to portray erroneously the Constitution as infinitely adaptable. In theory the concept/conception distinction does not make this claim, although the argument of this section is that in practice the Constitution's status as a charter embodying permanent principles of political justice is, in effect, jettisoned by the modern liberals.

To see how this is accomplished it is helpful to make the following distinction. A concept may be understood as a specific moral principle—specific, that is, in the minds of its authors—the application of which may yield different results, or conceptions, depending upon the circumstances and context in which it occurs. Or a concept may be understood, more abstractly, as appealing to what Dworkin terms "vague" notions, such as legality and equality.[38] Here the guidance provided by the framers of a constitution is much less than in the first instance, and it becomes the role of the Court to "revise these principles from time to time in the light of what seems to the Court fresh moral insight."[39] The conceptions that are derived from concepts thus understood represent the specific applications of modernized principles. This differs significantly from the first interpretation, where concepts, while perhaps broadly designed, are not vague in the sense that their essential meaning is discernible only in the light of fresh moral insight. Equality, for example, is indeed a vague concept, the meaning of which can be shaped to secure very different goals. For this reason it could not, standing alone, designate a constitutional concept from the first point of view; for here some greater direction—maybe "of opportunity"—is necessary to ensure that the Court, when applying such concepts, does not do violence to the fundamental principles constitutionalized by the authors of the document.

To illustrate this more concretely we should return to the discussion of the Madisonian system. The protection of rights, it has been suggested, was linked in *The Federalist* to the pursuit of a multiplicity of interests that is the precondition for political freedom. Not all scholars of the constitutional period attribute such high-minded motives to the framers, believing instead that their principal motivation was economic self-aggrandizement, not the protection of individual rights.[40] Both views, the one emphasizing the connection between political and economic liberty and the other stressing elite advantage, implicitly deny the assertion in Justice Holmes's *Lochner* dissent that the Constitution does not embody a particular economic theory.[41] Again, Madison in number 10: "The diversity in the faculties of men, from which the rights of property originate is not less an insuperable obstacle to a uniformity of interests. The protection of these faculties is the first object of government."[42] No mere rhetoric this; the language of the original Constitution clearly evinces this priority.

More specifically, the language of the document, the declared intentions of many of its authors, and the judicial opinions of some of its early interpreters reveal that the protection and preservation of property rights were perceived as perhaps the most important functions government could perform. As Justice Story put it, "The fundamental maxims of a free government seem to require that the rights of personal liberty and private property should be held sacred."[43] Indeed, the liberty associated with private property receives special textual recognition in the unamended Constitution (for example, Article I Section 10's prohibition against state impairment of the obligation of contracts), which suggests that economic liberty could easily lay claim to priority status in an eighteenth-century version of the preferred freedom doctrine. What is also suggested, in the language of number 10, is that while protecting the diverse faculties of men is essential to constitutional design, private property is an, if not *the*, essential good to be derived from such diversity. The "first object of government" is the protection of "diversity in the faculties of men"; this objective, however, must be seen as instrumental to the attainment of the end made possible by such diversity. Whether this end is to be described as political freedom or private property per se, property rights are ultimately decisive in assessing the framers' designs.

It is fair to say, then, that a broad agreement between opposing schools of thought would not be difficult to assemble on the following proposition: that some version of a right of property would have to be included on any list of liberties deemed essential by the framers of the Constitution. Certainly such a right is to be taken seriously. Yet, as several reviewers of Dworkin's work have correctly noted, it is a right to which Dworkin attaches only slight importance;[44] indeed, there is reason to interpret his somewhat elusive comments on the subject as affirming the nonexistence of a property right. "What can be said," he asks, "on the general theory of rights I offer, for any particular right of property?"[45] His answer proceeds by way of indicating how the curtailment of this right does not offend the principle of equal concern and respect (which we will look at later), and thus "the alleged right does not exist; in any case there can be no inconsistency in denying that it exists while warmly defending a right to other liberties."[46] Among the latter are the "distinct rights to certain liberties like the liberty of free expression and of free choice in personal and sexual relations."[47]

This is not the place to debate the preferred status of these rights, so for the purposes of the present argument let us assume that most people accept that justice in our contemporary political and social setting comports with Dworkin's priority preference (although in reality this acceptance cannot be assumed). Let us also assume that if the preferred rights are to enjoy the status of constitutional guarantees, they must be conceptually derived from some constitutional principle for, in both cases, the freedom of expression (which is not synonymous with speech) and the freedom of choice in personal and sexual relations are not grounded explicitly in the text of the document. For example, we might say, following Dworkin, that the right to freedom of choice in sexual relations (a right explored at great length in Richards's work), though not one of the rights acknowledged at the time by the framers, is nevertheless derivable from a more general concept that they constitutionalized.

Now it would seem from the concept/conception distinction (in both formulations) that two things follow. First, concepts (that is, general principles) are ultimately more fundamental than conceptions; and second, conceptions sanctified by the framers themselves, and still demanded by basic concepts, are, *at a minimum*, the equal in importance of conceptions more recently derived. The right of property is either, as Beard intimated, a constitutional concept that in itself provides the individual with trumping power to defend against intrusions upon something morally beyond the reach of popular majorities, or it is a conceptually based right that is specifically guaranteed to uphold the principle of political freedom (that is, the claim of *Federalist* number 10). In either case it is a right to be taken at least as seriously as those rights, unknown to the framers, but arguably consistent with general principles to which they adhered. Since Dworkin has not attempted to dispute the contemporary validity of the Madisonian argument, he is not justified in failing to recognize the right of property. This does not mean that the scope and substance of property rights requires judicial enforcement of conceptions contemporaneous with Madison's time; it does mean that there *is* an "inconsistency in denying that it exists while warmly defending a right to other liberties."

The point of all of this is not to chide Dworkin for being insufficiently respectful of private property or free enterprise. It is, rather, to suggest that the concept/conception distinction, at least as it functions in the liberal theory of law, offers a way of selectively ignoring original intent without blatantly appearing to do so. It allows one to inject one's own moral philosophy into the Constitution without abandoning a claim of textual fidelity.[48] It therefore provides grist for the scholarly mills of those who, like Raoul Berger, seek to confine constitutional interpretation to the narrowest textually grounded meanings and read the document as if it were a business contract.

Rights and Intentions

According to John Marshall,

> [I]ndividuals do not derive from government their right to contract, but bring that right with them into society. . . . This results from the right which every man retains, to acquire property, to dispose of that property according to his own judgment, and to pledge himself for a future act. These rights are not given by society, but are brought into it.[49]

Marshall's observation bears directly on the question of the derivation of rights. His is the classical natural rights position; rights are not a matter of societal determination but inhere in the nature of man. In his project of effecting a fusion between moral and constitutional theory, Dworkin fundamentally transforms this older understanding.

Nowhere is this better illustrated than in Dworkin's treatment of original intent, a treatment that makes clear what was only implicit in the consideration of property: conceptions represent specific applications of constitutional concepts or principles reflecting contemporary

currents in moral theory, rather than embodying permanent principles of justice mandated by the framers (who, for Marshall, have
constitutionalized preexisting natural rights). Initially Dworkin argues that "Judges cannot decide what the pertinent intention of the
Framers was . . . unless they make substantive political decisions of
just the sort the proponents of intention or process think judges
should not make."[50] And later he writes that

> Most of the delegates and congressmen who voted for the "broad"
> provisions of the Constitution probably did not have an interpretive
> intention that favored concrete intentions. There is no reason to sup-
> pose they thought that congressmen and state legislators should be
> guided by their, the framers', conceptions of due process or equality or
> cruelty, right or wrong.[51]

But what of the concepts? What interpretive rules apply to the
principles themselves?

"There is no stubborn fact of the matter—no 'real' intention fixed
in history independent of our opinions about proper legal or constitutional practice—against which the conceptions we construct can be
tested for accuracy."[52] Nothing, then, is fixed "against which" the
"conceptions we construct" are to be measured. In other words, the
concepts themselves are indeterminate (that is, to be determined by
judges or scholars), and the framers' views are not binding upon us.
Yet, unlike some who candidly disavow the notion of original intent,[53]
Dworkin retains the term while emptying it of any operational meaning. To wit: "there is no such thing as the intention of the framers
wanting to be discovered, even in principle. There is only some such
thing waiting to be invented."[54]

These comments suggest that the issue is not simply one of distinguishing between the discrete, immediate expectations of the framers
and the core principles of political justice to which they were committed. Since judges are invited to repudiate the framers on "a complex
issue of political theory," they thereby wield the authority to originate
the very concepts from which subsequent conceptions derive.[55] In
view of this position on original intent, one might wonder how
Dworkin can insistently exclude judicial discretion from the legitimate
realm of constitutional interpretation. Of course, the skeptic of
founding purposes will maintain that much, if not all, judicial use of
intent is necessarily discretionary, in that, according to this view,
intention is an elusive and largely unascertainable thing. This, however, goes well beyond Dworkin's position on these matters. In his
case, the denial of discretion, when placed beside the reflections on
framers' intent, clarifies the issue that has intrigued some scholars as
to whether or not Dworkin is a positivist.[56] His critique of Hart's

positivism effectively demonstrates the problems of separating law and morality; yet ultimately what the Constitution *is* on a specific question must be determined through reference to reigning moral theory. The Constitution is *not* what the judges say it is—thus no judicial discretion—but neither is it necessarily what the framers said it was. Hart's legal positivist follows the rules and, barring the occasional hard case, avoids discretionary decisions. Dworkin's moral positivist follows legal rules and the principles of contemporary moral philosophy; thus, even when confronted with the hard case, he or she can provide nondiscretionary, that is, nonidiosyncratic, answers.

> The constitution makes our conventional political morality relevant to the question of validity; any statute that appears to compromise that morality raises constitutional questions, and if the compromise is serious, the constitutional doubts are serious also.[57]

Dworkin's constitutional theory has a positivistic ring to it to the extent that the substance of constitutional law follows the dictates of conventional political morality; it has an antipositivistic ring to it to the extent that adjudication is limited by the interpretive parameters set by this morality.

For a contrast, it is illuminating to see what Joseph Story had to say in his *Commentaries* on roughly the same subject. Story is important, first because he was perhaps the foremost constitutional scholar of his generation, and second because his views reflect those of his colleague on the Court John Marshall. Marshall had written in *Ogden* v. *Saunders* that

> the intentions of the instrument must prevail; that this intention must be collected from its words; that its words are to be understood in that sense in which they are generally used by those for whom the instrument was intended; that its provisions are neither to be restricted into insignificance, nor extended to objects not comprehended in them, nor contemplated by its framers.[58]

For our purposes the words requiring closest attention are "those for whom the instrument was intended." By the most expansive interpretation this phrase refers to the people at any given time, for the document was clearly intended to serve the needs of future generations. Might this not be compatible with Dworkin's perceptions that the intention of the framers is not something to be discovered but invented? Thus we might say in this vein that in the late twentieth century the Constitution was intended for the people of this time, who are then free to provide the general words of the instrument with a meaning reflective of their needs, sentiments, philosophical orthodoxy, and so on. The Constitution is "the constitution of those living under it."[59] Should it not be interpreted to advance the vision of justice animated by the best thought of our day?

Story shows that this expansive rendering does violence to the rules of interpretation to which both he and Marshall were committed. He is not unrealistic about original intent: "It is not to be presumed, that, even in the convention, which framed the constitution . . . the clauses were always understood in the same sense, or had precisely the same extent of operation."[60] Nor is he inclined to recommend a policy of narrow interpretivism: "[N]o presumption of an intention to use the words [of the Constitution] in the most restricted sense necessarily arises."[61] He argues, however:

> Temporary delusions, prejudices, excitements, and objects have irresistible influence in mere questions of policy. And the policy of one age may ill suit the wishes, or the policy of another. The constitution is not to be subject to such fluctuations. It is to have a fixed, uniform, permanent construction. It should be, so far at least as human infirmity will allow, not dependent upon the passions or parties of particular times, but the same yesterday, to-day, and for ever.[62]

Dworkin would doubtless agree with Story's treatment of "mere questions of policy," the trumping power of rights (as grounded in principle) emerging from just such an understanding. For Story, however, it is not just utilitarian policy that is subject to "temporary delusions," and thus the fluctuations to which the Constitution may be subject implies no distinction between principle and policy. "[T]he rage of theorists to make constitutions a vehicle for the conveyance of their own . . . visionary aphorisms of government, requires to be guarded against with the most unceasing vigilance."[63] Story's rules of constitutional interpretation make quite clear that the way to guard against this threat is through scrupulous judicial fidelity to original intent. "When it is constitutionally altered, then and not until then, are the judges at liberty to disregard its original injunctions."[64] The Constitution is "not to be so construed, as to subvert the obvious objects, for which [it was] made; or to lead to results wholly beside the apparent intentions of those, who framed [it]."[65]

That these intentions are not always readily apparent is not an insight generated only recently. Story, as cited above, was aware of the magnitude of the problem. While insisting that contemporary history and contemporary interpretation would aid in the development of just conclusions,[66] he argues that more would be necessary. "In construing the Constitution of the United States, we are, in the first instance, to consider, what are its nature and objects, its scope and design, as apparent from the structure of the instrument, viewed as a whole, and also viewed in its component parts."[67] In other words, as

Charles L. Black and others have contended, inferences from structure assist in providing meaning to the text.[68] Ralph K. Winter has this in mind in arguing that "the court must seek to extrapolate from all the data the core principles of government underlying the provision and to elaborate those principles in a case-by-case process of adjudication."[69] If, then, an immediate expectation of the framers can be shown over time to be incompatible with *the framers'* own core principles, then and only then is a reversal of expectation legitimate. It should follow that if these principles are to be invented rather than discovered, then there would have to be a heavy presumption against any such reversal. Or, to put it slightly differently, if the intentions of the framers in regard to underlying principle are not ascertainable, then the judiciary should not innovate upon their, the framers', immediate expectations. Further, the immediate expectations of the framers cannot be ignored in extrapolating the essence of the core principles.

For example, the Fourteenth Amendment, according to many, reveals a clear legislative history to the effect that the elimination of segregated education, and segregation in general, was not among the objects of its framers. Michael Perry, for one, argues that unless one adopts a functional justification for noninterpretive review (as he does), this history means that decisions of the Court striking down segregation (including *Brown* v. *Board of Education*) are necessarily illegitimate.[70] Winter, on the other hand, seeking to defend interpretivism against the policy implications of noninterpretive review, functional or otherwise, draws a different conclusion.

> The immediate expectations of the Framers [of the Fourteenth Amendment] had been shown over time and in practice in the Court's own records to be quite inconsistent with the basic theory of the "equal protection" clause. For that reason, they had to be overridden.[71]

In what sense can this be viewed as anything but a repudiation of original intent; and moreover, how is it distinguishable from Dworkin's solution?

Two facts are initially important. First, the immediate expectations of the framers surely included the elevation in status of the black race, relative to the white race, as it emerged from the shackles of slavery. That this may have meant constitutionalizing only the protections of the Civil Rights Act of 1866, rather than full-fledged political and social equality, does not in itself answer the question of the nature of the framers' underlying principle. Second, the framers chose not to use the specific language of the Civil Rights Act, choosing instead the general language of Section 1 of the Amendment. If it is the function of the Court to determine original intent, then it must be proper for it to study carefully the historical context in which that intent expressed itself. In the case of the Fourteenth Amendment this means noting the obvious impact of institutionalized racism on both white attitudes and black preparedness to compete within a color-blind society. But conditions surely change, and what might have been an unrealistic expectation immediately after the abolition of slavery becomes quite realistic two or three generations later. No additional amendment to the Constitution is necessary, because nothing in the *language* of the Fourteenth Amendment precludes incorporation of a wider area of guaranteed protection.[72] And if the principled intention of the framers was to enhance the status of blacks vis-à-vis whites, then it seems consistent with such an objective for the judiciary to acknowledge changing sociopolitical realities as it goes about its business of constitutional interpretation. In any case, this is quite different from what Dworkin does, which is to define his concepts at such a high level of abstraction (and without historical verification) as to permit the substitution of a moral philosophy transcending both immediate expectations as to factual application *and* immediate intent as to the substance of principle.

Thus, the framers of the Fourteenth Amendment sought to prevent the relegalization of black people to the status of non-citizenship or only partial citizenship. They themselves did not determine that separation per se was a denial of equal legal capacity or full citizenship; but we, with the advantage of hindsight, having watched the institutionalization of Jim Crow and the development of dual school systems, see that separation is not compatible with the specific objectives of the framers, and therefore we abolish it on *their* authority. The legitimacy of interpretive innovation is to a significant degree determined by the level of specificity with which the judicial inquiry is begun.

In Chapter 6 we will examine Lincoln's theory of constitutional aspiration, which holds, among other things, that the founders anticipated, on the basis of practical considerations, delayed enforcement of rights that they intended ultimately to apply to all. Alexander Bickel's enquiry into the original understanding of the Fourteenth Amendment led him to see considerable merit in the argument that the framers of this amendment "emulated the technique of the original framers, who were also responsible to an electorate only partly receptive to the fullness of their principles, and who similarly avoided the explicit grant of some powers without foreclosing their future assumption."[73] For those who must always remember that it is, after all, a Constitution they are expounding, this intention carries a reminder that constitutional interpretation occasionally involves, or at least ought to, an element of aspirational striving—toward ends established and circumscribed by the specific purposes of the document's authors.

III. Conclusion

To highlight the transvaluative character of the recent jurisprudential efforts to apply contemporary liberal theory to constitutional law, a glance at Dworkin's essay on "Liberalism" is instructive. In it he makes a number of useful distinctions that clarify contemporary currents in American political thought. His object is to show that the "liberal conception of equality is a principle of political organization that is required by justice."[74] The argument is wholly consonant with the thesis in *Taking Rights Seriously*. It is, therefore, fair to say that the liberal conception of equality is essential to the liberal theory of law. At the root of this conception is the abstract right to equal concern and respect, which is also "understood to be the fundamental concept of Rawls's deep theory."[75] To guarantee this right, government is obligated to treat all its citizens *as equals*; that is, it must not allow differences of individual worth to determine the distribution of goods and opportunities.[76]

This is the principle Dworkin contends should form the basis for the Court's pronouncements on the people's rights under our constitutional system.[77] What does it require?

> The liberal . . . finds the market defective principally because it allows morally irrelevant differences, like differences in talent, to affect distribution, and he therefore considers that those who have less talent, as the market judges talent, have a right to some form of redistribution in the name of justice.[78]

The conservative, on the other hand, wishes to protect the unequal distribution of goods that may result from differential talent in the population by appealing to the "idea of rights to property," distinguishable, according to Dworkin, from the "liberal's civil rights."[79] To be sure, the liberal accepts some right to property—that degree of personal sovereignty essential to dignity—but rejects unlimited dominion over acquisition attributable to the special talents of the beneficiary, or what Rawls calls "the accidents of natural endowment."[80]

These special talents or accidental attributes are arbitrary from the moral point of view of modern liberal equality, and consequently represent threats to constitutionally protected rights that the judiciary is obliged to enforce.[81] No longer is the demand for rights a demand asserted against the arbitrary action of the state, but instead a claim upon the state to provide substantial material equality. Perceiving arbitrariness in this way, governmental action becomes a matter not of policy but of right or principle. Indeed, Dworkin's policy-principle distinction is useful here to summarize the difference between the old liberal constitutionalism and the new. The earlier variant permitted, within rather broad limits, governmental *policies* designed to advance a particular vision of social justice. Failure to do so did not necessarily cause anyone's rights to be encroached upon. The later interpretation requires a *principled* commitment to a particular vision of social justice, which, if left unattended, mandated judicial redress of arbitrarily inflicted wrongs. The innovation of the liberal theory of law lies not in its call for judicial activism, but rather in its deployment of a moral theory that ensures that there will be more judicial activism.

What is new in all of this is not the "fusion of constitutional law and moral theory" effected by Dworkin's jurisprudence; the fusion of natural law theory and early constitutional law is, after all, an oft-told tale.[82] What is innovative is the fusion of constitutional law and *contemporary* moral theory to legitimate an activist judicial role in enforcing the modern liberal rights agenda. This may be seen more clearly if, in conclusion, we consider our most important statement of rights—the Declaration of Independence.

As we have seen in the previous chapter, Morton White has shown that implicit in the language changes from Jefferson's rough draft to the final version of the Declaration are a number of important substantive changes. Perhaps the most significant is the one occurring after the listing of the famous trio of rights—life, liberty, and the pursuit of happiness. Recall that the rough draft reads: "that to secure these ends governments are instituted among men, deriving their just powers from the consent of the governed," whereas in the final version "ends" is replaced by "rights." White's argument was that the fundamental purpose of government changes from one of "aid[ing] and abet[ting] men in attaining ends proposed by God" to that of "making secure rights which have been given by God."[83] Or more simply, the change is from prescribing what government must do, to mandating what it cannot do.

When Dworkin insists on "taking rights seriously," he is in effect resurrecting Jefferson's rough draft and applying it to constitutional interpretation. The fundamental right to "equality of concern and respect," from which are derived such liberties as the freedom to choose a personal lifestyle, permits one to constitutionalize all the guarantees welcomed by the progressive-minded contemporary academic. To the extent that government fails to secure the *ends*, or results, flowing from this one basic right, the Court has the obligation to rectify the injustice. In this way does the transvaluation of liberal constitutionalism lead to the transformation of institutional function and responsibility.

CHAPTER 4

Hamilton, Positivism, and the Constitution: Judicial Discretion Reconsidered

THE TRANSVALUATION OF the Constitution has predictably aroused considerable concern. "We are entering," one noted judge and legal scholar has recently observed, "a period in which our legal culture and constitutional law may be transformed, with even more power accruing to judges than is presently the case."[1] But this, according to Robert Bork, is only part of the problem. There is also "the capacity of ideas that originate outside the Constitution to influence judges, usually without their being aware of it, so that those ideas are elevated to constitutional doctrine."[2] This, then, raises the question: "Why should constitutional law constantly be catching colds from the intellectual fevers of the general society?"[3]

The answer, Judge Bork believes, has largely to do with a general weakness of the law—the absence of a theoretical core that could provide intellectual resistance to outside influences, such as the currently fashionable moral philosophy found in today's law schools. Constitutional law, in particular, is extremely vulnerable to such influences; its frail intellectual structure provides an easy target for those seeking to place the constitutional imprimatur upon their own abstract moral commitments. Bork notes that "constitutional law has very little theory of its own and hence is almost pathologically lacking in immune defenses against the intellectual fevers of the larger society."[4]

Needless to say, Judge Bork is not content to sit idly by watching the Constitution succumb to infection. Judges must come to understand that the health of the Constitution depends upon their appreciation of the nontheoretical nature of the document. Thus, for example, our constitutional liberties "do not rest upon any general theory."[5] If, in other words, we accept the patient's absence of a theoretical core as a given, then that fact will not, in the end, facilitate the demise of the Constitution. The most effective medicine for the ills produced by an invasion of abstract moral theory is a commitment to seeing the Constitution as congenitally antagonistic to moral theory of any kind. Such is the commitment that one encounters in the constitutional scholarship of Raoul Berger.

Berger's writings possess two exceptional characteristics. They have the ability to attract the attention of the scholarly community as well as the general public. Also, they have a refreshing competence for providing new insights into subjects that have received ample, and seemingly exhaustive, scholarly investigation. In the process, Berger's detailed, meticulous examinations of original intent have a way of disturbing the most conventional of wisdoms of those engaged in legal research and legal practice. Among his recent works, *Government by Judiciary*[6] has evoked the strongest reactions.

This chapter will ignore what has aroused the greatest controversy concerning Berger's book—the author's contention that the Fourteenth Amendment has been transformed by the judiciary, in clear violation of the intentions of the amendment's architects, into a broad grant of authority for judicial policy innovation. It will focus upon Part II of Berger's study, where the author seeks to establish the true character of the Constitution and the consequent role that was prescribed for its official interpreters. It will argue that Berger's demonstration is only partly successful, and that, in particular, his portrayal of the Constitution as a positivistic legal document is quite misleading.

One preliminary caveat is in order. This chapter makes no claim to present a comprehensive response to the important issues raised in Berger's account. Rather, it will have as its specific focus the use to which Berger puts the writings of Alexander Hamilton in establishing the character of the prevailing constitutional jurisprudence of the founding period. Hamilton, of course, is for us a key figure; his defense of judicial review and the federal judiciary provides us with some of our keenest insights into the nature of the Constitution and the role of the Supreme Court. These insights, it will be contended, suggest that Berger is correct in his depiction of the misconstructions of modern realist commentators on the Constitution and the role of the Supreme Court, but seriously flawed in his own account of the theoretical underpinings of constitutional interpretation. He (and Bork) are appropriately concerned about judicial policy making through the application of principles of abstract moral theory. They err, however, in their denial of a core theory in the Constitution.

I. "The Rule of Law"

"For the Framers [the rule of law] was the essence of constitutional government."[7] Berger strongly affirms the framers' commitment, the essence of which was the obligation of government officials to stay within the constitutionally prescribed limits of their respective institutions. As applied to the courts this means that judges transgress the rule of law whenever they undertake to determine policy instead of adhering strictly to their assigned task, the policing of constitutional boundaries. Unlike those scholars whose rejection of "judicial legislation" can be traced to serious doubts about the legitimacy of judicial review, Berger harbors no uncertainty concerning the conformity of judicial review to the intentions of the founding fathers. But "judicial participation in legislative policymaking was unmistakably excluded."[8] Judicial review? Most assuredly yes. In the course of exercising this role, however, "the Justices' value choices may not displace those of the Framers."[9] Their task is a narrow, if important, one. They blatantly abuse their authority if they "revise the Constitution in the interests of 'justice.' "[10]

Berger makes it clear, however, that he is no fair-weather strict constructionist. For example, both Justice Frankfurter and Justice Black, who in different ways came to be identified with judicial self-restraint, are criticized by Berger for their partial adherence to appropriate norms of constitutional adjudication. Frankfurter's self-restraint grew out of a majoritarian deference to popularly based institutions, whereas Black's was grounded in a commitment to literalism in the interpretation of the constitutional text. Yet Berger says of Black that his record of "writing [his] predilections into the Constitution will long be unsurpassed."[11] He is more satisfied with Justice Frankfurter's record in this regard, but he finds the justice's "finely tuned antennae for ascertaining the inarticulate sentiments of the people" an unwarranted departure from the Constitution.[12] Berger, though, is closer to Black in his constitutional jurisprudence, although it is likely that he would have voted more often with Frankfurter if all three had sat together on the Court. Black also vigorously upheld the continuing sway of original intent, and while his reading of such intent was frequently erroneous (as, for example, in the case of the Fourteenth Amendment), he nevertheless dedicated himself in principle to the exclusion of sources of constitutional interpretation unrelated to the specific words of a written constitution. His jurisprudential credo could be summarized in the words of Jefferson, words that Berger is fond of quoting: "Our peculiar security is the possession of a written Constitution. Let us not make it a blank paper by construction."[13]

More specifically, Berger can be said to share Justice Black's contempt for the application of natural law precepts in constitutional interpretation. In the famous case of *Adamson* v. *California*, it was Black who urged, in pointed reference to the opinion of Justice Frankfurter, an abandonment of natural law, calling it "an incongruous excrescence on our Constitution."[14] Berger and Black are in complete agreement that resorting to natural law (or rights) notions enables the Court to free itself from the limits of a written Constitution.[15] Berger's scholarship, however, takes him well beyond Black's occasional critical remarks. His research leads him to conclude that the framers' support of the rule of law required that they separate natural law principles from the task of constitutional adjudication.

This is the contention that concerns us here. Indeed, it is Berger who quite properly challenges his readers: "proponents of 'natural law' must explain why the Founders, who manifestly excluded the judiciary from policymaking, who distrusted judicial discretion, even denied its exercise, could leave the barn door wide to unlimited discretion under natural law."[16] According to Berger, "the Founders were deeply committed to positivism, as is attested by their resort to written constitutions—positive law."[17] There is then, in this view, a necessary connection between positive law and positivistic jurisprudence. One who is dedicated to the first must also subscribe to the second. Written limits on power are not worth the paper they are printed on if they are enforced by judges who indulge in appeals to principles not explicitly provided for in the written document. Berger's key jurisprudential assumption is provocative and controversial, for there have always been scholars who would eagerly accept the virtues of positive law while concurrently rejecting the precepts of philosophical positivism. They would insist upon the binding character of written law with its attendant possibility for an ordered society, and also require that for such a society to be well ordered and thus legally obligating, its positive law must embody certain principles of justice derivable from nature.

John Austin's classic formulation of legal positivism—"The existence of law is one thing; its merit or demerit is another"[18]—would appear for Berger adequately to state the position of the founders. He portrays them as positivists who urged a strict separation of law from ethics and thus an identification of all positive law with justice. Not for them was there to be any theory of law that was grounded in a priori speculation, and that posited the idea of higher law transcending the world of empirical reality, from which objective, rational standards of justice could be derived. This is easily demonstrated, according to Berger, by reference to the writings of Alexander Hamilton, in particular his teaching in *The Federalist*.

II. "Neither Force nor Will"

To *will* something is to make a determination by an act of choice. Thus, Hamilton's famous statement that the judiciary "may truly be said to have neither FORCE nor WILL, but merely judgment"[19] is rightly interpreted by Berger to mean that judges with the power of judicial review were not intended to have discretion in matters related to policy-making. Those seeking inspiration from Charles Evans Hughes's dictum that "the Constitution is what the Supreme Court says it is"[20] will find no support for such a view in Hamilton. In this connection Berger calls attention to Hamilton's observation in *Federalist* number 81 that Congress had the authority to impeach members of the judiciary for "a series of deliberate usurpations on the authority of the legislature."[21] And as our leading student of impeachment, he reminds us that "these were no idle words, for both the English and the founders regarded 'usurpation' or subversion of the Constitution as the most heinous of impeachable offenses."[22]

If, then, the framers were careful to limit (Berger might say deny) judicial discretion, there still remains the question of what constitutes discretion. The distinction between "will" and "judgment" indicates that it is the abuse of discretion, rather than discretion per se, that Hamilton meant to delegitimate. Berger argues that the stricture against "usurpation" would be robbed of its force if judges were empowered "to enforce the wide-open spaces of 'natural law.' "[23] He agrees with Robert Cover that the term "constitutional positivism" describes the jurisprudential commitment of men such as Hamilton. Thus, Hamilton's denial of judicial will is consistent with "the tradition of positivism," a tradition that, according to Cover, "meant the judge ought to be will-less."[24] A judge who is *willful* is one who introduces an element of personal preference into his adjudication. Accordingly, in the view of Cover and Berger, judicial appeals to natural law principles were deemed impermissible as unwarranted intrusion of personal predilection upon the original will of the people, expressed in a written constitution.

Here, however, we encounter our first difficulty. The framers' commitment to constitutional positivism can be substantiated only if one antinomy—natural law/written constitution—and one identification—natural law = will—are established. If, on the other hand, natural law (natural rights would be more accurate) was viewed by the framers as being embodied *in* the Constitution, then it does not follow any longer that judges who appeal to such principles in the course of constitutional interpretation are necessarily abusing their discretion by acting willfully (to say nothing of committing an impeachable offense). Berger, who is devoted to the Constitution, is in essential agreement with those in our history who once denounced the document as a covenant with hell, in that both he and these abolitionists imagine judges appealing from the Constitution *to* higher law precepts of natural right. To be sure, the abolitionists would not have concurred in the perception of the subjective, idiosyncratic character of these precepts. They would have differed with Berger over the role of judges in a constitutional government while agreeing with his depiction of a positivistic constitution.

To support his argument about discretion, and in particular that the idea that judges could make law as an instrument of social change was alien to the thinking of the constitutional period, Berger calls our attention to the essay by Morton J. Horwitz (discussed earlier in the context of Pound's jurisprudence). Horwitz argued that in the eighteenth century, American common law rules were not regarded as instruments of legal change, and that when such change transpired, it was generally produced through legislation.[25] It was only in the early nineteenth century that common law judges began to assume some importance in directing the course of social change by framing doctrines in light of self-conscious consideration of social and economic policy.[26] The evidence Horwitz marshals lends substantial weight to Berger's observation that the original intent was to deny judges any discretion to innovate upon preexisting law.

It is, however, Horwitz's analysis of the factors accounting for the modest role expected of judges in the process of social change that is especially important here. Judges were not to exercise discretion in the application of common law rules because those rules were perceived as derivative from natural principles of justice.[27] They were, therefore, to be discovered, not made. Statutes, on the other hand, were acts of will, to be exercised within the legitimate discretion of the legislature.

> Where common law rules were conceived of as "*founded in principles, that are permanent*; uniform *and universal*," and where common law and natural law were interchangeably defined as "the Law which every Man has implanted in him," jurists would be unlikely to think of the common law as deriving its legitimacy from the will of the lawmaker.[28]

Horwitz's argument, then, amounts to this. The early denial of judicial discretion is directly traceable to the prevailing view concerning the natural law basis of common law doctrines. Judges could have no discretion with regard to these doctrines because they were permanent and immutable, unlike the will of individual judges. The change to instrumentalism in the nineteenth century coincided with a change in the prevailing attitude toward the common law. The new perception of the common law saw it as essentially an instrument of will, no longer embodying an eternal set of principles derivative from natural right.[29] Unless Berger is prepared to reject Horwitz's analysis of the underlying assumptions of the denial of judicial discretion (while accepting the demonstration of its denial), he cannot substantiate inferences of constitutional positivism from any intention to reject the appropriateness of willful adjudication.[30]

If we move from common law to constitutional law, it is instructive to consider for a moment this question of natural rights and judicial discretion in the work of that great Hamiltonian judge, John Marshall. Marshall, following Hamilton, insisted that "Courts are mere instruments of the law and can will nothing."[31] For those who see Marshall's judicial accomplishments as the realization of the chief justice's own particular political ideals, this denial of political discretion amounts to just so much rhetoric. Indeed, Marshall is a favorite example of legal realists in their demonstrations of the subjectivity that underlies all constitutional adjudication.[32] On the other hand, Marshall's jurisprudence has been viewed as embracing a "particular kind of politics," that of Lockean principles of political economy.[33] In this view, Marshall's interpretation of the fundamental law was not simply a matter of personal predilection but a commitment to what the chief justice held to be true—that is, objective, political perspective. Thus, in following the law, judicial discretion is guided by appropriate "general principles of law." There is no abuse of discretion here, for these principles of law are an integral part of the legal system. Moreover, to the extent that they represent commitments immanent within the document (rather than, as in Dworkin, an importation of contemporary modern philosophy), judges applying them exercise judgment, not will.

Berger, who of course is not a legal realist, goes only so far as to say that Marshall's allegience to the doctrine of natural law is debatable.[34] He seems comfortable with Justice Frankfurter's opinion that Marshall's references to natural law were "not much more that mere literary garniture . . . and not a guiding means for adjudication."[35] It is easy to see why, among other reasons, Berger adopts the position that so closely resembles that of the realists. To ˙view Marshall as having been serious in his commitment to natural right entails the consequence of accepting the judgment of our most important Supreme Court judge that there is no incompatibility between viewing the Constitution as a document embodying principles of natural rights and adhering to a definition of the judicial role as one involving judgment, not will. It might also require a reevaluation of Hamilton's constitutional jurisprudence, since realists and nonrealists alike accept the essential continuity of the two men in matters of constitutional interpretation.[36]

Without seeking finally to resolve the question of Marshall's commitment, an examination of his opinion in the case of *Ogden* v. *Saunders* may shed some light on the issue. It should perhaps be noted that Marshall was here writing in dissent where, it is often observed, a judge is relatively unconstrained in presenting his firmly held belief.

The specific issue before the Court was one involving the obligations of contract, and it is interesting (and perhaps significant to the present discussion) that Marshall's opinion begins with a statement about the judicial role in constitutional interpretation, one to which Professor Berger might give hearty assent. In it he addresses himself to the principles of construction that ought to be applied to the Constitution. These principles, he contends, are well known, having often been declared by the Court on previous occasions. The gist of them is that the intentions of the framers must prevail, that these intentions are to be collected from the words of the document, and that judges must interpret this language in the sense in which it was used by those for whom it was intended.[37]

The intentions of the framers are thus to be accorded the highest possible respect. It is therefore noteworthy when, later in his opinion, Marshall connects these intentions to his interpretation of the constitutional prohibition against states passing "any law impairing the obligation of contracts." He argues that the framers of the Constitution were intimately acquainted with the writings of "learned men, whose treatises on the laws of nations have guided public opinion on the subject of obligation and contract."[38] He then observes that the treatises he has in mind support his interpretation of the contract clause, and further that the framers viewed the subject in question in a like manner, as is clearly revealed by their language. Or, as is elsewhere stated in the opinion, the "obligation is not conferred on contracts by positive law, but is intrinsic."[39] What we know on the subject "evince[s] the ideal of a preexisting intrinsic obligation which human law enforces."[40]

Either Marshall meant what he said or he did not. If he did, then it is difficult to maintain, in the face of the above (and in similar statements in other opinions),[41] that Marshall's jurisprudential sympathies lay in the direction of constitutional positivism. Berger does not specifically say this about Marshall, and yet it is clear that the latter would have disagreed with Berger's characterization of the framers as constitutional positivists. Marshall's explicit opinion on the subject— one that he maintains expresses the sentiments of the framers as well—is that human law (that is, the Constitution) is intended to enforce certain preexisting natural rights. When, therefore, judges interpret the Constitution, they are not necessarily engaged in acts of will in appealing to and expounding these rights in order to reach a judgment in cases coming before them. And they are surely not committing an impeachable offense.

III. "The Spirit of the Constitution"

Marshall's testimony, important as it is, is not as significant as Hamilton's. Berger, rightly troubled by more recent judicial reference to "penumbras formed by emanations,"[42] wishes to dissociate Hamilton from this sort of orientation, and in the process to demonstrate that Hamilton's constitutional theory did not leave room for judicial application of the vagaries of natural law. Quoting from *Federalist* number 81, Berger claims that "Hamilton rejected the argument that the courts were empowered 'to construe the laws according to the *spirit* of the Constitution.' "[43] Then, quoting from *Federalist* number 78, he concludes that this rejection meant that judges were not to "substitute their own pleasure to the constitutional intentions of the legislature."[44] Here, Berger is clearly thinking of judicial application of natural law, for earlier he quotes approvingly from an opinion of Justice Miller in which the justice, in reference to natural law, maintained the inappropriateness of judges setting aside laws because of their "opposition to the spirit of the constitution."[45] The danger, according to Miller, is that this appeal to vague notions of abstract justice would permit judicial substitution of personal policy preference for the decisions of elected representatives. In the same context Berger indicates that Hamilton, referring again to the quote from number 81, repudiated "such obscurantist phrases as 'the spirit of our free institutions.' "[46]

Hamilton, to be sure, might very well have concurred with Justice Miller's reaction to the application of natural rights concepts by some of his colleagues on the Court. We must, however, take heed of Berger's cautionary remarks. "A common historicist fallacy is to import our twentieth century conceptions into the minds of the Founders."[47] If we examine the entire statement from which Berger infers Hamilton's rejection of judicial construction according to the "spirit of the Constitution," his rejection may not appear so categorical.

> There is not a syllable in the plan under consideration, which *directly* empowers the national courts to construe the laws according to the spirit of the constitution, or which gives them any greater latitude in this respect, than may be claimed by the courts of every state. I admit however, that the constitution ought to be the standard of construction for the laws, and that whenever there is an evident opposition, the laws ought to give place to the constitution. But this doctrine is not deducible from any circumstance peculiar to the plan of the convention; but from the general theory of a limited constitution; and as far as it is true, is equally applicable to most, if not to all the state governments.[48]

It should first be noted that Hamilton was here responding to the criticisms directed at the framers' plan for the Supreme Court by the opponents of the Constitution to the effect that "the power of constructing the laws, according to the *spirit* of the constitution, will enable the court to mould them into whatever shape it may think proper; especially as its decisions will not be in any manner subject to the revision or correction of the legislative body."[49] This is a serious charge, and obviously it could not be ignored by the defenders of the Constitution. But consider how careful and narrow is Hamilton's response. He does not say, as Berger would have us believe, that the Court may never construe the laws according to the spirit of the Constitution. Rather, he maintains (and chooses to emphasize) that the Constitution does not *"directly"* grant a power to the Court to invoke the spirit of the Constitution in its construction of the laws. Surely if he had wished to preclude any such invocation he would have omitted *"directly."* Instead, he implies that although the Constitution does not explicitly provide for such a power, it may nevertheless be inferred from the "general theory of a limited constitution." He does not anticipate that this will lead to the abuses projected by the opponents of the Constitution, an argument supported by the experience of the state courts. Moreover, he suggests the occasion where the spirit of the Constitution might well become an appropriate source for judicial construction. He indicates that where there is "an evident opposition" between enacted laws and the Constitution "the laws ought to give place." But as he could well have imagined, not all oppositions were likely to be "evident" from the text of the Constitution; thus it might, on occasion, be appropriate to go beyond the specific words of the Constitution *without* going beyond the Constitution itself. In other words, by appealing to the *spirit* of the Constitution.

It is necessary, however, to avoid stumbling into the historicist's fallacy. Berger's juxtaposition of the eighteenth-century "spirit of the constitution" with Justice Douglas's appeal to "penumbras formed by emanations" could suggest that the two phrases conveyed the same meaning and intent to those who articulated them. But the principles of natural rights, to which the spirit of the Constitution referred, and about which a general agreement existed, are not the penumbral emanations that provide the inspiration for activist-minded judges of today, or for like-minded constitutional theorists. Justice Douglas, after all, was the one judge who joined the dissenting opinion of Justice Black in *Adamson* v. *California*, an opinion that contains what is perhaps the most emphatic repudiation of natural law in the history of the Supreme Court.

Hamilton, on the other hand, as Clinton Rossiter wrote, "believed in the law of nature as a living presence."[50] His writings do not sustain Berger's observation that he repudiated such "obscurantist phrases as 'the spirit of our free institutions.' " For example, in *The Farmer Refuted* (1775), Hamilton wrote: "I will now venture to assert, that I have demonstrated, from the voice of nature, the *spirit* of the British constitution, and the charters of the colonies in general, the absolute non-existence of that parliamentary supremacy for which you contend."[51] In that same work he noted that "All lawyers agree that the *spirit* and *reason* of a law, is one of the principal rules of interpretation."[52] In his *Second Letter from Phocian* (1784) he commented, speaking of constitutions: "If the constitution were even silent on particular points those who are intrusted with its power, would be bound in exercising their discretion to consult and pursue its spirit, and to conform to the dictates of reason and equity."[53] Whether these remarks also represent Hamilton's thoughts about the Constitution created three years later we cannot say. If they do, and we have no reason to think that they do not, we must state it as Hamilton's understanding that judges (assuming they are among those intrusted with constitutional power) would be abusing their authority if they did *not* consult the spirit of the Constitution, which spirit, it is important to add, is informed by the dictates of reason and equity (that is, natural right).

It is worth noting here that Marshall, too, was not reluctant to invoke the spirit of the Constitution in the course of his constitutional adjudication. A review of his most important opinions reveals examples such as the following. In *Cohens* v. *Virginia*: "Will the spirit of the constitution justify this attempt to control its words? We think it will not."[54] And later: "While weighing arguments drawn from the nature of government, and from the general spirit of an instrument . . ."[55] In *Dartmouth College* v. *Woodward* he wrote:

> The case being within the words of the rule, must be within its operation likewise, unless there be something in the literal construction, so obviously absurd or mischievous, or repugnant to the general spirit of the instrument, as to justify those who expound the constitution in making it an exception.[56]

And finally, the oft-quoted line from *McCulloch* v. *Maryland*:

> Let the end be legitimate, let it be within the scope of the Constitution, and all means which are appropriate, which are plainly adapted to that end, which are not prohibited, but consist with the letter and spirit of the Constitution, are constitutional.[57]

Hamilton, like Marshall (and unlike Jefferson) had a fondness for quoting Blackstone. Thus, in *The Farmer Refuted*, he quotes the great English legal authority to this effect: "The first and primary end of human laws, is to maintain and regulate [the] absolute rights of individuals."[58] To be sure, the context of this appeal (and many others like it) was the movement for independence, not the writing or defense of the Constitution. The frequency of the appeal to natural rights understandably declined after independence was achieved. But to deny that these principles of natural rights were significant during the later constitutional period, one would have to assume that their importance in the earlier period was a matter of rhetoric and strategy rather than commitment. Having achieved independence, the Constitution that eventually emerged would accordingly not have as its end the maintenance and regulation of the absolute rights of individuals. It is a widely held article of historical scholarship that, at least during the early revolutionary period, the rights that constitutions were designed to protect were the inalienable rights possessed by all people by virtue of their common humanity. The position of constitutional positivism would therefore deny that a similar understanding prevailed in the minds of the framers of the Constitution in 1787.

Berger indicates that his study of the records of the Federal Convention "uncovered no intimations that natural law would empower judges to rise above the positive limitations of the Constitutions."[59] If, however, the Constitution was intended to *embody* the precepts of natural rights it should not be surprising that no statement exists sanctioning judicial appeal to sources external to the document. A more serious problem involves the silence of the framers in explicitly asserting the natural rights basis of the Constitution. Perhaps this silence reflects a general acceptance of, and acquiescence in, the truth of such an assertion. Or perhaps Edmund Randolph's explanation of why the Preamble—a logical place for this assertion—does not make mention of natural rights theory, is instructive for our purposes:

> A preamble seems proper not for the purpose of designating the ends of government and human politics—This . . . display of theory, however proper in the first formation of state governments, *is* unfit here; since we are not working on the natural rights of men not yet gathered into society, but upon those rights, modified by society, and *interwoven with* what we call the rights of states.[60]

It has, for example, been maintained similarly that the reason why judges, in later constitutional adjudication, were not always explicit in their application of natural rights was that such invocation was rendered superfluous by the implicit invocation of natural rights as a function of the fundamental law.[61] Moreover, since we are dealing with a theory that is not necessarily bound up with any particular constitutional provision but with the document as a whole (the "spirit of the Constitution"), it is not a matter of great surprise that we do not notice the mention of the theory while specific provisions were debated. In 1786, for example, John Adams claimed, in reference to the separation of powers, "It was not so much from attachment by habit to such a plan of power, as from conviction that it was founded in nature and reason, that it was continued."[62] The separation of powers is a structural attribute of the constitutional plan, not something mandated by any specific provision. And yet, if the testimony of John Adams one year before the Constitutional Convention is significant, the principal structural feature of our constitutional government is ultimately rooted in considerations of natural justice.

The anti-Federalist opponents of the Constitution *were* explicit in their references to natural rights doctrine. This was particularly the case in the context of their disappointment over the failure to include a bill of rights. The Federalists responded to the criticism using the same doctrine.[63] In this regard, Hamilton's rejoinder in *Federalist* number 84 is quite interesting. He provides a number of reasons why those concerned with liberty should not fear the Constitution for its omission of a bill of rights. But perhaps his most powerful argument appears, as we have seen in the previous chapter, when he maintains: "The truth is, after all the declamation we have heard, that the Constitution is itself in every rational sense, and to every useful purpose, A BILL OF RIGHTS."[64] Indeed, the unhappy possibility that a positive enumeration of the most fundamental rights would be given insufficient latitude weighed in favor of no enumeration at all. In other words, it can be argued that the natural rights that are to be safeguarded by a specifically enumerated bill of rights are already implicitly protected in the Constitution as a whole. Or, we might say, the proper assurance that liberty is indeed the object of the Constitution may be ascertained by consulting "the spirit of the Constitution."

IV. "The Sciences of Morals and Politics"

Hamilton begins *Federalist* number 31 with a statement that nicely reflects the mind of the eighteenth-century Enlightenment. Although he is not here writing about the judiciary, his remarks may illuminate some of his later reflections on this topic.

> In disquisitions of every kind there are certain primary truths of first principles upon which all subsequent reasonings must depend. These contain an internal evidence, which antecedent to all reflection or combination commends the assent of the mind. Where it produces not this effect, it must proceed either from some defect or disorder in the organs of perception, or from the influence of some strong interest, or passion, or prejudice. Of this nature are the maxims in geometry.[65]

Hamilton then indicates that similar maxims exist in ethics and politics; for example, that the means ought to be proportioned to the end. And finally there are other truths in ethics and politics

> which if they cannot pretend to rank in the class of axioms, are yet such direct inferences from them, and so obvious in themselves, and so agreeable to the natural and unsophisticated dictates of common sense, that they challenge the assent of a sound and unbiased mind, with a degree of force and conviction almost equally irresistible.[66]

It is, however, the case that in the "sciences of morals and politics,"[67] unlike the science of geometry, the truth of these axioms, and the inferences extending from them, are not always accepted. Hamilton insists that the certainty of the principles of moral and political knowledge is equal to that which prevails in mathematics. That this certainty is not always appreciated does not detract from the objective force of the moral and political principles, but only suggests a defect in the reasoner, owing to the triumph of his passions and prejudices. "Men upon too many occasions do not give their own understandings fair play; but yielding to some untoward bias they entangle themselves inwards and confound themselves in subtleties."[68] As we have seen, it is common to see in the writings of this period eloquent encomiums to Newton and Locke, with the scientific ideas of the first directly linked to the political ideas of the latter. Hamilton's suggestion is that while the truths of these two great figures were comparable, the world of Locke is somewhat more turbulent than that of Newton, in the sense that its defining truths are much more susceptible to the passions of men, and thus much less likely to be the basis of reasonable action.

What is necessary, it thus becomes clear, is that the Constitution must establish safeguards against the inevitable tendency of men to destroy or ignore these fundamental truths of morals and politics. Indeed, one could state this as the outstanding challenge confronting the new American science of politics.

The Federalist responds to this challenge in a number of ways. Hamilton's argument in number 78 for the permanent tenure of judicial offices is one familiar response. Such permanence is essential, according to Hamilton (and as noted by numerous commentators), in order to provide the judges with the independence necessary for responsibly interpreting fundamental law. Moreover,

> This independence of the judges is . . . requisite to guard the constitution and the rights of individuals from the effects of those ill humours which the arts of designing men, or the influence of particular conjunctures, sometimes disseminate among the people themselves, and which, though they speedily give place to better information and more deliber-

ate reflection, have a tendency in the meantime to occasion dangerous innovations in the government.[69]

In number 31 he speaks of the "passions and prejudices" that may deflect men away from moral and political truth. In number 78 he calls attention to "those ill humours" from which the Constitution must be guarded. *If* it is the case that the Constitution embodies these political and moral truths (for Hamilton this certainly is so in the case of the specific subject of number 31, the power of taxation); that is to say, if the Constitution *constitutes* testimony to some fundamental truths about human nature and political life, then it would seem to follow that judges are not simply "the bulwarks of a limited constitution against legislative encroachments,"[70] but are also the defenders of the timeless principles of morals and politics implicit in the document.

There is, of course, a big "if" involved in this particular interpretation. We are not, in other words, compelled by logic to accept the initial premise. At best, we can say the circumstantial evidence points in the direction of the premise. To wit: Hamilton's perception of the judges in number 78 as both vehicles for the communication of passionless reason and as mainstays of the fundamental law; his observation in number 31 that the passions may blind men to the truths of politics and ethics, truths that reason clearly demonstrates; and his warnings in number 78 against the ill-humors that reasoned judges must counteract. It is certainly plausible that Hamilton saw the connection between the arguments of the two papers, and that he would have been comfortable with the implication that the Constitution incorporates immutable principles of natural justice within the confines of its positive law.

It is also understandable, in view of our discussion in Chapter 2, why Berger's rejection of such an implication is consonant with broader scientific and intellectual trends. With the ascendance of quantum theory, relativity theory, and non-Euclidean logic, one was no longer safe in assuming an objective reality recognizable to all viewers. Quantum theory introduced notions of arbitrariness and indeterminism into the study of physical phenomena, and relativity theory suggested that how we see the universe depends upon where we see it from, that we simply cannot rely upon evidence within our immediate horizon to absolutize the concepts of space and time. And, needless to say, the attempt to absolutize or generalize the principles of right conduct through the medium of natural law no longer was persuasive. Those political truths that Hamilton saw as "so agreeable to the natural and unsophisticated dictates of common sense" lost all claim to scientific, to say nothing of constitutional, integrity.

V. Conclusion

The narrow focus of this chapter renders dubious and unreliable any sweeping conclusions. Although most scholars would acknowledge the importance of Hamilton in understanding the framers' views on judicial interpretation of the Constitution, he was never delegated by the framers to speak for them in matters of constitutional jurisprudence. So even if our interpretation of Hamilton's thought is persuasive, we would nevertheless have to qualify any conclusions regarding the intent of the founding fathers.

What we are entitled to say is that the alleged constitutional positivism of the authors and ratifiers of the Constitution is not supported by reference to the work of Alexander Hamilton. More specifically, we cannot infer from the framers' faith in a written constitution that they dismissed natural rights as a legitimate source for constitutional interpretation. An appreciation of Berger's warning against the dangers of judicial government does not require an acceptance of his views on the constitutional positivism of the framers. Hamilton's jurisprudential reflections should make us hesitate in equating adjudication that is informed by principles of natural rights with adjudication that is willful and inappropriately discretionary.

They should also make us hesitate in embracing Judge Bork's diagnosis of our constitutional problems. While Bork's analysis is intended to raise the level of our vigilance against the jurisprudential assaults of such as Pound and Dworkin, his argument, like Berger's, displays a rejection of traditional "natural rights" theory similar to those we have already encountered. Thus, for Bork:

> The judge can have nothing to do with any absolute set of truths existing independently and depending upon God or the nature of the universe. If a judge should claim to have access to such a body of truths, to possess a volume of the annotated natural law, we would, quite justifiably, suspect that the source of the revelation was really no more exalted than the judge's viscera. In our system there is no absolute set of truths, to which the term "political truth" can refer.[71]

It is understandable, in view of the radical revisions (amounting to rejections) of traditional natural rights theory undertaken by Pound and Dworkin, why Bork would view with suspicion any judicial deployment of truths dependent on "the nature of the universe." Better to deny the existence of any political truths (even those, presumably, that are "self-evident") than to encourage judges and their academic supporters to pursue their policy agendas under the legitimating banner of universal truth. Bork ultimately adopts a stance of moral skepticism as the only judicial posture consistent with the obligations of neutrality demanded by the Constitution.

This moral skepticism should remind us of Holmes, whose dissent in *Lochner* v. *New York* viewed the Constitution as agnostic on questions of economic philosophy. Bork agrees: "We now regard it as thoroughly old hat, passé and in fact downright tiresome to hear rhetoric about an inherent right to economic freedom or to economic property. We no longer believe that economic rights inhere in the individual because he is an individual."[72] Much like Pound, he suggests that property rights should be recognized "according to judgments of utility."[73] Dworkin, as we have seen, also denies the existence of an inherent right to property, although for him this denial does not (and *may* not) rest upon a utilitarian calculation. That, of course, is an important difference; yet in all three approaches we find a strong repudiation of the Lockean natural rights theory that was one of the sources for important constitutional interpretations of some of our earliest judges, most notably John Marshall.

It is easy to ignore all of this in view of more obvious points of disagreement, such as the fact that most contemporary followers of Pound advocate judicial activism, whereas Bork and Berger endorse judicial restraint. Pound was skeptical of the possibility of developing any absolute standard by which the law can determine the relative weight of the various claims that cry out for recognition. Not so different is Bork's position: "There is no principled way to decide that one man's gratifications are more deserving of respect than another's or that one form of gratification is more worthy than another."[74] This could lead one judge to seek to satisfy all claims and another to withhold all gratifications, each proceeding under the same principle of value-free constitutionalism. In both cases, however, constitutional aspiration, what Hamilton called the "spirit of the Constitution," becomes an object of antiquarian interest, essentially irrelevant to the task of interpretation.

CHAPTER 5

Making Sense of the "Unwritten Constitution"

"I AM PARTICULARLY INDEBTED to Robert Bork, the most effective critic of constitutional policymaking by the Supreme Court."[1] One might, upon encountering such a note of appreciation, imagine its author to be some young interpretivist scholar whose recently published work had been significantly influenced by the teachings of the old master. In fact, however, the debt of gratitude belongs to Michael Perry, perhaps the most emphatic among today's defenders of noninterpretive review and constitutional policy-making. Strange? Not really. For if one is seeking to legitimate an expansive role for the Supreme Court in terms of rights enforcement, there are real incentives to be found in embracing the constitutional analysis of a Robert Bork or a Raoul Berger. What decent person would not first repudiate interpretivism if a commitment to that theory of review required an abandonment of constitutional outcomes widely perceived as politically and socially progressive—including perhaps even *Brown* v. *Board of Education*? Appealing to sources external to the Constitution may not be so distasteful when the alternative of staying within the confines of the written document leads one inevitably to consistently unpleasant results.

This, then, raises the following questions:

> In reviewing laws for constitutionality, should our judges confine themselves to determining whether these laws conflict with norms derived from the written Constitution? Or may they also enforce principles of liberty and justice when the normative content of those principles is not to be found within the four corners of our founding document?[2]

In two oft-cited articles Thomas C. Grey has answered these questions, contending that judges who appeal to sources beyond the written document are acting as the framers wished. The implications of this conclusion are potentially far-reaching. Decisions of the Supreme Court considered questionable because of their lack of grounding in constitutional text might have their legitimacy enhanced if respected scholarly authority placed its imprimatur upon an extratextual or "noninterpretive" jurisprudence. If Grey is right, then free-wheeling judicial review can be justified even by reference to that most conservative of constitutional standards, the framers' intentions. Who then will take seriously the case for principled judicial restraint?

Grey claims that the natural rights tradition of the eighteenth century created a reservoir of legally binding principles that could be drawn upon by judges as an unwritten constitution, supplementary to the written one. Rejecting this approach, scholars such as Berger and Bork have argued that the natural rights tradition is (and was originally perceived to be) irrelevant to constitutional interpretation. This chapter defends an intermediate position: that the written Constitution was meant to embody the natural rights commitments of the framers. Therefore, judicial appeals to "higher law" are not justifiable when they lead to a distinction between written and unwritten constitutions, but they are justifiable insofar as they help explicate and illuminate the written words of the Constitution itself. From this perspective the positivists are correct in their insistence upon the exclusive authority of the written document, but fundamentally misguided in their understanding of the nature of this document, since, as we have seen, the written words do not preclude a natural rights content. Judges who accept the intermediate position stated above will not feel free to invoke ideas of natural justice that are not grounded in the constitutional text. Yet neither will they read that text as if it were a business contract or, worse, as an "unprincipled" document. If the Constitution is a set of rules and procedures, it is so in part because it flows out of a coherent and knowable, not arbitrary or ever-mutable, set of philosophic presuppositions.

At the outset we should note that all scholarly inquiry into the kinds of questions raised here should proceed in humble recognition of the largely circumstantial nature of the evidence at hand. Thus, for example, it is noteworthy (as well as a source of some considerable frustration) that at no time during the convention that framed the Constitution was there ever any mention of what the founders understood to be a jurisprudence fit for the interpretation of their creation. There are, of course, statements at the convention and elsewhere that may be taken to be strongly suggestive of jurisprudential preference, but conclusions based upon them must be qualified by the fact that they may represent only the views of individuals lacking authority to speak on behalf of the collective will that we like to designate original intent. With this caveat, we turn to the "unwritten Constitution."

I. Justice, Constitutionality, and James Wilson

Professor Grey has noted a characteristic American ambivalence: we tend to regard bad laws as unconstitutional, yet we also tend to regard judicial discretion as undemocratic and hence illicit.[3] He refers to this contradiction as the "Aristotelian dialogue that permeates American constitutional law."[4] Grey's side of this dialogue can claim distinguished lineage, "the idea of judicial review on the basis of an unwritten constitution [being] part of the common intellectual heritage of revolutionary Americans."[5]

One of the revolutionaries cited by Grey in this context is James Wilson, whose views command particular respect in light of his reputation as "the most learned and profound legal scholar of his generation,"[6] and whose contributions during the Constitutional Convention were exceeded only by those of James Madison. Wilson belonged to a group of scholar-statesmen—Jefferson and John Adams are others mentioned by Grey—whose legal argumentation on behalf of the binding character of the unwritten fundamental law supplemented the earlier polemics of such activists as Otis, Dulany, and Samuel Adams.[7] Grey is not alone in this judgment; according to Alfons Beitzinger, "The conclusion is not expressly drawn but it is quite evidently implicit in Wilson's reasoning—the judiciary must interpret the Constitution in light of the higher controlling law."[8]

That Wilson shared enthusiastically in the consensus regarding the existence of scientifically based moral principles deducible from immutable principles of natural justice is not in doubt. "The law of nature is immutable, not by the effect of arbitrary disposition, but because it has its foundations in the nature, constitution and mutual relations of men and things."[9] Within the consensus there were, to be sure, important differences. Wilson, as was pointed out in Chapter 2, adhered to the anti-Lockean moral-sense school of thought—but these differences did not overshadow what was ultimately fundamental, that governments are instituted to protect the natural rights of their people. What the connection between these rights and the Constitution was perceived to have been, however, and beyond that, what the intended role of the Supreme Court in this context was, are less clear.

The place to begin is the Constitutional Convention, where the argument for an extra-textual mode of interpretation must initially confront the debate over the so-called revisionary power. Madison's *Notes on the Federal Convention* inform us that on July 21 James Wilson moved that the National Judiciary be associated with the executive in the revisionary power. According to Madison, Wilson then remarked as follows:

> The Judiciary ought to have an opportunity of remonstrating against projected encroachments on the people as well as on themselves. It had been said that the Judges, as expositors of the Laws would have an opportunity of defending their constitutional rights. There was weight

in this observation; but this power of the Judges did not go far enough. Laws may be unjust, . . . may be destructive; and yet may not be so unconstitutional as to justify the Judges in refusing to give them effect. Let them have a share in the Revisionary power, and they will have an opportunity of taking notice of these characters of a law, and of counteracting, by the weight of their opinions the improper views of the Legislature.[10]

Madison himself supported Wilson by arguing that the revisionary power would be "useful to the Community at large as an additional check against a pursuit of those unwise and unjust measures which constituted so great a portion of our calamities."[11] It is interesting that the opposition, which eventually prevailed on this issue, shared in the assessment of the likely impact of the proposal. "It was making the Expositors of the Laws the Legislators," said Elbridge Gerry, "which ought never to be done."[12] And, added Luther Martin:

A knowledge of Mankind, and of Legislative affairs cannot be presumed to belong in a higher degree to the Judges than to the Legislature. And as to the Constitutionality of laws, that point will come before the Judges in their proper official character. In this character they have a negative on the laws. Join them with the Executive in the Revision and they will have a double negative. It is necessary that the Supreme Judiciary should have the confidence of the people. This will soon be lost, if they are employed in the task of remonstrating against popular measures of the Legislature.[13]

These comments are illuminating, if not entirely dispositive of questions concerning the jurisprudential significance of the higher law. Both sides assume the appropriateness of judicial review, which they understand as the authority to nullify legislative enactments that are unconstitutional. But they seem clear that a holding of unconstitutionality (as distinguished from an exercise of the revisionary power) is not to be based upon judicial assessments of the mere wisdom of legislation. The only way we can characterize Wilson, for example, as an advocate of an expansive policy-making judiciary is if we assume that, having lost the battle over the revisionary power, he altered his understanding of the constitutional role of the Supreme Court.

Not entirely clear, however, from Wilson's argument, are his views on a related issue of special concern to us. He indicates that the defense of constitutional rights is a judicial function, but he is not explicit as to whether the "unwritten constitution" is a source of these rights. In this connection a question is raised that goes to the heart of the positivist's interpretation of the Constitution. Wilson says: "Laws may be unjust, may be destructive; and yet may not be so unconstitutional as to justify the Judges in refusing to give them effect." It would matter greatly here if we could substitute the word "unjust," rather than "illegal," for Wilson's "unconstitutional." If we assume the former substitution to be consistent with Wilson's intent, then the sentence would convey the idea that some injustice is tolerable under the Constitution, as long as constitutional rights, which is to say, basic justice, are not threatened. The Court, in other words, cannot (without the revisionary power) guarantee a good society; it can, however, help to prevent a bad or corrupt one. Or to put it differently, if the Constitution were meant to embody the natural rights that government was obliged in theory to protect, then the content of these principles would define the amount of justice that the Court would defend through its power of judicial review. The alternative substitution, on the other hand, would confine the Court to the policing of constitutional boundaries, the securing of justice being at best only peripheral to the task of judging.

Wilson's law lectures provide additional insight into this matter. He addresses himself to a broad range of topics, including the vexatious issue that so preoccupied legal theoreticians during the struggle for independence—whether a legislative enactment contrary to common right and reason is nevertheless valid. Wilson, who was consistently more critical of Blackstone than his fellow framers, takes up the question by focusing on the English legal philosopher's contention (seemingly contradicted elsewhere in the *Commentaries*)[14] that no power existed that could control a parliamentary action contrary to reason. His rejection of this Blackstonian position accounts, in part, for the occasional associations of his name with the concept of an unwritten constitution. If in fact there were a power—the judiciary, according to Wilson—that could control Parliament, Wilson's readers might conclude that the source of this power must be an extra-textual one to which legitimate appeal could be made by judges acting in their official capacity. But a careful reading suggests difficulties in such an interpretation.

Wilson quotes a follower of Blackstone, who happens to be the latter's successor in the Vinerian chair at Oxford: "We must distinguish between right and power; between moral fitness and political authority. We cannot expect that all acts of legislators be ethically perfect, but if their proceedings are to be decided upon by their subject, government and subordination cease."[15] Wilson responds to this assertion by accepting the distinction between right and power, but adding that "I always apprehended, that the use of this distinction was, to show that power, in opposition to right, was divested of every title, not that it was clothed with the strongest title, to obedience."[16] On this premise he finds it shocking to imagine that "a thing manifestly contradictory to common reason" must be upheld by the Court.

Were this the end of the matter, a strong case could be made for Wilson's support of the unwritten constitution. But the specific context for his discussion here is a comparison of the British and American constitutional systems, one that leads him unequivocally to prefer the latter. This preference is attributable, according to Wilson, to the fact that in the United States the legislative authority is controlled by the superior law of the Constitution. All other law, such as the enactments of the legislature, must be deemed inferior, and therefore void when in conflict with the Constitution. Essentially this is the familiar claim of Hamilton's *Federalist* number 78 and *Marbury* v. *Madison*. But, unlike those two arguments, Wilson's lecture is not intended as a defense of judicial review. His purpose rather is to demonstrate the superiority of the American constitutional scheme by explaining how it effectively resolves the dilemma posed by parliamentary supremacy. Thus, the Supreme Court, in upholding the Constitution (and Wilson nowhere suggests he means anything but the written document), provides both a "noble guard against legislative despotism"[17] and a way of avoiding the implications of Blackstone's analysis—that the validity of law is not affected by its being contrary to right reason. By strong implication, then, the only way the Constitution could function in this role is if these principles of reason were themselves implicit in the document. One must, therefore, be cautious in ascribing to Wilson (and to others as well) positions on constitutional interpretation that may have applicability to the British situation, but which are at best anachronistic in the context of American improvements. Nothing, it bears emphasis, pleased Wilson more than that "the principles of our constitutions and governments and laws are materially *better* than the principles and governments and laws of England."[18]

At the conclusion of his comparison of constitutions, Wilson includes an eloquent encomium to the institution of trial by jury, describing it as one of the greatest blessings of liberty. Indeed, its contribution to the basic purpose of government—the securing of rights—is so great that "it should be placed on the most solid and permanent foundation."[19] Thus, it is a mark of the superiority of the American system over the British system that her trial by jury in criminal cases is "constitutional" and not merely "legal," that is, supported by the legislature.[20] Recalling Wilson's comments at the convention, we might infer from this that justice and constitutionality are related concepts, that the Constitution incorporates those attributes of justice essential for the protection of the people's natural rights. Appeals external to the charter are consequently obviated by the deliberate internalization of norms of right conduct.

What this means in the contest of the present Court, and in light of

Grey's concern that the judiciary not retreat from its role as an engine of social justice, is perhaps clearer now. The key distinction is between policy and right, and their connection to justice. The theory of natural rights that shaped much of the political thought of the founding generation represented a departure from traditional natural law theory—for example, the Christian version of Thomas Aquinas—in its minimalist objectives, all ultimately deducible from the right of self-preservation.[21] It provided the conditions for peace but abjured the quest for the good life. That quest, it was assumed, might be taken up individually or collectively as a matter of policy, and the constitutional system was built in anticipation of future efforts to contribute or add to the social justice of the system. Wilson's (and Madison's) statements at the convention are consistent with the observation in the law lectures that "Among all the terrible instruments of arbitrary power, decisions of courts, whetted and guided and impelled by considerations of policy, cut with the keenest edge, and inflict the deepest and most deadly wounds."[22] Considerations of policy may either advance or hinder the quest for justice; they must, however, not intrude upon the domain of the judges, whose guardianship extends to constitutional rights—the necessary but not sufficient condition for social justice. Much later, Justice Frankfurter was to insist repeatedly upon the distinction between constitutionality and wisdom, an insistence that clarified while it obfuscated.[23] Thus, it served as a healthy reminder that the constitutionality of a policy does not signal its desirability. At the same time it perhaps obscured the insight, derivable from Wilson, that the constitutionality of a policy does indeed connote its consistency with those minimum standards of justice that collectively represent a kind of constitutional wisdom.

II. Revolution, Judicial Review, and James Otis

> As to Acts of Parliament, an Act against the Constitution is void: an Act against natural equity is void: and if an Act of Parliament should be made, in the very words of this Petition, it would be void. The Executive Courts must pass such Acts into disuse.[24]

These defiant words of James Otis, taken from his famous argument in the *Writs of Assistance Case*, occupy a prominent place in American history; indeed, to John Adams they initiated the American Revolution.[25] Grey is only slightly less enthusiastic in his appraisal of Otis's arguments. For him, they serve to highlight the distinguished lineage of the unwritten constitution as a source for judicial decision-making. Otis's views were elaborated in his famous 1764 pamphlet, *The Rights of the British Colonies Asserted and Proved*, which, according to

Grey, "suggests not only that legislative authority should be subject to theoretical legal restraints, but also that those restraints should be enforceable in court."[26]

If there is an inflation of Otis' importance in Grey's evaluation of his contribution to our constitutional tradition, it is only very slight, for indeed Otis should be viewed as a figure of substantial significance. But what he ultimately demonstrates is not that our written constitution is supplemented by an unwritten one. Instead, Otis shows the necessity, in a system such as ours, of a written constitution of a particular kind. This interpretation of Otis embraces twin assumptions that have been adverted to in the discussion of Wilson: first, that a written document is compatible with natural rights interpretation; and second, that the appeal to an unwritten constitution in the political context of parliamentary sovereignty (that is, where there is no written constitution) serves as a weak, and probably erroneous, precedent for such an appeal where this political context has been repudiated.

To see how Otis's appeal to the unwritten constitution permits us ultimately to reject such a concept in constitutional adjudication, we begin with a perplexing ambiguity in his famous speech. Constitutional historians have understood Otis' appeal to the English constitution in large measure as an effort to condemn certain acts of Parliament as offensive to the principles of nature that give life to the fundamental law.[27] With this, Grey, of course, agrees. But the relationship of these principles to judicial action does not evoke the same consensus. Grey, for example, interprets Otis as suggesting the enforceability of natural law constraints by courts. Bernard Bailyn, on the other hand, doubts this was his intent:

> Otis did not mean that courts could nullify statutory enactments, but only that the courts, in interpreting statutes in cases that come before them, may indicate their belief that "the Parliament have erred or are mistaken in a matter of fact or right. . . ." Courts, Otis meant, are like public-spirited citizens, who have the obligation "to show [Parliament] the truth," but they have no authority to impose compliance; only Parliament could declare what is and what is not law.[28]

In other words, the courts, precluded from institutional equality by the doctrine of parliamentary sovereignty, could not, as under the later doctrine of judicial review, legally enforce their constitutional objections; they could only voice them publicly and hope that their arguments would be sufficiently compelling to induce change. This assessment comports with the English experience with the fundamental law, which, according to the leading student of the subject, was not connected to the practice of judicial review.[29] In seventeenth-century

England the idea of fundamental law essentially stood for "the principle that politics is subordinate to ethics, and . . . that in the last resort rebellion or revolution may be morally justifiable."[30] Whether or not Otis represents a departure from that tradition is the point at issue between Bailyn and Grey. In condemning the principle of taxation without representation as a violation of "the law of God and nature," did Otis in fact seek *judicial* nullification of the law contravening the unwritten constitution?[31]

Interesting and intriguing as this question is, fortunately it does not need to be resolved here. If Bailyn is correct, it is nevertheless possible that the Americans later borrowed from the tradition of appealing to principles of natural justice and equity, while they were institutionalizing their own unique practice of judicial review. And if Grey's version is correct, it does not follow that the previous assumptions about judicial prerogatives still applied after adoption of a written constitution establishing more or less coequal branches of government. As in judging, so in scholarly commentary about judging: the best precedents come from a factual context that parallels the present one.

Assuming, *arguendo*, that Grey has succeeded in capturing Otis's intent, the fact remains that our earliest judges were functioning in a political-constitutional context fundamentally different from the setting within which Otis delivered his famous sentiments. As Grey astutely notes, "The new practice of establishing a written constitution, drawn up by a special representative convention and ratified by the people, influenced the place of unwritten law in constitutional theory."[32] What the influence was, Grey leaves unaddressed.[33]

Perhaps the most significant contextual difference is the demise of parliamentary sovereignty, although Grey, once again challenging Bailyn, claims that the eighteenth-century theory of legislative supremacy had very little influence in the colonies.[34] This is not to say that the doctrine was unimportant; for even if it failed to persuade the Americans, it certainly shaped their constitutional arguments, specifically their assertions of supremacy for the fundamental law. Grey reminds us that the "idea of an enacted constitution was relatively novel in 1760, while the idea of the ancient unwritten constitution compounded of custom and reason was comfortable and familiar in the English-speaking world."[35] This is true enough, but it tells us little or nothing about the status of the unwritten constitution after our revolutionary success and subsequent legitimation of the written Constitution.

Several decades ago Edward S. Corwin asked why legislative sovereignty did not establish itself in our constitutional system, and his response speaks directly to the issue before us.

In the American *written Constitution,* higher law at last attained a form which made possible the attribution to it of an entirely new sort of validity, the validity of a *statute emanating from the sovereign people.* Once the binding force of higher law was transferred to this new basis, the notion of the sovereignty of the ordinary legislative organ disappeared automatically, since there cannot be a *sovereign* law-making body which is subordinate to another law-making body.[36]

Corwin's understanding is consistent with the findings of Sylvia Snowiss, whose fresh look at the historical evidence distinguishes three distinct periods in the early evolution of the American practice of judicial review, and succeeds in generating insights that bear upon the issue of the unwritten constitution.[37] She shows that during the first period (from independence to the publication of *Federalist* number 78), judicial review was still affected by the Blackstonian teaching on legislative omnipotence. While the explicit Blackstonian dogma was not acceptable, it nevertheless shaped the contemporary debate between those who supported legislative supremacy against judicial power and those who appealed to the same fundamental law tradition that had attracted James Otis. This latter position held laws violating commonly accessible standards of political right to be void, but their illegality was not connected to a judicial determination to that effect. Thus, violation of the fundamental law had political significance, but the judiciary was not yet in a position to enforce pronouncements of voidness against legislative excess. During the second period (roughly from number 78 to *Marbury* v. *Madison*), the written Constitution emerged as a "vehicle for the explicitness of American fundamental law," thereby providing the basis for a decisive rejection of Blackstonian legislative supremacy.[38] The explicitness, clarity, and public nature of the fundamental law removed the principal theoretical impediment in the way of judicial enforcement of it; deference to legislative judgment on matters of constitutionality no longer seemed institutionally justified. The point is best articulated in Judge Tucker's opinion in the 1793 Virginia case of *Kamper* v. *Hawkins.*

This sophism [legislative sovereignty] could never have obtained a moment's credit with the world, had such a thing as a written Constitution existed before the American revolution. . . . What the *constitution* of any country *was* or rather *was supposed to be,* could only be collected from what the *government had at any time done*; what had been *acquiesced* in by the people, or other component parts of the government; or what had been *resisted* by either of them. Whatever the government, or any branch of it had *once done,* it was inferred they had a *right* to do it *again.* The union of the legislative and executive powers in the same men, or body of men, ensured the success of their usurpations; and the judiciary having no *written Constitution* to refer to, were obliged to *receive* whatever *exposition* of it the legislature might think proper to make. But, with us, the Constitution is not an "ideal thing, but a real existence: it can be produced in a visible form": its principles can be ascertained from the living letter, not from obscure reasoning or deductions only.[39]

This observation does not convey precisely the point Corwin, who emphasized higher law, was making; it (as well as Snowiss's point) suggests, however, an interpretation of judicial review difficult to reconcile with extra-textual sources for constitutional adjudication. The written Constitution emerges in this synthesis as a document appealing to potentially contradictory jurisprudential aspirations. Thus, the constitutional positivist's yearning for order, predictability, and certainty are addressed by the codification of the fundamental law. But this codification cannot be viewed as valid simply as a result of its parchment form; it must (and does) satisfy the natural law proponent's insistence upon ethically grounded fundamental law. The traditional connection between fundamental law and right reason (Corwin's higher law) is maintained through the absorption of principles of natural justice in the charter itself. Had, in Judge Tucker's words, "such a thing as a written Constitution existed before the American revolution," then Otis's speech, we may speculate, might have impressed his contemporaries less as a revolutionary appeal (recall John Adams' reaction) than as a conventional and legal assertion of natural rights. When the principles of natural rights have, in effect, been constitutionalized in written form, they transform revolutionaries into judges; that is, they replace rebellion with judicial review.

In his *Letters of Fabius*, the conservative revolutionary John Dickinson allows us to reflect more deeply upon this point.

> If it be considered separately, a *constitution* is the *organization* of the contributed rights in society. *Government* is the *exercise* of them. It is intended for the benefit of the governed; of course can have no just powers but what conduce to that end: and the awfulness of the trust is demonstrated in this—that it is founded on the nature of man, that is, on the will of his *Maker*, and is therefore sacred. It is then an offence against Heaven, to violate that trust.[40]

This excerpt makes much the same argument as the Declaration of Independence, but makes more explicit the relationship between constitutional law and natural rights. Where there is no agent to enforce the sacred trust that underlies the Constitution, the clear implication, as in the Declaration, is that revolutionary action may be necessary to restore justice to the civil community. What is justice under a constitution?—the "*organization* of the constituted rights in society," rights founded on the nature of man. Under a written constitution this organization exists for all to observe; but judges, under the Federalist theory of judicial review, bear a special responsibility to declare what the law (organized rights) is and to enforce its content against transgressors—those, in other words, who dare to offend against Heaven.[41] In so doing the judges civilize politics, thus obviating the necessity for revolutionary activity.

In short, the eighteenth-century doctrine of natural rights, especially the theory associated with John Locke, always contained revolutionary implications, and yet the same doctrine formed the basis for legitimate government. It was at once a radical and a conservative theory. For Otis, the judicial appeal to these principles served the revolutionary purpose of galvanizing sentiment against an illegitimate governance. On the other hand, the practice of judicial review involves the judiciary in a legitimizing role or function, the purpose of which is preservation, not change. Take, for example, the observation quoted earlier from Hamilton's *Federalist* number 84. "The truth is, after all the declamations we have heard, that the Constitution is itself in every rational sense, and to every useful purpose, A BILL OF RIGHTS."[42] Why not, then, enumerate them in detail? Because, as Herbert Storing has noted, such rights, while they provide the ultimate source and justification for government, can also threaten government.[43] "Even rational and well-constituted governments need and deserve a presumption of legitimacy and permanence. A bill of rights that presses these first principles to the fore tends to deprive government of that presumption."[44] The Hamiltonian argument was that the enumeration of rights was necessary in a political setting where the absence of a written constitution required some alternative method of limiting royal or parliamentary prerogative; that the American Constitution was itself a bill of rights, in that its grant of limited government was an articulation of those first principles upon which these familiar declarations of rights rested. Thus, by enforcing the language of the written Constitution, judges were indeed defending the same principles of right conduct represented in a declaration of particulars.

Ultimately, of course, the Federalists reconciled themselves to a bill of rights, a development that does not affect the argument here. The Hamiltonian logic was not repudiated; judges were simply provided with greater specificity in enforcing constitutional guarantees. Why, we must ask, need judges appeal to sources external to the document when those sources have, as it were, been internalized? Moreover, these sources were not, as they have become in the twentieth century, subjectively defined and interpreted—recall that they constituted a *science* of morals. "The analogy," Otis declared, "between the natural, or material, as it is called and the moral world is very obvious."[45]

Lysander Spooner, the abolitionist constitutional theorist, suggested years later that "no one can know what the written law is, until he knows what it ought to be."[46] Judges operating within the moral consensus of the eighteenth century knew what the written law was, because they understood it to be a statement of what ought to be. But they possessed, as we have seen in the discussion of Wilson, a minimalist natural rights philosophy, meaning that the Constitution should not be seen as a guarantor of social justice but rather of conditions necessary for any just society.[47] Or, as John Dickinson put it, "A good constitution promotes, but not always produces a good administration."[48]

III. The Supreme Court and the First Principles of Fundamental Law

On August 22, 1787, a brief debate occurred at the Constitutional Convention over the ex post facto change. Oliver Ellsworth of Connecticut contended that "there was no lawyer, no civilian who would not say that *ex post facto* laws were void of themselves. It can not then be necessary to prohibit them."[49] James Wilson concurred, claiming that inserting a constitutional prohibition would "bring reflexions on the Constitution—and proclaim that we are ignorant of the first principles of Legislation, or are constituting a Government which will be so."[50] In opposition, Williamson of North Carolina indicated that "such a prohibitory clause is in the Constitution of N. Carolina, and tho it has been violated, it has done good there and may do good here, because the Judges can take hold of it."[51] From this debate Grey concludes that "the validity of judicial review on the basis of unwritten first principles was supported as a matter of course by two important delegates, and implicitly disputed by no one."[52]

How plausible is this interpretation? Does not Williamson's argument indicate that, at least in his judgment, judicial review on the basis of unwritten first principles might fail because it would not provide the judiciary with something they "can take hold of"? Perhaps this is only an indirect critique of the unwritten constitution, but how direct are Wilson and Ellsworth in affirming the principle ascribed to them by Grey? For example, Wilson's statement can just as easily be seen as an early formulation of Hamilton's bill of rights argument, to the effect that any enumeration of rights is superfluous in light of the incorporation of principles of natural right within the document as a whole. Thus, by singling out ex post facto laws, the framers might expose themselves to the unfair insinuation that this protected area represented the extent of their knowledge and understanding of first principles. And Ellsworth's comment simply seems to affirm the accessibility of the science of morals to ordinary understanding without indicating any opinion on the appropriate interpretive role of the Supreme Court.

Like the Bill of Rights, the ex post facto clause found its way into the Constitution. (Wilson and Ellsworth were joined only by Johnson of New Jersey in voting against its inclusion.) It was not long before it became a subject of judicial attention, and ultimately of scholarly concern. Let us consider some of the leading cases on which Grey relies, beginning with *Calder* v. *Bull.* Justice Samuel Chase's opinion in *Calder* v. *Bull* has figured prominently in the scholarly treatment of the uses of natural law in the American constitutional context.[53] It is typically juxtaposed with Justice William Iredell's opinion in the same case to present a classic debate on the validity of natural law jurisprudence. At the outset, however, it should be noted that all the justices on the Court agreed that the Connecticut statute alleged to have offended the ex post facto clause was not unconstitutional.

Chase begins his examination by carefully limiting its scope. "The sole inquiry is whether this resolution or law of Connecticut . . . is an *ex post facto* law, within the prohibition of the federal constitution."[54] He then delivers himself of certain eloquent sentiments that do indeed demonstrate his attachment to the orthodox natural rights position.

> The purposes for which men enter into society will determine the nature and terms of the social compact; and as they are the foundation of the legislative power, they will decide what are the proper objects of it. The nature, and ends of legislative power will limit the exercise of it. This fundamental principle flows from the very nature of our free republican governments, that no man should be compelled to do what the laws do not require; nor to refrain from acts which the laws permit. There are acts which the federal, or state legislature cannot do, without exceeding their authority. There are certain vital principles in our free republican governments, which will determine and overrule an apparent and flagrant abuse of legislative power. . . . An act of the legislature (for I cannot call it a law), contrary to the great first principles of the social compact, cannot be considered a rightful exercise of legislative authority. The obligation of a law, in governments established on republican principles, must be determined by the nature of the power on which it is founded.[55]

The critical sentence is that which denies the status of law to any legislative act "contrary to the great first principles of the social compact." This can be construed as an appeal to higher law outside the Constitution only *if* the great first principles of the social compact have not been incorporated within the document. It is significant that we find Justice Chase turning immediately to the specific language and intent of the constitutional prohibition, which he interprets narrowly in terms of its "technical"[56] meaning. The result is a denial of its application to private rights of property or contract; the clause was meant to apply, he claims, only to criminal matters. What is more, "Every law that takes away or impairs rights vested [which this one did], agreeable to existing laws, is retrospective, and is generally unjust, and may be oppressive."[57] But the fact that a law may be somewhat lacking in justice does not deprive it of constitutionality if it is not so deficient as to offend that basic level of justice guaranteed by the Constitution. We see, in short, an illustration of the point made earlier, that the Constitution is no guarantor of good law, or even just laws, but only laws that are compatible with the great first principles of republican, that is, free government.[58]

To the extent that Justice Iredell's concurring opinion (criticizing "speculative jurists" who hold "that a legislative act against natural justice must, in itself, be void")[59] was directed against Justice Chase, it does not do complete justice to his colleague's position. Iredell surely differs from Chase; but, to use Grey's terminology, it is not a question of interpretivism versus noninterpretivism. Iredell writes that a law "within the general scope of [a legislature's] constitutional power" cannot be pronounced void by the Court "merely because it is, in their judgment, contrary to the principles of natural justice."[60] To which Chase might have replied that, if intended for him, the observation is internally contradictory, because a law within the scope of constitutional power could not be contrary to the principles of natural justice. Iredell was an early constitutional positivist, believing in a separation of natural and constitutional law, although his commitment to written constitutions has caused him mistakenly to be understood as representing the jurisprudential orthodoxy of his times.[61] It was Chase, and not Iredell, who stood for the received opinion in the formative years of the constitutional system.

The case of *Wilkinson* v. *Leland* is less well known but similarly instructive. Here, too, the Court upheld a statute against a claim that it violated the ex post facto clause. Justice Story's opinion contains language reminiscent of Justice Chase's earlier opinion.

> That government can scarcely be deemed to be free, where the rights of property are left solely dependent upon the will of a legislative body, without any restraint. The fundamental maxims of a free government seem to require that the rights of personal liberty and private property should be held sacred.[62]

The case is also noteworthy for the fact that the statute in question came from Rhode Island, which according to Story, was "the only

state in the Union which has not a written Constitution of government, containing its fundamental laws and institutions."[63] This became a central issue in the complicated litigation involving a legislative
ratification of a probate action that the defendant claimed exceeded
the authority of the state government. The legislation was acknowledged to be retrospective, but in a state without a written constitution,
how does one determine whether such a law is invalid?

The Court heard two quite different answers to this question.
Whipple, counsel for the plaintiff in error, argued:

> No other limit to the power of the legislature of Rhode Island is known,
> than that which is marked out by the Constitution of the United States.
> If any clause in that instrument is expressly or virtually infringed by the
> confirmatory act of 1792, such a violation would render the act a nullity.
> The national constitution being the only limitation, the court has no
> right to pronounce a law of Rhode Island void, upon any other ground.
> It has been said in England, that an act of Parliament, contrary to the
> principles of natural justice, would be void. Such an opinion in reference
> to a law of state, has never been intimated in the court.[64]

To this, Webster, counsel for the defendant in error, replied:

> It is of no importance to the question before the court, whether there
> are restrictions or limitations to the power of the legislature of Rhode
> Island, imposed by the Constitution. If, at this period, there is not a
> general restraint on legislatures, in favor of private rights, there is an
> end to private property. Though there may be no prohibition in the
> Constitution, the legislature is restrained from committing flagrant acts,
> from acts subverting the great principles of republican liberty, and of
> the social compact.[65]

Ultimately, of course, the case had to be decided on the basis of an
interpretation of the federal Constitution; but this debate, while
perhaps not critical to the outcome, is nonetheless worth some reflection here. Whipple's argument, for example, is more subtle than it
may first appear. His rejection of the principle of voidness, used
earlier by Otis, has an important implicit qualification. The Court, he
argues, has never accepted the formulation that, in the absence of an
express prohibition, *a law of state* that violates principles of natural
justice is to be considered void. This leaves open the possibility that a
law of the federal government *would* be a nullity if it contravened such
principles. Thus, sixty-five years after Otis made his declaration, the
Supreme Court was still hearing faint repetitions of his argument, but
the context had changed dramatically. How much so is marked by the
fact that Whipple's interpretation of the only constitution relevant to
the state of Rhode Island is confined to the specific language (and
underlying intentions) of the document. Indeed, his examination of

the ex post facto clause follows precisely Chase's reasoning in *Calder* v. *Bull*. There is no extra-textual interpretation of the federal Constitution, although this Constitution is the only documentary restraint upon the federal government—a government, according to the legal document, which inferentially is limited by the principles of natural justice. Thus, it follows that these principles must be embedded in the written fundamental law; that, in other words, the validity of Otis's appeal no longer relies upon the unwritten constitution.

Whipple's legal brief would not command this much attention were it not for the fact that Justice Story's opinion is in essential agreement with it. Story nowhere accepts Webster's broad claim regarding the unwritten constitution, choosing instead to find Rhode Island limited only by the express limitations of the federal Constitution. "We cannot say, that this is an excess of legislative power, unless we are prepared to say, that in a state, not having a written Constitution, acts of legislation, having a retrospective operation, are void."[66] His reference, then, to the "fundamental maxims of a free government" must be seen in the context of an opinion that first refuses to embrace an explicit formulation of the concept of an unwritten constitution and then provides a technical, some might say narrow, interpretation of the ex post facto clause of the written Constitution. It is difficult, in short, to see *Wilkinson* v. *Leland* as supportive of Grey's thesis.

The famous case of *Fletcher* v. *Peck*, containing the Court's first interpretation of the contract clause, does appear to have an opinion based upon the unwritten constitution. Justice Johnson's separate opinion states: "I do not hesitate to declare, that a state does not possess the power of revoking its own grants. But I do it, on a general principle, on the reason and nature of things; a principle which will impose laws even on the Deity."[67] Chief Justice Marshall's opinion for the Court, on the other hand, demonstrated a commitment to principles of natural right without abandoning the written Constitution. The state of Georgia, he claims,

> was restrained, either by general principles which are common to our free institutions, or by the particular provisions of the Constitution of the United States, from passing a law whereby the estate of the plaintiff . . . could be constitutionally and legally impaired and rendered null and void.[68]

Admittedly, the reference, in a separate clause, to general principles, might convey a commitment to extra-textual interpretation.[69] Yet in *Ogden* v. *Saunders*, another famous contract clause case, Marshall indicates that "the framers of our Constitution were intimately acquainted with the writings of those wise and learned men, whose treatises on the laws of nations have guided public opinion in the subjects of obligation and of contract."[70] It would be logical to assume that the "particular provisions of the Constitution," adverted to by Marshall in *Fletcher*, framed as they were by statesmen knowledgeable in the treatises that formulated the "general principles," were indeed intended to incorporate those strictures within the specific language of the relevant clauses. For the judge most closely identified with both the written Constitution and the institution of judicial review, Marshall's opinion in *Fletcher* v. *Peck* advances the rationale for judicial power suggested earlier, that such power substituted for a revolutionary appeal to principles of natural justice.

Terrett v. *Taylor*, another case involving contract rights, is inconclusive on the question of the unwritten constitution. Justice Story does say:

> That the legislature can repeal statutes creating private corporations, or confirming to them property already acquired under the faith of previous laws, and by such repeal can vest the property of such corporations exclusively in the state . . . we are not prepared to admit; and we think ourselves standing upon the principles of natural justice, upon the fundamental laws of every free government, upon the spirit and letter of the Constitution of the United States, and upon the decisions of most respectable judicial tribunals, in resisting such a doctrine.[71]

But the opinion is quite ambiguous on the role that "natural justice" plays in deciding the case. One recent study, for example, suggests that the reliance on natural justice was at most an alternative holding, perhaps meant to express moral outrage at a statute that violated the Constitution.[72] Unlike Justice Johnson's opinion in *Fletcher*, which explicitly relies on natural justice independent of the written charter, Story speaks of these principles in the same sentence in which he cites "the spirit and letter of the Constitution of the United States." Perhaps the passage was analogous to a First Amendment opinion citing the Declaration of Independence and the works of Tom Paine, without meaning to imply that these documents would be legally sufficient substitutes for the constitutional text. Be that as it may, the ambiguity of Story's formulation renders problematic any final assessment of the case in the present context.

Finally, there is Justice William Paterson's opinion in *Vanhorne's Lessee* v. *Dorrance*. In it we are treated to an explicit consideration of the written Constitution, one that provides a fitting conclusion to this chapter. Near the beginning of his opinion, Justice Paterson asks, "What is a Constitution?"[73] This question occurs immediately after an inquiry into the authority of Parliament.

> In England, the authority of the parliament runs without limits, and rises above control. It is difficult to say, what the constitution of England

is; because, not being reduced to written certainty and precision, it lies entirely at the mercy of the parliament. . . . Some of the judges in England have had the boldness to assert, that an act of parliament, made against natural equity is void; but this opinion contravenes this general position, that the validity of an act of parliament cannot be drawn into question by the judicial department: it cannot be disputed, and must be obeyed. The power of parliament is absolute and transcendent; it is omnipotent in the scale of political existence. Besides, in England, there is no written Constitution, no fundamental law, nothing visible, nothing real, nothing certain, by which a statute can be tested. In America, the case is widely different.[74]

It is interesting to note Paterson's nonrecognition of British fundamental law and its relationship, in his estimation, to the absence of a written constitution. This takes on greater significance when, in response to his query about the nature of a constitution, he avers: "It is the form of government, delineated by the mighty hand of the people, in which certain first principles of fundamental laws are established."[75] Here, in brief, is the rejoinder to Grey's thesis. The written Constitution of the United States is the documentary embodiment of the fundamental law, of the first principles of government. When, in the next several paragraphs, Paterson invalidates the Pennsylvania statute at issue, declaring it to be "inconsistent with the principles of reason, justice, and moral rectitude" as well as "contrary both to the letter and spirit of the Constitution,"[76] there is no question that these two sources of adjudication are inextricably linked in his mind, that the written Constitution contains *within it* the principles of justice for which the noninterpretivist seeks external justification.

IV. Conclusion

The debate over the unwritten constitution, interesting as it is for the historian of ideas, should also be appreciated for its practical implications in contemporary constitutional adjudication. Grey, who argues for the judicial enforceability of "theoretical legal constraints," is quite explicit in articulating the practical tendencies of his jurisprudential position.[77] We should understand that in the context of the modern Court's increasingly expansive definition of the scope of judicial review,[78] the judicially enforceable unwritten law promises even more extensive constitutional innovations than might otherwise occur. Thus, for example, judges applying Grey's analysis to a "fundamental interest" claim under the Fourteenth Amendment might readily perceive the wisdom and logic of going beyond the explicit text (and discernible intent) of the Constitution to evaluate the legitimacy of the claim and its corollary expectation of heightened judicial scrutiny.[79] Whether or not that is a good thing, the legitimation of the unwritten constitution, and the judicial mode of interpretation associated with it, surely makes the judiciary a more obvious participant in the governmental pursuit of a socially just society.

In the end, perhaps, the best question to be raised in this context, is one put forward by Grey himself.

> Conceding the natural-rights origins of our Constitution, does not the erosion and abandonment of the eighteenth-century ethics and episte-mology on which the natural-rights theory was founded require the abandonment of the mode of judicial review flowing from that theory? Is a "fundamental law" judicially enforced in a climate of historical and cultural relativism the legitimate offspring of a fundamental law which its exponents felt expressed rationally demonstrable, universal and immutable human rights?[80]

That Grey's answer to his question is affirmative is indicated by his sympathy for the role of the contemporary Court as "expounder of basic national ideals of individual liberty and fair treatment, even when the content of these ideals is not expressed as a matter of positive law in the written Constitution."[81]

This is a role with considerable attraction for constitutional theo-rists. That the Supreme Court possesses certain unique institutional advantages when it comes to articulating fundamental societal beliefs and ideals is an assumption long held by many students of American politics. The Court's absence of electoral accountability enables the justices to act as spokesmen for a public morality that may or may not enjoy popular approval at any given time. The judges, Publius de-clared, would be "too far removed from the people to share much in their prepossessions."[82] As we reap the benefits of a pluralistic political system that makes a virtue of our differences, it is helpful—some would say necessary—that there be institutional expression for the ideas and goals that provide definition and purpose to us as one people.

Indeed, it has been shown that our earliest Supreme Court judges took advantage of their privileged positions to act as "republican schoolmasters," a role through which they sought to safeguard the legal and political principles of the regime.[83] With the text of the Constitution and the national laws as their educative guides, they viewed their constitutionally assigned task as involving more than a strict interpretation of the law. Today the judges are urged to per-form in a similarly educative mode; it is, in fact, suggested that a role of this kind constitutes the only viable justification for noninterpretive review.[84]

The suggestion comes from Michael Perry, who, like Grey, advises judges to go beyond the Constitution for answers to adjudicative problems. Perry sees the Court as an official agent of moral evolution, serving a "people committed to ongoing moral reevaluation and moral growth."[85] However, unlike the case of the early circuit-riding judges, the expounding of national ideals that Perry and Grey argue to be essential to the mission of the Supreme Court is a function of noninterpretive review. Whether or not we are a people committed to ongoing moral reevaluation, the Constitution, according to the older view, is not; that is, it is the embodiment of certain permanent principles of political justice, whose meaning does not reflect what is thought by some to be evolution in our moral understanding. The commitment to a written constitution is, to be sure, a commitment to the rule of law; but it is also a commitment to *the* principles embodied in the document, principles whose articulation is one of the central tasks of judicial statesmanship.

Justice Paterson, who also believed in the role of the Court as expounder of national ideals (or, more accurately—because they were rooted in nature—supranational), adhered to a conception of judicial review that differs from Grey's not on the basis of any disagreement over the validity of natural rights, but on the extent to which these rights were incorporated within the written document. Hence, Paterson's conclusion:

> The constitution of a state is stable and permanent, not to be worked upon by the temper of the times, nor to rise and fall with the tide of events: notwithstanding the competition of opposing interests, and the violence of contending parties, it remains firm and immovable.[86]

To a great extent the future of constitutional law will reflect the competition between these alternatives: judicial aspiration and constitutional aspiration.

CHAPTER **6**

Abraham Lincoln
"On This Question of Judicial Authority": The Theory of Constitutional Aspiration

ANY SERIOUS CONSIDERATION of the nature and extent of the Supreme Court's judicial authority involves a parallel inquiry into the meaning of the Constitution. From Hamilton's early forays into the field of judicial review to the most recent explorations, most notably in the work of John Hart Ely,[1] the elaboration of important statements or theories of judicial review have been predicated on more or less clear renderings of constitutional purpose and design. This chapter will examine one such effort, that of Abraham Lincoln, whose famous argument on the limits of judicial supremacy provides the occasion for students of public law to piece together a coherent and illuminating constitutional theory. It is one that is responsive to the question raised by Lincoln in his third debate with Stephen Douglas: "What do you understand by supporting the Constitution of . . . the United States?"[2]

As part of this examination the chapter will discuss Ely's thoughtful and widely acclaimed analysis, an analysis that, we will argue, represents a sharply divergent perspective on judicial review from that supported by Lincoln and suggests the distance we have traveled in a century of constitutional jurisprudence. Although Lincoln nowhere undertakes anything like the systematic analysis of judicial review found in *Democracy and Distrust*, his numerous reflections on a variety of legal and political issues enable one to formulate a Lincolnian legal philosophy, which in the succeeding pages will be characterized as the theory of constitutional aspiration. In this theory, the Supreme Court plays a prominent, though far from exclusive, role in the national striving to fulfill the substantive ideals of the Constitution and the Declaration of Independence.

Lincoln's theory demonstrates that, while providing an aspirational focus for constitutional interpretation, these substantive ideals do not provide boundless interpretive possibilities. This is of considerable significance, since, as we have already seen, the idea of aspiration may easily fuel the ambitious designs of those seeking to improve upon the work of the founders. For example, a recent inquiry into the meaning of the Constitution quite properly concludes that "the Constitution embodies our aspirations."[3] Yet improperly it says of the Constitution that "to be the supreme law it purports to be, its ways must continually be reaffirmed as descriptive of our best current conception of an ideal state of affairs."[4] Thus, the substantive content of constitutional aspiration is rendered mutable, dependent, as Dworkin might say, upon a fusion of constitutional law and contemporary moral theory. For Lincoln, there is also need for reaffirmation, specifically of the nexus between constitutional law and the moral theory of the founders. Only in the framework of this particular association may the Constitution be understood to embody the nation's aspirations.

I. The Denial of Unqualified Finality

On June 26, 1857, Abraham Lincoln ensured himself a place in the judicial process anthologies of the twentieth century. On that date in Springfield, Illinois, Lincoln joined the company of Thomas Jefferson and Andrew Jackson in suggesting that the policies of the Supreme Court do not create any politically important binding obligations for the coordinate branches of the federal government. Thus, the Congress was not compelled to adhere to the policy declared by the Court in *Dred Scott* v. *Sanford*. It was a necessary, if risky, venture for Lincoln, who exposed himself to the charge of attempting "to bring the Supreme Court into disrepute among the people."[5]

It is important here briefly to repeat this frequently cited tale as the basis for describing an interpretation of Lincoln's constitutional jurisprudence. The tale is one that "has served to haunt the Court every since."[6] Or at least such is the view of Jesse H. Choper, who, in his recent treatise on judicial review, understands Lincoln's response to the *Dred Scott* decision as an "encouragement to disobedience [that has] long outlived the conditions that generated its birth."[7]

Had it been the case that Lincoln's policy on compliance with *Dred Scott* constituted an "encouragement to disobedience," or worse, an incitement to mob violence (as Douglas alleged),[8] it would have stood as a repudiation of his own oft-stated belief on the subject of legal obligation. As a young man Lincoln, in his Lyceum Address, urged "a strict observance of all the laws,"[9] a theme that found repetition during his subsequent political career. In that same speech, however, Lincoln acknowledged the possibility of bad laws, and in what might be seen as an anticipation of the *Dred Scott* controversy, he argued that such laws "should be repealed as soon as possible," although "for the sake of example, they should be religiously observed."[10]

The consistency of Lincoln's views may be established if a contrast is made between the Springfield statement and Ronald Dworkin's interpretation of legal obligation that begins from a similar premise. Dworkin's defense of civil disobedience includes a paraphrase of Charles Evan Hughes. "We cannot assume . . . that the Constitution is always what the Supreme Court says it is."[11] Eventually this leads him to conclude that "if the issue is one touching fundamental personal or political rights, and it is arguable that the Supreme Court has made a mistake, a man is within his social rights in refusing to accept that decision as conclusive."[12]

The point of Lincoln's address and much of the subsequent debate with Douglas was precisely that the Constitution is not necessarily what the Supreme Court says it is. What is it, then, and what obligations or entitlements follow from its judicial misinterpretation? The second part of the question is answered in a way that distinguishes Lincoln from Dworkin, in that the individual is not justified in refusing to accept the conclusiveness of judicial decisions, although implicitly he is encouraged to vote for representatives who would dispute Justice Jackson's much quoted aphorism about the Court being infallible because its decisions are final. These are Lincoln's words: "Judicial decisions have two uses—first, to absolutely determine the case decided, and secondly, to indicate to the public how other similar cases will be decided when they arise."[13] And from the First Inaugural:

> I do not forget the position assumed by some, that constitutional questions are to be decided by the Supreme Court; nor do I deny that such decisions must be binding in any case, upon the parties to a suit, as to the object of that suit, while they are also entitled to very high respect and consideration, in all parallel cases, by all other departments of the government. And while it is obviously possible that such decision may be erroneous in any given case, still the evil effect following it, being limited to that particular case, with the chance that it may be over-ruled, and never become a precedent for other cases, can better be borne than could the evils of a different practice.[14]

No counsel to, or justification of, disobedience—civil or otherwise—can be inferred from Lincoln's observations here, or in those that immediately follow on the subject of the political responsibilities of elected officials. While Douglas, then, was surely wrong in depicting Lincoln as an encourager and condoner of disobedience, his charge that Lincoln was engaged in an attempt to discredit the Court cannot so easily be dismissed. Indeed, to the extent that the work of the Taney Court had wrought real damage, the Court had to be discredited, at least in the eyes of those who Lincoln felt misunderstood the Court's role in the interpretation of constitutional principles. His return to Jefferson's "departmental" approach to judicial review (or at least a variant thereof) enables us to gain insight into Lincoln's perspective on the question that is our principal concern—what is the Constitution?

As Don E. Fehrenbacher has noted, Lincoln had apparently given no thought to the meaning of judicial review prior to having been compelled to do so by the *Dred Scott* decision.[15] When he confronted the issue—and in his frequent restatement of his position—he tended to downplay the significance of his stand, claiming that "all that I am doing is refusing to obey it [*Dred Scott*] as a political rule." He went on: "If I were in Congress, and a vote should come up on a question whether slavery should be prohibited in a new territory, in spite of that *Dred Scott* decision, I would vote that it should."[16] Nothing very novel about this, Lincoln maintained; after all, Jefferson and Jackson had made similar claims, and as early as 1850 Senator Salmon P. Chase had denied that Congress was bound by decisions of the courts.

The examples of Jefferson and Jackson were not completely apposite, and Douglas, for example, was correct in pointing out that in the case of Jackson, the Court's ruling on the constitutionality of the bank, while disputed by Jackson, was resisted only after the bank charter had expired and the proposition had been urged to create a new bank. "Is Congress bound to pass every act that is constitutional? Why, there are a thousand things that are constitutional, but yet are inexpedient and unnecessary, and you surely would not vote for them merely because you had the right to?"[17] Lincoln's view may also be seen as not claiming quite as much as Jefferson, who had argued for the presidential authority to decide what laws or decisions would or would not be enforced.[18] Nevertheless, in "limiting the scope and denying the finality of the decision," Lincoln positioned himself unambiguously in the tradition of Jefferson and Jackson.[19]

As interpreted by Lincoln, the denial to the Court of an unqualified finality on constitutional questions was entwined with the theory of self-government. Thus,

> if the policy of the government, upon vital questions, affecting the whole people, is to be irrevocably fixed by decisions of the Supreme Court, the instant they are made . . . the people will have ceased to be their own rulers, having, to that extent, practically resigned their government, into the hands of that eminent tribunal.[20]

Nowhere does Lincoln question the legitimacy of judicial review, and his comment should not be construed as a Jeffersonian assault on the counter-majoritarian implications of that institution. The key words here are "the instant they are made." Fehrenbacher's assessment that "The *Dred Scott* decision as of June 1857, according to Lincoln, was in an intermediate phase between promulgation and legitimation"[21] is exactly right.

For additional support of this conclusion we can go back to 1839 and a speech given by Lincoln, in which he expresses himself on the constitutionality of the national bank.

> We have often heretofore shown . . . that a majority of the Revolutionary patriarchs, whoever acted officially upon the question, commencing with Gen. Washington . . ., the larger number of the signers of the Declaration, and of the framers of the Constitution, who were in the Congress of 1791, have decided upon their oaths that such a bank is constitutional. We have also shown that the votes of Congress have more often been in favor of than against its constitutionality. In addition to all this we have shown that the Supreme Court—that tribunal which the Constitution has itself established to decide Constitutional questions—has solemnly decided that such a bank is constitutional. Protesting that these authorities ought to settle the question—ought to be conclusive, I will not urge them further now.[22]

Several themes in this statement anticipate the Lincoln reflections on judicial authority precipitated by the *Dred Scott* crisis. First, there is a clear acknowledgment of the appropriateness of having constitutional questions decided by the Supreme Court. But while the Court has a role to perform in this regard—indeed a special one ordained by the Constitution—the case for the constitutionality of the bank does not rest alone on John Marshall's word. It is only after Lincoln has cited the affirmation of the bank's constitutionality by the revolutionary patriarchs with connections to the Declaration and the Constitution, along with various votes of Congress, that he mentions the Supreme Court. This parallels his reaction to *Dred Scott*, where he calculates the authoritative weight of judicial decisions in light of such factors as their unanimity (or lack thereof), adherence to a clear line of precedents, consistency with legal public expectation, accuracy in the use of historical facts, and perhaps most important, their continuity "with the steady practice of the departments throughout our history."[23] In the presence of all these factors it would be "factious, nay, even revolutionary, to not acquiesce in it [*Dred Scott*] as a precedent."[24]

One should also note here the emphasis Lincoln attaches to the oath to uphold the Constitution. It reminds one of Marshall's argument in *Marbury* v. *Madison*, an argument effectively countered by Judge Gibson in *Eakin* v. *Raub*, who pointed out that since judges were not unique in the oath they take, they cannot claim that it legitimizes a special judicial entitlement for constitutional interpretation. Lincoln is as serious about the oath as Marshall, but, without accepting Gibson's denial of judicial review, he adopts the logic of the latter's position. Thus, he echoes his 1839 sentiments with this post–*Dred Scott* query: "Can you, if you swear to support the Constitution, and believe that the Constitution establishes a right, clear your oath, without giving it support? Do you support the Constitution if, knowing or believing there is a right established under it which needs specific legislation, you withhold that legislation?"[25] The answer is quickly forthcoming: "There can be nothing in the words, 'support the Constitution,' if you may run counter to it by refusing support to any right established under the Constitution."[26]

But why? Does one always have an affirmative obligation to advance the cause of constitutional rights? Did, for example, the passage of the Voting Rights Act of 1965 mean that congressmen, who had served in Congress in the years since the passage of the Fifteenth Amendment, through their inaction had violated their constitutional oath? That seems preposterous, but when, if ever, *does* an act of omission implicate a legislator in such a violation? Lincoln's answer would seem to be that the failure to *respond* to the action of some other agency that undermines constitutional rights makes such acquiescence culpable. If, in the case of the Supreme Court, a decision that cannot be deemed "fully settled"[27] announces a general policy incompatible with the principles of the Constitution, the decision must be opposed. On the other hand, a fully settled decision *is* consistent with the Constitution and, therefore, is politically as well as legally obligatory. It remains to be seen what understanding of the Constitution informs this perspective; how, in other words, the limits of judicial supremacy are traceable to the nature of the constitutional document.

II. The "Apple of Gold" and the "Picture of Silver"

The *Dred Scott* case has provided many lessons for statesmen and scholars over the years. John Hart Ely draws this conclusion: "*Judicial* attempts to cement fundamental values in the Constitution have [not succeeded]. That *Dred Scott* v. *Sandford* did not prove durable is the grisliest of understatements."[28] That the Supreme Court *ought* not to be involved in the business of substantive values is a principal theme in Ely's constitutional scholarship. His presentation of this theme is fresh and insightful; however, in its basic thrust, it is in essential harmony with prevailing orthodoxy in constitutional jurisprudence. As we shall see, this places it in contradiction to Lincoln's legal philosophy, and also serves nicely to illuminate it by comparison.

As with Lincoln, Ely's teaching on the judicial authority is bound up with his commitment to self-government.

[N]either that which would grant our appointed judiciary ultimate sovereignty over society's substantive value choices nor that which would refer such choices to the beliefs of people who have been dead for over a century—is ultimately reconcilable with the underlying democratic assumptions of our system.[29]

Lincoln, too, as we have seen, viewed as inappropriate the conferring upon the judiciary of "ultimate sovereignty" in these matters, and he also acknowledged the necessity of limiting the authoritative voice of the founding fathers. "I do not mean to say we are bound to follow implicitly in whatever our fathers did. To do so, would be to discard all the lights of current experience—to reject all progress—all improvement."[30] But there is a difference in tone that sets Lincoln apart from Ely, a difference that eventually illuminates the key jurisprudential difference between the two. Lincoln continues: "What I do say is, that if we would supplant the opinions and policy of our fathers in any case, we should do so upon evidence so conclusive, and argument so clear, that even their great authority, fairly considered and weighed, cannot stand."[31] The reason for Lincoln's greater deference is that for him the commitments of the founders—the "beliefs of people who have been dead for over a century"—are of central importance in contemporary interpretation of substantive constitutional values.

Before establishing this point in Lincoln, let us turn to Ely. His objective is to avoid the pitfalls of "interpretivism" and "noninterpretivism." The former, as we have seen, is a variant of positivism that confines judges to enforcing norms grounded in the written Constitution, and the latter, the opposing view that counsels judges to go beyond the document for sources of adjudication.[32] Ultimately Ely supports "a participation-oriented, representation-reinforcing approach to judicial review,"[33] which he understands to be consistent with the basic commitment of the framers to process and structure rather than to the preservation of specific substantive values. The framers, according to this view, abjured the temptation to provide justice with an enduring meaning, instead deciding that they could best serve the ends of a liberal society by ensuring the openness of the governmental process. Consequently, "preserving fundamental values is not an appropriate constitutional task."[34]

It is in Ely's rejection of one of the noninterpretivist approaches—natural law—that the significance of his work for present purposes chiefly lies. Speaking of natural law, he declares that "the idea is a discredited one in our society . . . and for good reason."[35] He quotes Ruberto Unger's claim that "all the many attempts to build a moral and political doctrine upon the conception of a universal human nature have failed."[36] Those wondering if this qualifies the founders for failure will learn from Ely that the belief that the Constitution should be informed by natural law was not the majority view of the principal architects of our political system.[37] Their frequent references to natural law and natural rights should be understood in light of their immediate political predicament and not as reflective of an abiding faith in a system of ultimate truth. Take, for example, the Declaration of Independence:

> The Declaration of Independence was, to put it bluntly, a brief (with certain features of an indictment). People writing briefs are likely, and often well advised, to throw in arguments of every hue. People writing briefs for revolutions are obviously unlikely to have apparent positive law on their side, and are therefore well advised to rely on natural law.[38]

This, perhaps, more than any other observation in Ely's treatise, reveals the great gulf dividing his constitutionalism and Lincoln's.[39]

On his trip from Illinois to Washington to assume the presidency, Lincoln delivered a brief speech in Philadelphia's Independence Hall. In it he declared, "I have never had a feeling politically that did not spring from the sentiments embodied in the Declaration of Independence."[40] He then wondered out loud about what had kept the country together. "It was not the mere matter of the separation of the colonies from the mother land; but something in that Declaration giving liberty, not alone to the people of this country, but hope to the world for all future time."[41] He concluded his remarks by pledging his efforts toward saving the country, without abandoning the great principle in the Declaration that justified its continued existence.

For Lincoln, then, the significance of the Declaration is not its status as a brief for the "separation of the colonies from the mother land." It is, rather, in the principles in the document, principles that for Ely are noteworthy only for their historical and rhetorical importance. On another occasion Lincoln claimed that "The assertion that 'all men are created equal' was of no practical use in effecting our separation from Great Britain; and it was placed in the Declaration, not for that, but for future use."[42] All of this makes it clear that Lincoln was deeply committed to the natural rights philosophy inserted in the Declaration and to the political principles deducible therefrom. But what is the significance of this commitment for constitutional interpretation?

An uncharacteristically metaphorical comment of Lincoln's sheds light on this question. In a "Fragment on the Constitution and the Union," Lincoln, speaking of the principle of liberty set out in the Declaration of Independence, says:

> The assertion of that *principle* at *that time*, was *the* word, *"fitly spoken"* which has proved an "apple of gold" to us. The *Union* and the *Constitution*, are the *picture* of *silver*, subsequently framed around it. The picture

was made, not to *conceal*, or *destroy* the apple; but to *adorn*, and *preserve* it. The *picture* was made *for* the apple—*not* the apple for the picture.[43]

In Ely, the Declaration and the Constitution are two discrete and independent documents (or events); the former best understood as one of those noninterpretive natural law sources that should not inform constitutional judgment. Lincoln, on the other hand, sees the principles of the Declaration as providing the core meaning to the Constitution. To exclude these principles from constitutional adjudication is hardly imaginable. Without the Declaration's principle of liberty we could have established our independence, "but *without* it, we could not . . . have secured our free government, and consequent prosperity."[44] The Declaration, of course, did not establish a government; the Constitution did that. Thus, the government established by the Constitution can remain free only if the commitments of the Declaration are realized. It is but a small leap to the conclusion that those who in their official responsibilities are sworn to uphold the Constitution (and hence the free government it is intended to establish) are not misguided should their interpretive judgments rely upon the natural rights precepts of the Declaration.

Lincoln would doubtless argue that this reliance upon natural rights is not, strictly speaking, a noninterpretive jurisprudential choice, in that the Declaration's principles are implicit in the written folds of the Constitution. Judges, for example, would not be going beyond the constitutional document in seeking sources for interpretation; rather they would be appealing to extrinsic language to clarify meanings intrinsic to the Constitution. Here, despite the obvious differences in approach to natural rights, there is also a level of agreement between Ely and Lincoln. Ely, in his effort to steer a middle course between the shoals of interpretivism and noninterpretivism, advances a theory of judicial review stressing representational and participatory goals that are deemed implicit in constitutional structure and intent. As in Lincoln, the document reflects a purpose and design that, even if not always explicitly manifest, ought to have a decisive bearing upon the course of constitutional development. The achievements of the Warren Court, for example, especially in the related areas of voter qualifications and malapportionment, are evaluated highly by Ely as vindications of the philosophy underlying the Constitution.[45]

This general level of agreement, however, supports divergent understandings. Ely insists upon the distinction between process and substance, arguing that, with rare exceptions, the Constitution, in its explicit provisions and its implicit purpose, guarantees procedural fairness, not substantive ends. His distinction reminds one of Lon. L. Fuller's differentiation between "external" and "internal" moralities of law; the latter being essential for a just society, and involving "the integrity of the channels of communication by which men convey to one another what they perceive, feel, and desire."[46] It may also remind one of Justice Stone's footnote in *United States* v. *Carolene Products Co.* Indeed, this most famous of all legal footnotes occupies a central position in Ely's constitutional jurisprudence. As Ely correctly interprets it, Stone asks us

> to focus not on whether this or that substantive value is unusually important or fundamental, but rather on whether the opportunity to participate either in the political processes by which values are appropriately identified and accommodated, or in the accommodation those processes have reached, has been unduly constricted.[47]

Lincoln saw the relationship of substance and process differently, and he might have agreed with Walter F. Murphy's observation that in the Constitution's hierarchy of values, "substantive goals take precedence over process."[48] The difference is much more than semantic in nature. Take, for example, Lincoln's opposition to the Kansas-Nebraska Act, which had achieved what the *Dred Scott* decision later gratuitously accomplished—the repeal of the Missouri Compromise prohibiting slavery in the territories. Douglas's doctrine of popular sovereignty, the theoretical support for the legislation, was viewed as a pernicious doctrine by Lincoln precisely *because* it provided "the opportunity to participate . . . in the political processes by which values are appropriately identified." Even had blacks participated in great numbers in the decision regarding their status as free men, Lincoln would have opposed the process. His opposition was grounded in purely substantive considerations—slavery was irreconcilable with the liberty that the Constitution, following the Declaration, was bound to protect.[49] Moreover, it is worth noting, in light of the stronger presumption of constitutionality granted by footnote number 4 of *Carolene Products Co.* to legislation touching upon economic matters, that the core of Lincoln's objection to slavery was expressed in terms of the right to property: "in the right to eat the bread, without leave of anybody else, which his own hand earns, *he* [the Negro] *is my equal . . . and the equal of every living man.*"[50]

Slavery, it is interesting to note, is a subject that Ely discusses as one of the few exceptions to his account of the founder's disinterest in protecting substantive values. He argues that slavery stood nearly alone in being singled out by the original Constitution for protection, just as now, with the Thirteenth Amendment, *non*slavery is notable as an exception to the essential thrust of the document.[51] "[A]n understandable squeamishness,"[52] he maintains, accounts for the absence of the word in the original charter, a fact that Lincoln attaches much greater significance to, linking it to the founders' intention to place slavery on the course of ultimate extinction because of its incompatibility with republican principles.[53] This attachment is, of course, related to what we have already seen in Lincoln, the special place of the Declaration of Independence in constitutional interpretation. Thus, the concession made by the founders to the exigencies of the moment constitutes a glaring exception to the free government that the natural rights principles of 1776 clearly mandated. It is, therefore, not surprising that Ely, who does not take these principles seriously (at least in constitutional terms), would find that it is only *after* the addition of the Civil War amendments that the Constitution can be construed as valuing "nonslavery." These alternative perspectives will be useful later in completing our interpretation of Lincoln's reaction to the *Dred Scott* decision.

Before returning to that unfinished business, however, there is one further important difference that is connected to Ely's commitment to the jurisprudence of *Carolene Products Co.* Ely maintains:

> The approach to constitutional adjudication recommended here is akin to what might be called an "antitrust" as opposed to a "regulatory" orientation to economic affairs—rather than dictate substantive results it intervenes only when the "market," in our case the political market, is systematically malfunctioning.[54]

This marketplace metaphor is familiar to our constitutional law, most notably from the famous *Abrams* dissent of Justice Holmes. In his famous opinion, Holmes asserts that "the best test of truth is the power of the thought to get itself accepted in the competition of the market."[55] For Holmes, like Ely, the "market" occupies a prominent place in his constitutional adjudication; it is, in fact, "the theory of our Constitution."[56]

In an examination of Ely's First Amendment theory, one is not surprised to find it consistent with this stated market approach, that is, respectful of the process-substance distinction of *Carolene Products Co.*

> If the First Amendment is ever to begin to serve its central function of assuring an open political dialogue and process, we must seek to minimize assessment of the dangerousness of the various messages people want to communicate.[57]

The state may restrict speech only if done to avert an evil, or "specific threat," and only if done "independent of the message being regulated."[58] Inasmuch as the Constitution is not concerned with substantive goals, and judges are not to seek enforcement of fundamental values, this approach to the First Amendment is the only reasonable one consistent with these assumptions.

What is the approach consistent with Lincoln's alternative assumptions? Nineteenth-century constitutional history contains very little First Amendment adjudication or reflection, and Lincoln's writings are no exception. But we do gain certain insights into the question. For example, in the fifth debate with Douglas, Lincoln was confronted by the frequently repeated charge that the Republican party was a sectional party, the evidence for which was its reluctance to campaign in certain regions of the country. Lincoln's response may profitably be contrasted with the "market" theories of Holmes and Ely.

> [I]t may be true of this country, that in some places we may not be able to proclaim a doctrine as clearly true as the truth of democracy, because there is a section so directly opposed to it that they will not tolerate us in doing so. Is it the true test of the soundness of a doctrine, that in some places people won't let you proclaim it? . . . Is that the way to test the truth of any doctrine?[59]

Douglas was as much of a legal positivist as Holmes, and had he responded in a nonpolitical context, he might well have seen Lincoln's query as other than the rhetorical thrust Lincoln had obviously intended. Lacking the commitment to self-evident principles of natural right, he, like Holmes, would have found it difficult to avoid the conclusion that, yes, to some extent that *is* the way to test the truth of any doctrine. Holmes, of course, would have insisted on the right to proclaim the opinion, but Lincoln's deeper point certainly is that the marketplace's predictable rejection of his doctrine in those hostile areas is no evidence of the untruthfulness of the message.

What is at issue here are profound differences about how to define a liberal society. Ely, we have every reason to believe, would have been an enthusiastic supporter of Lincoln's message, while, however, insisting upon a policy of tolerance of opposing views. Such a policy represents a principled commitment to procedure, based upon the assumption that a free society may not endorse an official or public orthodoxy. Lincoln's vision of a free society does allow for official orthodoxy; not any, of course—only the truths of the Declaration will do. In principle, therefore, he can be both liberal and intolerant, defining as subversive those ideas that are repugnant to the moral consensus necessary to support a liberal polity.[60] In practice, Lincoln's intolerance did not embrace legal sanctions;[61] but notice, for example, how illiberal Lincoln can sound from the perspective of the other liberalism. In his Cooper Institute Address, for example, he discussed the morality of slavery, and indicated the centrality of the issue to the nation. "If slavery is right, all words, acts, laws, and constitutions against it, are themselves wrong, and should be silenced, and swept away."[62] On the other hand if, as the Republicans believed, it is wrong, then, Lincoln suggests, the same reasoning and implications follow.

On another occasion Lincoln said of the Republicans that they "think slavery is wrong; and that, like every other wrong which some men will commit if left alone, it ought to be prohibited by law."[63] But since words spoken for slavery are also wrong, it follows that they, too, ought to be prohibited. Again, Lincoln does not in fact advocate this as a policy, but his comments, taken together, suggest that a free society has the right (perhaps the obligation) to employ public authority to assert and establish the illegitimacy of certain ideas.

III. Constitutional Aspiration

It was not as a precursor of modern legal realism that Lincoln wrote in some notes for a law case that "*Legislation* and *adjudication* must follow, and conform to, the progress of society."[64] Ten years earlier, in 1848, he had used these words in speaking of the amending process.

> As a general rule, I think, we would [do] much better [to] let it alone. No slight occasion should tempt us to touch it. Better not take the first step, which may lead to a habit of altering it. Better, rather, habituate ourselves to think of it, as unalterable . . . The men who have made it . . . have passed away. Who shall improve, on what *they* did?[65]

In neither case was Lincoln referring to slavery or the Supreme Court, yet these seemingly conflicting sentiments have bearing "on this question of judicial authority."[66] To appreciate this, one should note that there is, in fact, no conflict here; for although in the first instance Lincoln appears as an advocate of change in the law, and in the second of resisting change in our constitutional law, these statements are easily reconcilable, and in their reconciliation is the essence of Lincolnian constitutionalism.

We have first to recognize what it is adjudication and legislation must conform to, and then what it is *they* (the founding fathers) did. It is not *changes in society*, but *progress of society*, that Lincoln appeals to as guidance for judges and legislators. The distinction is important, as seen in this observation of Bertrand Russell: "Change is one thing, progress is another. 'Change' is scientific, 'progress' is ethical; change is indubitable, whereas progress is a matter of controversy."[67] It is thus important to distinguish between change and progress when, as is so often the case, the two do not coincide.[68] To make this distinction it is necessary to have a fixed standard against which progress can be assessed. Clearly, for Lincoln this standard is the Constitution and the timeless principles it embodies. This explains his desire to have the

Constitution perceived as "unalterable," a conviction strengthened by his belief in the impossibility of improving upon the work of the document's authors. The fusion of constitutional law and moral theory does not, as in Dworkin, await achievement; rather, it requires reaffirmation.

The progress of society, then, may be conceptualized as the advancing realization of constitutional ideals. Lincoln's admission that if he were in Congress he would ignore the *Dred Scott* decision makes sense in these terms. The Missouri Compromise represented progress; *Dred Scott* did not. As a legislator he would not be conforming to the progress of society if he obeyed the decision of the Court as a political rule. To repudiate the act prohibiting slavery in the territories would be tantamount to repudiating constitutional ideals traceable to the Declaration. To be sure, the Missouri Compromise was a compromise; that is, it did not fully realize the self-evident truth of the Declaration. In this regard, however, it is worth contemplating some remarks of Lincoln, wherein he discusses the object of the signers of the Declaration of Independence.

> They meant simply to declare the *right*, so that the *enforcement* of it might follow as fast as circumstances should permit. They meant to set up a standard maxim for free society, which should be familiar to all, and revered by all; constantly looked to, constantly labored for, and even though never perfectly attained, constantly approximated, and thereby constantly spreading and deepening its influence, and augmenting the happiness and value of life to all people of all colors everywhere.[69]

We might profitably place these lines beside language from the Constitution that Lincoln was fond of quoting, but which receives only slight attention today. Article IV declares, "The United States shall guarantee to every State in this Union a republican form of government." Officers of the United States are the agents of this guarantee, and thus to comply with their oath to uphold the Constitution, they must work toward the establishment in practice of that "standard maxim for a free society" enunciated in the Declaration. Laws—and this includes decisions of the Supreme Court as well as congressional enactments—must be legally obeyed whether they are progressive (in conformity with ethical right) or retrogressive (not in conformity); but in the long run it is only those of the former kind that will be able to command permanent obedience. For this reason it is essential that retrogressive law be challenged politically, and that the doctrine of immediate finality—judicial or legislative—be restricted with vigor and conviction. It has been persuasively and correctly argued that Lincoln's reaction to *Dred Scott* was consistent with "The animating genius of the Founders' vision [which] was that each and every institution could be freed—in fact, allowed to be 'active'—because the activity of each branch could, within the internal structure of power, be watched, balanced, and checked."[70] What needs to be added is that the vision that leads to this structural design is itself informed, Lincoln would argue, by substantive principles of natural justice that represent the ultimate justification for our institutional arrangement and the internal dynamics associated with it.

This is the theory of constitutional aspiration. Archibald Cox has written that "the aspirations voiced by the Court must be those the community is willing not only to avow but in the end to live by."[71] Lincoln saw the Constitution as both a legal code and a statement of the ideals which we as a people chose "in the end to live by." When as president he needed to defend some of his extraordinary (and constitutionally suspect) actions, he said that he "felt that measures, otherwise unconstitutional, might become lawful, by becoming indispensable to the preservation of the constitution, through the preservation of the nation."[72] In going out of his way to argue for the legality of his actions he acknowledges the status of the Constitution as a legal charter, and in specifying the preservation of the document and the nation (dedicated to a certain proposition) as the goal of his actions, his thoughts, it seems fair to say, were not far from the "apple of gold" imagery of the "Fragment on the Constitution and the Union."

In this case he was defending his actions as president. Constitutional law could not be viewed as incompatible with constitutional ideals. Very different was his situation in the 1850s when, as an outsider, he could see very clearly how some interpretations of constitutional law were undermining constitutional ideals or goals. To the extent that these interpretations remained unchallenged, our official aspirations would be left malevolently unattended. Because these aspirations are ultimately political—that is, they define us as a polity, legal interpretations that impinge negatively upon them must always be open to political challenge. Hence Lincoln had no choice but to respond to *Dred Scott* in the way that he did.

Recall, however, Lincoln's statement that, when "fully settled," decisions of the Supreme Court ought to be accepted legally and politically. How is this reconcilable with the foregoing analysis? Can we assume, for example, that all such decisions will be consistent with the great ends expressed by the Constitution? How do we know that our acquiescence in a fully settled decision will not hinder our efforts to respond progressively to constitutional aspirations? To answer these questions, let us imagine *Dred Scott* to have been a fully settled decision; in other words, one satisfying Lincoln's criteria for finality. Not only would it be a decision consistent with a clear line of precedents and legal public expectation, but it would also be consistent with historical facts and the historic practice of coordinate political institutions. To imagine *Dred Scott* as a fully settled decision means imagining a country not worth defending.

This seems, at least, to be Lincoln's point. Recall his remarks where he indicates that if all his criteria were satisfied it would be "factious, nay, even revolutionary, to not acquiesce in it [*Dred Scott*] as a precedent." Indeed, it would be revolutionary to resist such a decision, and moreover, morally justifiable and consistent with the teaching on revolution in the Declaration of Independence. And so we are brought back once again to the "apple of gold." In our constitutional system a fully settled decision, properly understood, would have to be consistent with the Declaration, and thus compatible with constitutional aspirations.

There is, of course, the possibility of improper understanding. What we imagined about *Dred Scott* was in fact believed. Lincoln's objective was to prevent Douglas (whose understanding was distorted in this way) from succeeding "in moulding public sentiment to a perfect accordance with his own—in bringing all men to endorse all court decisions, without caring to know whether they are right or wrong."[73] Why?

> In this age, and this country, public sentiment is every thing. *With* it, nothing can fail; *against* it, nothing can succeed. Whoever moulds public sentiment, goes deeper than he who enacts statutes, or pronounces judicial decisions. He makes possible the inforcement of these, else impossible.[74]

Public sentiment is everything in the practical sense that meaningful compliance with official decisions is dependent upon it, and in the broader philosophical sense where popular sovereignty (not, of course, Douglas's caricature) is a derivative, as Corwin once suggested, of the natural right of people to select their own governing institutions.[75] Earlier we noted that Lincoln's denial of an unqualified finality to Supreme Court decisions involving constitutional questions was bound up with his commitment to self-government. This needs to be clarified by reference to the theory of aspiration.

In a republican polity the realization of substantive ideals must engage the people as active participants in a common quest. The Court may have a special role in this process, but it was never intended for that institution to go it alone. Archibald Cox's insight, that constitutional adjudication depends upon "a delicate, symbiotic relation" where "the Court must know us better than we know ourselves,"[76] captures a good deal of what is involved here. But what the Court knows about us, or our better selves, is itself shaped in important ways by how we understand ourselves. Thus, it was Lincoln's view that *Dred Scott* was made possible by the public sentiment formed by the widely promulgated doctrine of indifference regarding the morality of slavery, and that the decision in turn had the potential for preparing the public mind for an even more objectionable ruling. The only way to break this destructive cycle and to redirect public sentiment (and thus eventually the Court as well) toward the fulfillment of constitutional aspirations was through the initiative and efforts of nonjudicial institutions. For Congress not to accept the Court's decision as a political rule meant holding out the possibility that public sentiment could once again become firmly attached to those animating principles of natural justice that gave the polity its distinctive character. Public sentiment *is* everything; in the end, it is the consent of the governed that undergirds the legitimacy of the constitutional polity.

IV. Conclusion

Lincoln's understanding of the Constitution breaks very little new ground; in all important respects it follows in the natural rights tradition of the eighteenth century. His principal contribution to our constitutional jurisprudence lies in the adaptation of this understanding to the practice of judicial review. *Dred Scott* v. *Sandford* was only the second case in which the Supreme Court invalidated congressional policy, and it was the first occasion where legislation of any importance was involved. John Marshall had chosen wisely in selecting a rather trivial section of a law dealing with judicial matters to create the precedent for judicial review. The luxury of insignificance did not present itself to Lincoln; instead, our most profound national crisis rendered unavoidable reflection on the great unresolved dilemma of judicial review—how to respond to a deviant decision of a deviant institution.[77]

Lincoln's response, to ignore the decision as a political rule, was predicated on the view that those sworn to uphold the Constitution have an obligation to advance the cause of constitutional principle, to the end of realizing the ideals of the Declaration of Independence. Thus he articulated a constitutionism that, in contrast to the theory espoused by John Hart Ely, aspires to substantive as well as procedural ends. Ely's interpretive approach expresses eloquently the spirit of the modern intellectual era, one that is extremely skeptical of the possibility of deriving answers that are correct according to some absolute standard of justice.

What, however, in Lincoln's approach is different from those contemporary theories that claim also to derive right answers, and for that reason are objects of Ely's critical skepticism? The answer is to be found precisely in the fact that Lincoln's understanding of the Constitution does *not* break new ground. Thus, his reliance upon the natural rights tradition of the eighteenth century—exemplified by his repeated application of the Declaration—means essentially that all people possess the natural right to be governed only with their own consent. This is distinguishable from the view that "taking rights seriously requires [according] demands or wants the status of rights, as if, by natural right, a person consents to be governed on the condition that his wants be satisfied."[78] In aspirational terms the difference amounts to this: Lincoln's constitutional theory requires the political realization of the self-evident fact of human equality, which means that the Constitution aspires to a state of affairs where *arbitrary* infringements upon the rights of people to govern themselves do not exist. It does not require that the specific aspirations that at any given time may be pursued under the authority of self-governance be constitutionally mandated.

CHAPTER 7

Constitutional Theory and
the Dilemma of Judicial Finality

So numerous indeed and so powerful are the causes, which serve to give a false bias to the judgment, that we upon many occasions, see wise and good men on the wrong as well as the right side of questions, of the first magnitude to society. This circumstance, if duly attended to, would furnish a lesson of moderation to those, who are ever so much persuaded of their being in the right, in any controversy.[1]

THUS SPEAKS PUBLIUS in the opening essay of *The Federalist*. His insight serves to frame the central question of this chapter: What can be done when the "wise and good" justices of the Supreme Court declare themselves on the wrong side of an important question?

This question has recently been raised in Congress as well, where an important subcommittee has held extensive hearings on legislation introduced by members who are persuaded that the Supreme Court made a tragic mistake in its 1973 abortion ruling. The congressmen are in essence raising the issue Lincoln forced us to consider by his opposition to the *Dred Scott* decision. It is, of course, the issue of judicial finality, which, according to Harry Wellington, is the one "more than any other question posed by majoritarian theory, that proponents of judicial review must address."[2]

Lincoln's approach to this problem in jurisprudence and democratic theory was guided by what we have referred to as his theory of constitutional aspiration. Fundamental to the theory was an understanding of the Constitution as a document embodying principles of natural right that find explicit articulation in the Declaration of Independence and implicit recognition in the language of the Constitution itself. While accepting the doctrine and practice of judicial finality, his adherence was contingent upon two qualifications: that a distinction be made between compliance with judicial decisions by the parties to the immediate case and acceptance by other political actors of the binding character of a ruling as applied to future actions; and that finality, in this second, political sense, was not, in questions of fundamental principle, a matter of declaration so much as achievement. Doubtless for some, this demonstrates Lincoln's denial of

113

judicial finality; for Lincoln, however, the real denial was that the Constitution is what the judges say it is.

The constitutional theory that informs Lincoln's understanding of finality is distinguishable from all the theories discussed in the previous chapters. In addition to Ely, the approaches of Pound, Berger, Grey, and Dworkin may be seen in varying degrees as differing from Lincoln's position on constitutional interpretation. We might expect, therefore, that their respective positions on the question of judicial finality would also differ from Lincoln's. Only Raoul Berger, however, has written in any detail on the subject. The others have at best made oblique references to the issue, although Grey and Ely have sent letters to the aforementioned congressional subcommittee setting out their views on what they see as the threat to the finality doctrine represented by the proposed legislation. As a vehicle for clarifying and summarizing the various constitutional theories that have dominated contemporary American jurisprudence, this chapter will spell out the implications that each of these legal philosophies has for the binding character of judicial decisions. It will also address directly the relevant language of S. 158, the bill providing that human life shall be deemed to exist from conception.

I. Perspectives on Judicial Finality

A Brief Recapitulation

Despite fundamental differences in approach and philosophical commitment, a sort of negative consensus unites the several theorists we have considered. They all represent the modern rejection of the natural rights tradition that influenced the development of our early constitutional experience. That tradition was the political face of the scientific revolution of the seventeenth century. Eventually, however, its self-evident principles of political justice become anything but self-evident as the modern era witnessed the crumbling of the consensus that once supported the old "science of morals." Thus, Pound sees in the jurisprudential application of natural rights an impediment to progress and social happiness; Berger holds with deep suspicion a source of constitutional adjudication that enables the Court to free itself from written constraints; Grey opens up the concept to a post-consensus, pluralistic infusion of modern values; Dworkin meets Pound's objections by retaining the old forms of natural rights but substituting a new content; while Ely finds an invalid obstruction to the democratic process in the judicial incorporation of fundamental values into the constitutional text. In each case the theorist makes a decisive break from the epistemological assumptions guiding the prevailing constitutional orthodoxy of late eighteenth century American legal thought.

Of course, there are differences in degree and emphasis. Pound, Berger, and Ely are explicit and emphatic in their rejection of natural rights jurisprudence, the latter two denying, contrary to Pound, that they were rejecting an important commitment of the framers. Grey and Dworkin wish to retain a role for the Court as counter-majoritarian expounder of national ideals; thus they must separate themselves from the sociological positivism of Pound, whereby the Court pursues its function by being responsive to external demands, and they must part company from the constitutional positivism of Berger and Ely, which leads to a relatively reduced role for the judiciary in the active pursuit of a socially just society.

A Note on Finality

The power of the Supreme Court to issue final and binding interpretations of the Constitution is commonly viewed as a necessary corollary of judicial review. Indeed, the Court itself has pointedly noted that it is "supreme in the exposition of the law of the Constitution."[3] Nevertheless, the many occasions when the Court has overruled an earlier interpretation is vivid testimony to the problematic character of its oft-proclaimed supremacy. A characteristic reflection on human nature appearing in *Federalist* number 22 speaks directly to the dilemma posed by judicial finality.

> There are endless diversities in the opinions of men: We often see not only different courts, but the Judges of the same court differing from each other. To avoid the confusion which would unavoidably result from contradictory decisions of a number of independent judicatories, all nations have found it necessary to establish one paramount to the rest—possessing a general superintendence, and authorized to settle and declare in the last resort, an uniform rule of civil justice.[4]

Inevitably one is reminded of Justice Jackson's familiar aphorism that "We are not final because we are infallible, but we are infallible only because we are final."[5]

The case for judicial finality, then, cannot rest upon a presumption that the Court's interpretation of the Constitution will necessarily be correct. That the accuracy of its views can be relied upon more safely than those of the other governmental institutions is rarely contested any longer, and indeed was an important theme in Hamilton's classic defense of judicial review. But unless one adopts the other famous judicial aphorism—that "the Constitution is what the judges say it is"—then the case for judicial finality must in the end rest as much upon the obvious desirability that constitutional issues be conclusively settled, as that they will be rightly settled.

There has always, however, existed a tension between the finality of judicial judgments and the coequality of the three branches of government, a tension increased by the presence of electoral accountability in the two nonjudicial branches. Thomas Jefferson perhaps best symbolizes early opposition to judicial monopoly over constitutional determinations. His advocacy of a departmental approach to judicial review represents the most public expression of an uneasiness that was reflected in contemporaneous debate and discussion. Thus, James Wilson:

> We are now led to discover, that between these three great departments of government, there ought to be a mutual dependency, as well as a mutual independency. We have described their independency; now let us describe their dependency. It consists in this, that the proceedings of each, when they come forth into action and are ready to affect the whole, are liable to be examined and controlled by one or both of the others.[6]

At the Pennsylvania Ratifying Convention, Wilson, immediately after referring to the judiciary's right to refuse to carry out an unconstitutional law, said: "In the same manner the President of the United States could shield himself and refuse to carry into effect an act that violates the Constitution."[7]

The debate over finality persists throughout our history. For example, Donald G. Morgan, in an important study of the relations between the Court and the Congress, summarized a 1958 congressional debate over legislation in this way:

> One position conceived of constitutional questions as technical in nature, suited for the courts, and calling for only cursory attention in Congress. The other conceived of the Constitution itself as a subtle collection of principles and rules, rooted in part in the understandings of the people and developed in part by the representative body. The former minimized and the latter elaborated a duty and power in members of Congress to examine constitutional issues for themselves.[8]

This lacks the dramatic quality of a Jefferson-Marshall confrontation over judicial review, but it does illustrate the continuing resistance to the identification of the Constitution with the Supreme Court. While it emphasizes a popular component or influence in constitutional interpretation as justification for congressional involvement, such involvement may also be grounded in a sense of obligation to constitutional principles whatever their source of definition. Thus, the oath to uphold the Constitution on the part of coequal members of the government renders problematic the total exclusion of any one branch from the process of constitutional interpretation.

Roscoe Pound

His reading of William James's essay "The Moral Philosopher and the Moral Life" led Roscoe Pound to observe that "this seems to me a statement of the problem of the legal order."[9] As I have argued elsewhere, Pound's legal philosophy builds systematically upon James's philosophical premises, chief among which is that in ethics, as in physics, there is no final truth.[10] It is this absence of finality that suggests Pound's jurisprudential position on judicial finality.

Pound's rejection of the founders' commitment to natural rights philosophy had important potential implications for the role of the judiciary. It established a strong basis for a more activist Court; that is, one more responsive to the demand of societal change and improvement. But without any final truths to establish a fixed standard by which judges, in the language of the Declaration, "secure rights," the business of adjudication, including constitutional interpretation, was to be viewed as an open-ended process that had its analogue in the methodology of the natural sciences. This meant that judicial outcomes, like scientific findings, were always subject to revision in the light of experience; it meant too that judges, like scientists, possessed the unique expertise and training to preside over this revision. And as we have seen, such constraints upon the judicial role as might extend from the separation of powers would not be expected to constrain Pound, whose esteem for the separation principles was as low as it was for traditional natural rights.

Thus it is logical to infer, from Pound's general position, affirmation for the principle of judicial finality, provided, of course, that the legitimacy of the Court's authority to reexamine its own decisions in the context of changing circumstances is not denied. Harry Wellington, who follows Pound and Cardozo in advocating judicial deference to the "moral ideals of the community,"[11] provides insight into sociological jurisprudence's perspective on finality. He argues that "In the most substantive of constitutional cases there is always doubt about finality at the time of decision because there is always the possibility of judicial mistake and the inevitability of social change."[12] It is only "when the Justices are right about the moral ideals of the community [that] their decisions become settled and accepted."[13] Thus, for example, the finality of the *Brown* decision was not effectively achieved until the values articulated by the Court gained general acceptance.[14] Until that time the decision enjoyed at best a "provisional" status, by which Wellington seems to suggest a symbiotic relationship between the Court and the community, a mutual dependence of one upon the other that defines the limits of the judicial function.

It is interesting, in light of our discussion of Lincoln's constitutional theory, to note Wellington's use in this context of the term "aspiration." He employs it to emphasize the central importance of the community's ideals to his conception of the judicial role.[15] Unlike Lincoln's view, the object of constitutional aspiration is not represented by some fixed standard, but rather evolves with changes in the social mores. The Court, which in Cardozo, for example, is well suited to discern the constitutional implications of the social mores, is also assigned, in Wellington's understanding, the role of adapting constitutional principles to societal change. Thus, "at least where principles are involved, mistakes can be discovered and mistaken decisions amended by normal judicial processes."[16] It is significant for our purposes to note that Wellington uses *Roe* v. *Wade* to illustrate his argument.

Briefly, Wellington's point regarding the decision is that it may in retrospect be seen as mistaken, because subsequent Court action sustaining restrictive abortion-financing legislation reveals that the initial ruling had been based upon an erroneous interpretation of the moral ideals of the community. "When the Court recognizes it has made a mistake [as it has done here] it should, in the appropriate case, rectify the situation."[17] That appropriate case, we might add, has been reviewed, and the Court, contrary to Wellington's implicit expectations, has seen fit decisively to reaffirm its *Roe* decision.[18] The "normal judicial processes" have thus not succeeded in reversing what many view as a grievous error, and it is difficult at this point to refer to anything in Wellington's (and Pound's) theory to deny finality to the 1973 decision.

In the previous chapter we observed that Lincoln's use of aspiration implied a distinction between change and progress. Because the basis of this distinction—immutable principles of natural right embodied in the document—is omitted in Pound's jurisprudence, the finality of a constitutional decision must ultimately rest upon the transient tides of public sentiment. This does, indeed, incorporate change into the process of constitutional adjudication, but it leaves progress subject to shifting standards of public morality, rather than to criteria implicit in the document.

This was a point well understood by Alexander Bickel, whose Burkean distrust of abstract theory placed him in opposition to a constitutional jurisprudence predicated on principles of natural right, but whose commitment to the "enduring values" of society implied a respect for such principles to the extent that they were an important source of societal ideals. (It is no surprise that the hero of his most important book, *The Least Dangerous Branch*, is Lincoln.) Bickel, like Pound, rejected a mechanistic conception of the separation of powers. This rejection, however, did not eventuate in the projection of an avowedly legislative role for the Court; instead, it served to legitimate a collaborative role for the branches of government in seeking to realize the aspirational ideals embodied in the polity's enduring values.[19]

> The functions [of the branches of government] cannot and need not be rigidly compartmentalized. The Court often provokes consideration of the most intricate issues of principle by the other branches, engaging them in dialogues and "responsive readings"; and there are times also when the conversation starts at the other end and is perhaps less polite. Our government consists of discrete institutions, but the effectiveness of the whole depends on their involvement with one another, on their intimacy, even if it often is the sweaty intimacy of creatures locked in combat.[20]

Being an agent of change differs from being an agent of progress. The latter entails realizing constitutional aspirations, a function so fundamental that formally to relegate it to a specific institutional base diminishes its transcendant importance. As Bickel put it in his concluding paragraph of *The Supreme Court and the Idea of Progress:*

> The true secret of the Court's survival is not, certainly, that in the universe of change it has been possessed of more permanent truth than other institutions, but rather that its authority, although asserted in absolute terms, is in practice limited and ambivalent, and with respect to any given enterprise or field of policy, temporary. In this accommodation, the Court endures. But only in this accommodation. For, by right, the idea of progress is common property.[21]

Bickel was never quite clear on the substance of society's enduring values, but his constitutional jurisprudence, unlike Pound's, provides a principled basis for qualifying the finality of judicial judgments. Constitutional aspirations, then, are common property in two senses: they express particular ideals uniting us as one people, and they exist as goals to be aspired to by all who occupy positions of public trust.

Ronald Dworkin

In the previous chapter we contrasted Dworkin's position on civil disobedience with Lincoln's reflections on legal obligation, noting that the possibility of judicial error leads Dworkin to support individual resistance through noncompliance, and Lincoln to encourage political resistance through legislation. Both appear to deny the position of unqualified judicial finality, and both strenuously object to the identification of constitutional meaning with judicial interpretation.

There is, however, reason to apprehend a fundamental incompatibility between the contemporary "liberal theory of law" and Lincoln's position on judicial finality. It arises principally in regard to the role of

Congress and amounts to this: that the counter-majoritarian premise of the rights thesis effectively excludes meaningful participation by the legislative branch in the dialectical interpretive process leading to conclusive constitutional judgment. Thus, the principle/policy distinction, developed by Dworkin to legitimate an activist judicial role in the protection of individual rights, has the effect also of delegitimating congressional involvement in the collaborative political process prescribed by the theory of constitutional aspiration.

Recall, in this context, Richards's use of the rights thesis and its "institutional correlate . . . of judicial supremacy which enforces a catalogue of human rights against majoritarian institutions which tend to be utilitarian."[22] In a letter to the Senate Subcommittee on Separation of Powers, Richards puts his theoretical argument into practice. Thus, he writes:

> [M]y considered view is that the proposed statute would be an unconstitutional contraction of the constitutional rights established in *Roe* v. *Wade* and its progeny. In my view, the forms of fact-finding, which are alleged to justify S. 158, are not, properly understood, the kind of Congressional investigation which can justify an expansion of constitutional principles beyond those established by the Supreme Court. . . . The Supreme Court's judgment rests on an interpretation of constitutional values, which no amount of putative fact-finding by Congress can here—consistent with *Marbury* v. *Madison*—undercut.[23]

Viewed in conjunction with the earlier statement, the Court's interpretation of constitutional values acquires a privileged (which is to say, final) status through the institutional correlate of the rights thesis. To challenge the Court's construction of constitutional values or principles implies an assault upon judicial supremacy in rights cases. In terms that Dworkin might apply, Congress's assertion of an independent voice in matters of constitutional principle represents a basic confusion regarding its proper function in the structural design of the national government.

It is instructive here to ponder the case of Madison, whose assumptions about majority rule, as we have seen, suggest a less prominent profile for the Court than the one projected by the liberal theory of law. Madison's views on judicial review have been thought by some scholars, including Berger, to be inconsistent; others, most notably Corwin, find them coherent and of the first importance in discerning founding intention. Berger, for example, sees as "confused"[24] Madison's thoughts expressed in a 1788 letter to a Mr. Brown. Madison had written:

> In the State Constitutions and indeed in the Federal one also, no provision is made for the case of a disagreement in expounding them;

and as the Courts are generally the last in making ye decision, it results to them by refusing or not refusing to execute a law, to stamp it with its final character. This makes the Judiciary Department paramount in fact to the Legislature, which was never intended and can never be proper.[25]

Corwin, while not denying the appearance of some inconsistency in Madison's various statements on judicial review, argues that these views, taken together, indicate Madison's belief that the Constitution has not settled all important questions related to judicial review.[26]

On the question of judicial finality, Madison, of all the participants in the debate over the removal power, was the most outspoken advocate of congressional involvement in constitutional interpretation. Indeed, Berger acknowledges that "but for Madison, majority and minority were united in recognition of the courts' right to the last word."[27] Actually, Madison did not deny the Court's authority to decide questions of constitutionality; but his interest in recording a clear statement of Congress' assessment of constitutional meaning is understandable in the terms we derived earlier from *Federalist* number 10.

When our perception of the Court as an essentially counter-majoritarian institutional force is softened by an appreciation of the sociopolitical constraints that significantly reduce the dangers implicit in majority rule, then our toleration of some legislative involvement in constitutional interpretation should increase. The need, in other words, to exclude all majoritarian participation, for fear of incurring inevitable encroachments upon constitutional rights, is mitigated by an awareness of the safeguards built into the political process. This in no way establishes an equality between the branches with respect to the ultimate finality of constitutional determinations. It does, however, allow us to counter monopolistic claims on behalf of the judiciary that are based upon institutional prerogatives rooted in the principle/policy distinction.

It also suggests a link between Madisonian theory and Lincoln's theory of aspiration. Recall the significance of Lincoln's observation that "*Legislation* and *adjudication* must follow, and conform to, the progress of society."[28] From the perspective of constitutional ideals, the Missouri Compromise was a progressive enactment nullified by a retrogressive judicial decision. Lincoln's position was that Congress's obligation was to respond progressively; that is, in support of the Constitution and the principles it embodied. Madison's Constitution opens the way for adjudicative *and* legislative pursuit, along separate but interactive tracks, of the principled ends toward which we as a society aspire. Henry M. Hart, Jr., has argued that "the political branches . . . retain at all times the crucial ability to force the Court to reexamine in new contexts the validity of the Constitutional positions it has previously taken."[29] This ability would be of little consequence if there were not a general acceptance, within the legislative branch and without, that the arena of constitutional principle is not the exclusive preserve of the judiciary. Madison's theory does what Dworkin's does not: it legitimates political engagement in matters of constitutional principle.

Raoul Berger

The Finalist generally takes the position that the only political process which can be constitutionally used for the purpose of overcoming an undesired judicial interpretation of the Constitution is that of constitutional amendment. From the point of view of those who deny the necessary identity of the judicial version of the Constitution with the Constitution, this position, of course, simply begs the question whether the Constitution needs amending, and in view of the extremely undemocratic method which the Constitution provides for amendment, such question-begging is extremely hazardous.[30]

The author of this observation, Edward S. Corwin, placed himself among those critical of the Finalist's position, believing that the issue of judicial finality had not been resolved, or even seriously addressed, by the architects of judicial review. Raoul Berger, on the other hand, is as confident of the founding intent concerning finality as he is of the framers' commitment to judicial review.

In particular, Berger is persuaded that any significant role for Congress in determining matters of constitutionality was incompatible with founding conceptions of constitutional government. The experience of the framers had led them to fear legislative despotism, and they were not about to legitimate loopholes from which popular tyranny might emerge. Berger, however, is best noted for his scholarly assaults on judicial imperialism; thus the question arises as to why he is determined to preclude any dilution of judicial hegemony over constitutional interpretation. The answer, in part, is related to his jurisprudential rejection of natural rights and the "spirit of the Constitution."

For Berger, as we have seen, the role of the Court is to police the constitutional boundaries drawn by the written document, not to enforce any political truths implicit in the Constitution or external to it. "As the Fathers conceived it, the judicial role was to 'negative' or set aside unauthorized action rather than to initiate policy."[31] The Court's policy-making role was to be as narrow as was the Congress' role in constitutional interpretation. "In an atmosphere crackling with distrust of Congress, it is significant that advocates of judicial review cast the courts in the role of nay-sayer, with never a hint that they were to serve as a 'leader' of public opinion."[32] Indeed, it was the limited scope of judicial review that justified the judicial monopoly over constitutional interpretation.

We may illustrate this point by reference to the famous debate in the first session of the First Congress over the president's power to remove major executive appointees. Most of the discussion focused upon whether a bill that conferred upon the president the authority unilaterally to remove the head of the department of foreign affairs was constitutional. And a significant part of that discussion was concerned with the issue of Congress's responsibility in considering constitutional questions. While various views were expressed, one study concludes that "a dominant theme in the debate was that legislative consideration of such questions, instead of being a discretionary power, was a moral and constitutional duty."[33] With the possible exception of Madison (an important one to be discussed later), this consensus did not question the finality of the judicial determination of constitutionality.

The debate on the matter was the first of many to occur in Congress over the years. The leading student of the subject has, as we have seen, summarized the two principal positions. They bear repeating.

> One position conceived of constitutional questions as technical in nature, suited for the courts, and calling for only cursory attention in Congress. The other conceived of the Constitution itself as a subtle collection of principles and rules, rooted in part in the understanding of the people and developed in part by the representative body. The former minimized and the latter elaborated a duty and power in members of Congress to examine constitutional issues for themselves.

This analysis once again calls to mind Lincoln's position, which justified an activist congressional role on the basis of the legislator's oath to support the Constitution, and through it, the principles of the Declaration. Although the source of principle was for Lincoln rooted not so much in the "understandings of the people" as in the original will of the people, the implications for constitutional interpretation are quite similar. Thus, contrary to Berger's preference for a "technical" conception of the document over one requiring inquiry into underlying substantive principles, the alternative conception both increases the likelihood of judicial error and broadens the consequences attendant on such error. For the nonjudicial coequals within the federal tripart system, the argument for nonparticipation in constitutional determinations weakens as the scope and seriousness of these exercises increases. This point may, but need not, lead one to Jefferson's departmental concept of judicial review and its denial of the interpretive finality of the courts. The departmental view, one should add, was not, despite the frequent linking of his position with Jefferson's, Lincoln's understanding of judicial finality.[34] The latter's theory of constitutional aspiration accepted nonjudicial participation in the process by which judicial finality was ultimately achieved. To the extent that all branches were involved in the common enterprise of attempting to realize constitutional ideals, they all had a responsibility to defend, in appropriate ways, their best understanding of these ideals.

It is instructive here to return to our original point of contrast with Berger: Hamilton's theory of the judicial power. In *Federalist* number 81, Hamilton makes the following observation:

> It is not true . . . that the parliament of Great Britain, or the legislatures of the particular states, can rectify the exeptionable decisions of their respective courts, in any other sense than might be done by a future legislature of the United States. The theory neither of the British, nor the state constitutions, authorizes the revisal of judicial sentence, by a legislative act. Nor is there anything in the proposed constitution more than in either of them, by which it is forbidden. In the former as well as in the latter, the impropriety of the thing, on the general principles of law and reason, is the sole obstacle. A legislature without exceeding its province cannot reverse a determination once made, in a particular case; though it may prescribe a new rule for future cases. This is the principle, and it applies in all its consequences, exactly in the same manner and extent, to the state governments as to the national government, now under consideration. Not the least difference can be pointed out in any view of the subject.[35]

Berger cites this comment to dispute the views of Leonard Boudin, who had earlier argued that the framers had not intended to establish judicial review. Boudin claimed that this passage contradicted Hamilton's defense of judicial review in number 78, and that number 81 was much more representative of the preponderant evidence in support of his conclusion. Berger's critique correctly establishes the flaws in this argument; but in doing so it never acknowledges that Hamilton, who as we have seen took seriously the "spirit of the Constitution," did not categorically reject a legislative role in constitutional interpretation. Indeed, was it not Lincoln's position that "A legislature without exceeding its province cannot reverse a determination once made, in a particular case; though it may prescribe a new rule for future cases"? Berger thus goes too far when he says: "How Boudin could distill from No. 81 the proposition that Hamilton asserted the power of Congress to change a constitutional interpretation passes understanding."[36] There is no question of Hamilton's support of judicial review, nor is there evidence to doubt his commitment to judicial finality. But as in Lincoln's view, and probably for the same reason, the legislative branch could not be foreclosed from seeking to change a grievously misguided constitutional interpretation. Hamilton makes clear that there are various ways to rectify an "exceptionable decision" of the Court. "General principles of law and reason" preclude any solution that denies the finality of a judicial determination in a particular case; but the political process provides alternative means for seeing to it that the Constitution is not necessarily what the judges say it is.

The difference between Corwin and Berger on the question of finality, is, in the end, as much a jurisprudential as it is a historiographical disagreement. Corwin lacked Berger's positivistic suspicions of natural rights; thus, he could not be satisfied with the amendment process as the necessary route to overturning an undesired judicial interpretation of the Constitution. To be sure, the option of impeachment exists, but as John Marshall wrote in a letter to Samuel Chase, "A reversal of those legal opinions deemed unsound by the legislature would certainly better comport with the mildness of our character than [would] a removal of the Judge who has rendered them unknowing of his fault."[37]

Thomas C. Grey

"Justice is the end of government. It is the end of civil society. It ever has been, and ever will be pursued, until it be obtained, or until liberty be lost in the pursuit."[38] But what is justice? The author of these lines in *Federalist* number 51 could have provided an answer broadly representative of the view of his founding compatriots; but, as Thomas Grey has reminded us, "Intellectually, the 18th century philosophical framework supporting the concept of immutable natural rights was eroded with the growth of legal positivism, ethical relativism, pragmatism, and historicism."[39] Grey nevertheless wishes to enlist the judiciary in the pursuit of a socially just society. His observation shows, however, that he appreciates the complexity and riskiness of this assignment in the modern era.

Although he has written in opposition to S. 158, Grey's understanding of judicial finality is not immediately evident from his scholarly writings. Yet it is possible inferentially to conclude that his defense of the unwritten constitution, and the mode of adjudication associated with it, would lead him to a position of extreme circumspection in regard to nonjudicial institutional involvement in constitutional interpretation. Assuming that the most likely objection to Grey is that his constitutional theory encourages judges to roam freely in search of that version of the unwritten constitution that best accommodates contemporary visions of justice, he might understandably be reluctant to strengthen the force of the objection by including additional governmental actors in the same practice.

On the other hand, the bold, potentially far-reaching noninterpretive review advocated by Grey would seem, in a constitutional democracy, to cry out for some form of popular check or safeguard. Michael Perry, for example, whose functional justification for noninterpretive adjudication does not claim to fulfill the expectations of the founders, insists that the principle of electorally accountable policy-making be satisfied as a condition for adopting the aggressive judicial approach that he, Grey, and others support. His method for satisfying this condition is the controversial jurisprudence-limiting power of Congress traceable to Article III of the Constitution. This enables Congress to exercise political control over noninterpretive review by preventing the federal judiciary from enforcing value judgments not constitutionalized by the framers.

Without addressing the considerable doubts raised over the constitutionality of legislation restricting federal jurisdiction, and without examining the efficacy of this strategy as a method of political control, we may nevertheless suggest certain theoretical implications of the proposal. Initially it is worth noting that restricting the jurisdiction of the federal courts does nothing to reverse a particular decision of the Supreme Court—*Roe* v. *Wade*, for example—but, in fact reinforces its finality by denying the Court the opportunity to reverse itself. It is a method of political control stemming much more obviously from political, rather than constitutional, considerations. Congress in effect declares to the Court (and its electorate) that it no longer wants the federal judiciary mucking around in the fields of abortion, or busing, or school prayer, or whatever. Constitutional questions surrounding these policy issues remain unresolved—a functional response to a functional provocation. In a sense this is altogether appropriate, or at least symmetrical: trans-constitutional stimulus triggering trans-constitutional response.

If the Congress may silence the Court through its Article III authority, why should not the principle of electoral accountability also entitle it to reverse the Court? Perry anticipates this question, and his response is revealing. As a noninterpretivist he is perhaps himself not persuaded by his initial reflection that there is no explicit constitutional authorization for such a power, and so he quickly moves on to the following argument.

> Were Congress to be conceded the power to reverse, we would come to view the Court, in its noninterpretive role, as a sort of delegate to Congress much as a court in its common-law role is a delegate of the legislature, which may revise the common law. Such a change in the relationship between Congress and the Court would tend to undermine

the very inter-institutional tension—the dialectical interplay between Court and Congress—that is the reason to value noninterpretive review in the first place. The moral authority of the Court's voice would be diminished; its opinions would be essentially only advisory.[40]

This is a strong argument, although rarely does one encounter the bold proposition that Congress has the authority to reverse, by act of legislation, a judicial decision. (S. 158 is incorrectly described by Perry in this context as *reversing Roe* v. *Wade.* That is the ultimate hope of its sponsors, but the legislation itself would not accomplish that end.) It is, however, the noninterpretive underpinnings of Perry's constitutional theory—or, in Grey's terms, the reliance upon an unwritten constitution—that requires giving serious thought to something as radical as outright reversal.

Thus, only when the legitimacy of noninterpretive review is conceded do we need to provide a direct, electorally accountable check to judicial power. If the Court is going to make policy in accordance with extra-constitutional values, then Congress must possess the wherewithal to prevent or reverse decisions that are incompatible with its own views on policy and values. If, on the other hand, we do not concede the legitimacy of noninterpretive review, then congressional intervention is justified by the obligation to support the Constitution, rather than the need to provide a popular check to the policy-making of an unelected branch of government. This in turn allows us to imagine less drastic forms of congressional involvement than either reversal, which Perry rightly must reject, or prevention, which has the perhaps ironic effect of sustaining judicial finality. As we shall see shortly, an intellectually coherent dialectical relationship between Court and Congress presupposes a constitutional theory in which commitment to intra-constitutional principle legitimizes nonjudicial participation in an interpretive process pointing toward settled constitutional meaning.

John Hart Ely

"[O]ur society does not, rightly does not, accept the notion of a discoverable and objectively valid set of moral principles, at least not a set that could plausibly serve to overturn the decisions of our elected representatives."[41] It presumably follows from Ely's understanding that a similar implication applies in the opposite direction: no moral principles could plausibly serve to qualify the finality of a judicial decision. If the preservation of fundamental values is not, as Ely claims, an appropriate judicial task, then resistance to a constitutional decision on grounds of its offensiveness to an "objectively valid set of moral principles" is not an appropriate legislative task. Thus, for example, Lincoln's call for congressional action in response to *Dred Scott* was predicated upon the assumption that the Constitution embodied substantive principles of natural right, which required nurturing and defense on the part of all those charged with high governmental responsibility.

What about a situation where the Court performs egregiously by its failure to advance the cause of a "participation-oriented representation-reinforcing" polity? In many cases the question of judicial finality would be largely academic—for example, where a legislature has the authority to remove the obstacles to the democratic process that the Court has itself declined to remedy; or where the Court *has* removed an obstacle and the Congress disapproves. Surely resistance, under Ely's theory, could not be justified in the interests of what in effect would be a nonparticipation representation-retarding cause. Thus, a one-person, one-vote ruling by the Court could not be upset by congressional support for a some-people, two-vote scheme of legislative apportionment.

Ultimately, however, it is the issue of trust that would appear to signal the Ely approach to judicial finality. "[O]ur elected representatives are the last persons we should trust" with the securing of representational rights under the Constitution.[42] Ely's view parallels Jesse Choper's functional analysis of the role of the Supreme Court, which holds that "in continuing vigorously to exercise its power of judicial review over [individual rights] issues, the Court is performing its vital role in American democratic society—the role for which it is peculiarly suited and for which all other government institutions are not."[43]

A healthy distrust of popular institutions is certainly prudent, particularly in relation to the protection of individual rights. As we have seen, however, the founders, while similarly prudent in these matters, did not on this account establish rigid functional divisions of labor between the Court and popular institutions. Because they did not view the Court as unique in its capacity to safeguard individual rights, their constitutional theory did not foreclose the possibility of nonjudicial institutional involvement in matters of constitutional interpretation.[44] But when the level of distrust directed, for example, at the legislative branch is so high that one assumes a basic unfitness in responsibly acting on certain matters of great constitutional importance, then it becomes difficult to imagine effective qualifications of judicial finality emerging from the popular institutions. Why sanction an interpretive role for a branch of government understood to be unsuited for such work?

In this regard, the inferences we have drawn are similar to what was said about Dworkin. In the case of Ely there is one additional consideration. The case for an unqualified judicial finality also stems from the fact that the judges are "experts on process," and for Ely it is process, rather than substance, that is the essence of constitutional law. Thus, it is not simply a negative functionalism—distrust of legislative justice—that legitimizes an exclusive role for the Court; the expertise of the Court in precisely those areas that matter most creates a compelling positive claim for supremacy by the federal judiciary.

II. S. 158: Congress and the Court

One's perspective on finality illuminates the issue of institutional responsibility in the determination of constitutional meaning. From one perspective, which we might refer to as declaratory, or static, the Court has a monopoly over such determinations; from another, the aspirational, it can accommodate itself, even invite, congressional involvement in the interpretive process.

A glance at the dictionary reveals the word "final" to mean a state of affairs "not to be altered or undone: conclusive"; as well as a condition "of or relating to the ultimate purpose or result of a process."[45] Standing alone, the first of these meanings may remind us of a person in authority who announces, concerning some activity, "that's final!"— perhaps accompanying the declaration with the phrase "like it or not." An emphasis, however, on the second meaning yields a state of finality connoting culmination or fulfillment. What is "not to be altered or undone"?—that which has realized its truest self, its "ultimate purpose."

Without certain assumptions about the aspirational content of the Constitution, judicial finality is left unqualified by the second dictionary rendering, so that constitutional interpretations are conclusive upon declaration by the Supreme Court. The fact that a majority in Congress may regard a given interpretation as unconstitutional, as, in the most extreme instance, a repudiation of animating constitutional ideals, does not legitimate congressional efforts to develop an alternative interpretation. That would call into question the finality of judicial judgments and more broadly undermine assumptions basic to the stability of the legal system.

This issue is well exemplified by the 1982 debate over S. 158, the so-called "Human Life Bill." The first two sections of this legislation read as follows:

Section 1. (a) The Congress finds that the life of each human being begins at conception.

(b) The Congress further finds that the fourteenth amendment to the Constitution of the United States protects all human beings.

Section 2. Upon the basis of these findings, and in the exercise of the powers of Congress, including its power under section 5 of the fourteenth amendment to the Constitution of the United States, the Congress hereby recognizes that for the purpose of enforcing the obligation of the States under the fourteenth amendment not to deprive persons of life without due process of law, each human life exists from conception, without regard to race, sex, age, health, defect, or condition of dependency, and for this purpose "person" includes all human beings.[46]

Another controversial section seeks, under the authority of Article III of the Constitution, to withdraw federal court jurisdiction in cases involving or arising from state laws or municipal ordinances restricting or regulating abortions. Testimony on this two-pronged assault upon *Roe* v. *Wade* was voluminous, featuring prestigious names from both the scientific and legal communities. The discussion here will focus on sections 1 and 2 quoted above.

These sections deeply disturbed a number of the witnesses at the hearings. For Senator Moynihan, for example, the "legislation constitutes a direct assault upon the constitutional processes and concepts of the U.S. Government."[47] It is one thing for "Congress [to] set in motion a process for amending the Constitution, but with respect to the interpretation of the words of the Constitution, the Court is the supreme branch of Government."[48] Archibald Cox described S. 158 as an unprincipled, radical attack upon "the foundations of our Constitution."[49] Senator Hatch, an outspoken opponent of the *Roe* decision, and the principal author of a constitutional amendment seeking its reversal, pointed out that

> Even if S. 158 was not more than a Congressional attempt to get the Court to take another look at its 1973 decisions, there would still be no basis for the Congress to "advise" the Supreme Court on the "proper" meaning of the Constitution. The role of the Congress is to legislate.[50]

This latter sentiment finds expression also among those not sharing Senator Hatch's ideology or specific views on abortion. Thus, according to Laurence Tribe, "Congress is empowered only to *make laws*, not to lobby or advise the courts."[51]

The proponents of the bill sought to minimize the challenge to the Court's authority. Thus the subcommittee's report emphasized that "The purpose of this legislation is not to impair the Supreme Court's power to review the constitutionality of legislation, but to exercise the authority of Congress to disagree with the result of an earlier Supreme Court decision based on an investigation of facts and on a decision concerning values that the Supreme Court has declined to address."[52] Without denying the ultimate finality of the Court's decisions, the subcommittee majority rejected any expectation of automatic deference to judicial interpretation of the Constitution. As they portrayed it, their efforts were directed toward the end of establishing responsible dialogue between Congress and the Court. Needless to say, a reversal of *Roe* was seen as the best possible outcome of this dialogue.

In addition, a credible case could be made that, wittingly or unwittingly, it was the Court, not the Congress, who had initiated the dialogue. Depending upon one's perspective on the issue, the Court in *Roe* was either refreshingly candid or transparently disingenuous in its declaration of incompetence to decide the vexing question of when human life begins. But since humility of this kind, sincere or not, is rare in Washington, it might have been anticipated that at least some congressmen would see as only natural their filling of the vacuum left by the Court's admission. Hence Section I(a)'s finding that human life begins at conception, far from representing an assault upon the integrity of the judicial process, complements and supports this process by providing vital information to guide the Court's further deliberations on the constitutional questions involving abortion.

Yet S. 158 does more than fill a vacuum. Section I(b) proceeds to interpret the Fourteenth Amendment's guarantees as extending to all human beings, and thus, as Section 2 makes explicit, broadens the meaning of the Fourteenth Amendment's operative word "person" in a way that brings it into direct conflict with the Supreme Court's decision. Justice Blackmun's opinion for the Court had severed the issue of personhood from the determination—or nondetermination—of the origins of human life, essentially agreeing with those who urged a postnatal condition as a prerequisite for constitutional protection. The connection between (a) and (b) is made clear in the subcommittee's report.

> A congressional determination that unborn children are human beings and that their lives have intrinsic worth and equal value will encourage the Court to reexamine the results and reasoning of *Roe* v. *Wade*. . . . The Court's view of the relative weight of the interests of the unborn child was necessarily influenced by the Court's professed inability to determine whether the unborn child was a living human being. It is difficult to believe that the Court would again balance the respective interests in such a way as to allow abortion on demand, if the Court were to recognize that one interest involved was the life of a human being.[53]

In short, faced with an unambiguous declaration on the humanity of the fetus, the Court would find it very difficult to persist in its denial of personhood to prenatal life.

Of course, it just might persist in spite of the Congress's intervention, a possibility that led to opposition from some of *Roe's* detractors, who viewed S. 158 as too weak. The political and legal reality of S. 158 is that it leaves the outcome in *Roe* v. *Wade* untouched; although it certainly anticipates modification, and ultimate reversal, in the future. Conceptually it represents a stage in the politics of rights, a variation on Stuart A. Scheingold's argument that rights-oriented decisions of the Supreme Court are best construed as political resources that *begin* a process leading to progressive social change. Eventually political mobilization transforms the initial proclamation of rights into the actual enforcement and realization of rights. "Since rights carry with them connotations of entitlement, a declaration of rights tends to politicize needs by changing the way people think about their discontents."[54] The decision of the Court, then, is the crucial moment in a dynamic that ends only with the attainment of a reality that incorporates the values of our political-constitutional creed.

Similarly, congressional intervention on behalf of a particular constitutional interpretation of rights may also be construed as a political resource pointed toward eventual progress. The Court here must be understood as a political institution in the broad sense that it is responsible to a mobilization of resources pushing it to a greater approximation of constitutional ideals. "The assumption is that our rights are reflected in, protected by, and consistent with the basic tendencies of American politics—allowing, of course, for some inevitable slippage between reality and aspiration."[55] This does not mean that any such mobilization, whether or not it includes congressional input, will or should influence the Court, only that the Court must allow itself to remain open to persuasion in regard to the possible narrowing of the gap between reality and aspiration in constitutional adjudication.

Nothing, then, obliges the Court to embrace the Congress's alternative rendering of constitutional meaning. By the same token, however, nothing precludes Congress from counterposing its own version of constitutional meaning in a situation where a judicial decision is viewed as destructive of that meaning. One would hope that this sort of legislative activity would occur only infrequently and—to be at all effective as a political resource it would have to be—reserved for those instances when widespread conviction exists that fundamental constitutional rights have been abrogated by the Court. As a matter of constitutional theory, however, it is difficult to understand why a legislative finding at variance with a judicial determination, but which is not binding upon the Court or anyone else, is a dangerous threat to the constitutional system, as was frequently alleged.

For example, in a letter to the subcommitee considering S. 158, Laurence Tribe claimed: "At stake . . . is not simply an attack . . . on the binding effect of the Constitution, as construed by the Court, upon those whom the people elect to public office—those whose oaths to uphold the Constitution as the supreme law of the land can be enforced in no other way than through Supreme Court review."[56] Tribe's argument recalls Stephen Douglas's challenge to Lincoln. A congressman's oath to uphold the Constitution implies an obligation to accept the binding effect of the Constitution, *as construed by the Court*. This means either that the Constitution is what the Supreme Court says it is or that the supremacy of the Constitution is contingent upon absolute deference to judicial interpretation, correct or incorrect, of the document. Lincoln had also relied upon the congressional oath, but for him the binding character of the Constitution symbolized by the oath required that a distinction be made between the principles of the document and the construction of those charged with applying the text in specific cases. Tribe's position does not require passive resignation in the face of grossly distasteful Supreme Court decisions; his view (and that of many others who testified) is that "the only way to undo a proposition of constitutional law is by constitutional amendment, not by legislative redefinition of constitutional language."[57] Indeed, the amendment procedure illustrates quite well that the framers did not want a simple majority of legislators defining and redefining the Constitution at their pleasure.

Ultimately the Constitution of *Dred Scott* was altered through amendment, and it is likely that if the right to an abortion is to be read out of the Constitution, an amendment will be necessary. While those advocating this change may come to see this as something demanded by political realities, it is important to understand why it is not demanded by the logic of constitutional theory, as Tribe and others have suggested. Or more precisely, it is important to appreciate why the logic of a constitutional theory that embodies an aspirational component grounded in fixed principles of political justice does not compel one to insist upon new constitutional language.

Let us imagine here that Hamilton's argument in number 84 had prevailed, that his case against including a bill of rights had persuaded his contemporaries to drop their plans to amend the Constitution. Now let us suppose that in a subsequent case involving a claim to a right, one which Hamilton had believed was protected by the unamended Constitution, the Supreme Court announced that no such protection could be found in the document and therefore the claim must fail. No doubt someone at this point would have approached Hamilton with the following sort of argument. "Look here, Mr. Hamilton. Evidently you were wrong in your claim about the

Constitution—that the Constitution was itself a Bill of Rights, and all of that. And we were foolish to have allowed you to persuade us of your point. So now you must join us in our belated efforts to amend the Constitution as originally proposed, for the Supreme Court has clearly repudiated your understanding. The Constitution, as I suspected all along, does not guarantee our right to be protected against unreasonable searches and seizures." What might Hamilton have said in response? How would the author of *Federalist* number 78, the classic justification of judicial review, have reacted to the Court's rejection of his argument in number 84?

Hamilton might very well have thought it expedient at this point to join in the efforts of his colleagues; but on principle it is possible to imagine the following rejoinder: "No doubt what I have to say will be seen as a further manifestation of Hamilton's monumental ego, but I assure you that the issue involved here is of transcendent importance, involving principles of political justice that dwarf us all. You say that the Supreme Court has repudiated my argument, and that therefore the Constitution does not include the guarantees I have maintained it does. I must reject this formulation, with its dangerous implication that the meaning of the Constitution is identifiable with the most recent Court decision; to join you would give tacit support to a constitutional theory that has no place in our political system. Let me explain.

"My contention in number 84 that the Constitution protects certain rights, though no specific enumeration was included in the document, is consistent with views that I have long espoused regarding our fundamental law. Thus, in the past I have appealed, for example, to the 'spirit of the Constitution,' intending to invoke principles of natural right whose embodiment in the Constitution demands attention by those responsible for its interpretation. The Court, however, has seen fit to ignore these principles, and we are asked to accept their judgment as final.

"Indeed, I have seen my own words used as support for this view, number 78 being quoted rather liberally in the press to stimulate interest in your amendment plans. 'The interpretation of the laws,' I wrote in that number, 'is the proper and peculiar province of the courts.'[58] And from this, you may wonder, in light of all the recent attention given this observation, whether I am not being inconsistent in declining to acknowledge as ultimately authoritative the interpretation of the Supreme Court. I do not think so, as my discussion of that essay will presently show.

"In the first place you must recall that my purpose in number 78 was to affirm the necessity of judicial review, and in so doing, establish the superiority of the Constitution to ordinary law. In declaring acts void that are 'contrary to the manifest tenor of the constitution,' the courts defend a most vital principle, that 'No legislative act . . . contrary to the constitution can be valid.'[59] Can it now be maintained that a judicial act contrary to the Constitution is valid? To be sure, as I indicated in my essay, there are good reasons to suppose that an independent Court will be more reliably scrupulous in its adherence to the Constitution than an elected legislature; but this relative advantage hardly establishes the infallibility of the judiciary, nor the illegitimacy of legislative opposition in the face of judicial decisions deemed violative of constitutional principle.

"Nowhere in number 78 do I claim that the interpretation of the fundamental law is a uniquely judicial responsibility. The passage that is so often quoted refers specifically to the laws passed by the legislature, where, of course, 'the constitution ought to be preferred to the statute.'[60] Notice my argument three paragraphs later, where, appealing to nature and reason, I say: 'They teach us that the prior act of a superior ought to be preferred to the subsequent act of an inferior and subordinate authority; and that, accordingly, whenever a particular statute contravenes the constitution, it will be the duty of the judicial tribunals to adhere to the latter, and disregard the former.'[61] Is it not implicit in your position that when a judicial decision contravenes the Constitution, the legislature must adhere to the former and disregard the latter? Surely it was not my intent to suggest that the institution of judicial review established the equivalent authority of the Court and the Constitution. So if the Court, like the Congress, is subordinate to the Constitution, and since members of both institutions are sworn to uphold the superior authority of the fundamental law, does it not follow from the logic of number 78 that ultimate finality in judicial interpretation of the Constitution is not to be reflexively conferred upon every constitutional judgment of the highest tribunal?

"In short, then, my answer to you is that my continued adherence to the constitutional views voiced in number 84 obliges me at this point to decline your invitation. I would not want the inference to be drawn from my support of an amendatory agenda that I now concede, as a political fact, the interpretation of the Constitution set forth by the judges of the Supreme Court. Rather, I choose to work with those in the legislature, who share my beliefs, to persuade the Court to reverse itself. Of course, should this effort fail I may ultimately have to join you, but at least then my decision will be rightfully perceived as expediential rather than principled."

These imaginary remarks provoke one to recall Hamilton's reflections on legislative checks and balances, the judiciary, and the science of politics cited in Chapter 2. "They are means," he declared, "and powerful means, by which the excellences of republican government may be reformed and its imperfections lessened or avoided."[62] The "excellences" and "imperfections" of republican government may be seen now in aspirational terms, given substance by the scientific and epistemological context of the eighteenth century, and expressive of the unified purpose underlying the institutions of our national government. From Hamilton to Douglass to Lincoln to King, this purpose meant realizing the ideals at the core of our understanding of republican government.

III. Conclusion

"To be an American . . . is an ideal; while to be a Frenchman is a fact."[63] Samuel Huntington employs this observation of Carl Friedrich to support an argument for the uniqueness of the American national identity—its political rather than organic character. One can speak of the "American Creed"—a set of core political values (liberty, equality, individualism, democracy, and the rule of law under a constitution)— in a way that one cannot speak of a British Creed, a French Creed, or an Italian Creed. Where other societies have created national identities out of language, ethnicity, culture, religion, or some combination of these organic characteristics, Americans, Huntington maintains, have nothing important in common, no cementing unity, without the complex amalgam of goals and values that constitute the American Creed.

> The United States came into existence at a particular moment in time— July 4, 1776—and it was the product of a conscious political act based on explicit political principles. "We hold these truths to be self-evident," says the Declaration. Who holds these truths? Americans hold these truths. Who are Americans? People who adhere to these truths. National identity and political principle were inseparable.[64]

Identity and principles find their official expression in the Constitution; therefore the document becomes, in effect, the basis of community. "In other countries, one can abrogate the constitution without abrogating the nation. The United States does not have that choice."[65] Thus the treatment and resolution of constitutional questions assumes a significance in the United States that is perhaps unique: the articulation, preservation, and perpetuation of the ideals and aspirations that define the national character.

This task, however, is complicated by the potential contradictions embodied within the creed. The relatively unsystematic state of the political ideas forming the creed, and hence the difficulty of ordering them in relation to each other, produces the possibility of deriving a variety of identities, the outcome depending upon the emphasis one attaches to this or that individual value. As we have indicated earlier, this concern is particularly relevant in the modern era, where strong pressures exist to perceive antinomies in ideas such as liberty and equality, individualism and democracy, and majority rule and minority rights. Huntington notes that the configuration of the several commitments that make up the substance of the American Creed varies in shape and form from individual to individual. He also notes that for most people they are, in the end, always in some kind of balance, with no value given absolute priority over any other. "The checks and balances that exist among the institutions of American politics are paralleled by the checks and balances that exist among the ideas of the American Creed."[66]

This checking and balancing parallelism suggests a model for an institutional structure of constitutional interpretation compatible with the aspirational dimensions of constitutional design. In this model the Court exercises the principal responsibility for constitutional interpretation, a responsibility involving, in Alexander Bickel's formulation, the articulation of the society's "enduring values."[67] But to entrust the meaning of the Constitution, the definition of American national identity, to an exclusive judicial monopoly, is risky business indeed. The stakes, as Huntington suggests, are enormous. If, for example, the egalitarian strand of creedal aspirations is weighted too heavily by the Court, so that the equilibrium of the whole is upset, then should there not be some institutional mechanism to give effective voice to the libertarian filament in our constitutional constellation? If our commitment is to the constitutional principles that in the end define us as a people, then we must direct our energies to the support of those structures of interpretation that can best realize such lofty and consequential commitment. This may sound obvious, but, to paraphrase Holmes, education in the obvious is more important than elucidation of the obscure.

CHAPTER **8**

Conclusion: "To Seize the Permanent"

"IT IS ESSENTIALLY ACCURATE to say that the Court's preoccupation today is with the application of rather fundamental aspirations."[1] Few today would find fault with this observation made by Felix Frankfurter in 1957. As a general proposition, a judicial function involving the application of fundamental aspirations is compatible with the jurisprudential perspectives of a wide range of constitutional theory. But this compatibility would not likely survive Frankfurter's elaboration of the judicial guidelines associated with aspirational applications. The function requires the "habit of curbing any tendency to reach results agreeable to desire" and "a disposition to be detached and withdrawn."[2] These are moral qualities, Frankfurter indicates, that "are desirable in all judges, but . . . indispensable for the Supreme Court."[3] Why? "Its task is to seize the permanent, more or less, from the feelings and fluctuations of the transient."[4]

Thus, the type of aspirations that are properly the business of the Supreme Court are ones relating to what is permanent in constitutional adjudication. That, no doubt, is what makes them "fundamental." Those aspirations whose wellspring is located in the transient desires of the moment are, or should be, of no direct concern to constitutional interpretation. This has two possible meanings: first, that while it is certainly appropriate for judges to accommodate aspirations flowing from the desires of the moment (by not creating unnecessary constitutional obstacles to their fulfillment), the existence of desire should not create judicial obligations for gratification mandated by the Constitution; and second, that judges should resist the temptation to follow any currently fashionable moral system that would deflect them from the central task of "seizing the permanent" or, as has been suggested in the previous pages, realizing constitutional aspiration.

This is all well and good, but by this point the patient reader is probably anxious to have several related matters addressed directly. They fall generally under the question "So what?" Perhaps the most important could be put in terms of the following objection: assume that what has been earlier maintained is true, that the Constitution embodies a particular theory of natural rights, which theory contains most, if not all, of the substance of constitutional aspiration. Of what relevance is this to those concerned with issues of contemporary constitutional interpretation? Does it make a difference? Indeed, *can* it, if we also acknowledge that appeals to natural rights no longer retain the prestige or credibility that they did in the past? Moreover, since few constitutional disputes turn on issues addressed by eighteenth-century natural rights theory, how can such theory be expected to instruct us in regard to judicial decisions?

We might respond to these queries by first recalling an important distinction. Constitutional aspirations refer to the aspirations of the Constitution. What saves this bit of triteness from utter banality is the further point that these aspirations do not contain a specific blueprint or vision for what our society should become. Thus what the Constitution aspires to will leave considerable space for the political application of additional aspirations, concerning which the document is basically agnostic. These latter aspirations may not contradict constitutional design, which consists of the fundamental principles that determine, in effect, the type of regime we may *not* become. Indeed, this sort of negative formulation of aspirational content is consistent with the natural rights theory that is its most important source.

Thus, some of the criticism that is understandably produced by the advocacy of necessarily fuzzy concepts of natural justice might be minimized if we establish appropriate interpretive boundaries for adjudication. To say that eighteenth-century political philosophy is useless in the context of contemporary constitutional jurisprudence is only correct if one chooses to ignore a critical fact, that this philosophy was not intended to have specific application to many important constitutional questions. Whether or not, for example, the legislative veto is constitutional must be resolved according to language, principles, and precedents that do not reach the level of natural rights consideration.

Similarly, the fact that there is often no present consensus on social aspirations is a problem only if we erroneously identify such aspirations with constitutional requirement. A review of a recently published collection of essays criticizes the author, Laurence Tribe, for proposing that "constitutional choices" be "based on a vision of what 'we' wish our society to become."[5] Unfortunately, the critique claims, in the issues argued in the courts " 'we' do not ordinarily hold a single vision of the society 'we' wish to become, let alone how best to move toward any such goal."[6] The objection to Tribe's argument is, in essence, that he confuses the particular social aspirations of some with the commitments mandated by the Constitution.

This objection, however, does not hold against constitutional aspiration rightly understood. Here it is not a matter of a judicial determination of what "we" aspire to as a society; but rather of an effort by judges to retrieve, where relevant, the constitutional aspirations of the framers. In so doing they will need to consult, and to reflect upon, the natural rights principles of these framers, and ultimately to ask themselves how it is possible for them, as judges, to interpret—understand and apply—our fundamental law if they reject, or simply are ignorant of, its presuppositions. Surely this was Lincoln's view at the time when the Supreme Court, and particularly its chief justice, seemed so tragically uninformed about the Constitution's underlying principles.

The example of Lincoln, as instructive as it is, nevertheless raises a problem. If there is anything today that unambiguously stands as a violation of natural rights principles, it is the institution of slavery. Now that we no longer have that evil to contend with, what further jurisprudential role can be anticipated from a theory of constitutional aspiration that is dependent upon these principles? Will not any other applications be inherently controversial?

There are two ways to respond to these questions. The first is to acknowledge that, yes, we are unlikely to secure anything approximating a consensus on the application of natural rights arguments to any important constitutional issue before the court. This was, of course, also true in Lincoln's day with respect to the issue of slavery, and it is true, moreover, with respect to all imaginable approaches to the sorts of questions that today's Supreme Court agrees to decide. If an issue gets to the Court it is by definition highly controversial, and its resolution, on whatever grounds, will be viewed by many as indefensible.

But this response is evasive. It does not confront, for example, Raoul Berger's claim that natural law approaches inevitably raise the specter of judicial subjectivity, allowing judges to shield their personal agendas behind the banner of ultimate reality. This claim has force even if, as we have argued, Berger is mistaken regarding the historic nexus between eighteenth-century natural rights theory and the origins of the Constitution. One might choose to accept our alternative historical account while still finding wisdom in the warning that more harm than good is the probable result of an insistence that this history provide standards for governing contemporary constitutional adjudication.

But should one make this choice? Perhaps, but only if there is no hope of revitalizing constitutional aspiration, in which case the appropriate response is to consider ways of cutting our losses. The loss that would be most difficult to replace is the general guidance that the aspirational commitments of the framers provides to those responsible for interpretive constitutional judgments. These commitments provide an intellectual context that both sets limits and suggests possibilities for judicial consideration of difficult constitutional cases. It is easy to dismiss natural rights theory as providing glittering generalities that are essentially useless. The generalities (if one insists on discussing them in this way) can be important, however, in initiating a line of inquiry that, when brought to bear upon specific constitutional questions, may help produce wise decisions.

A wise decision is one that, at a minimum, is consistent with constitutional aspiration, which is to say that it does not contradict the core principles of the liberal constitutional polity. Judges should be encouraged to place claims that are asserted before the Court within the broader political framework of the fundamental law. This may narrow the possible bases of decision, suggesting the implausibility of certain lines of argument or the viable options contained within others. If the issue, for example, calls for the recognition or nonrecognition by the Court of a right that is not explicitly guaranteed in the Constitution, the first question raised should be: Is the alleged constitutional right of a type that displays a consistency with the constitutional conception of individual rights? The natural rights philosophy underlying this conception has been aptly summarized:

> The form of our rights is that they are primarily *rights to do, keep, or acquire things* and corresponding *rights not to have things done to us or taken from us*. . . . Securing rights in this conception is a matter of providing security for enjoyment or pursuit, not of providing the desired objects of the rights themselves.[7]

Constitutional provisions, such as due process or equal protection, should then have their applicability to the case at hand assessed in the light of this basic rights orientation, an orientation that expresses a broad commitment to the type of polity the Constitution aspires to have.

This is, of course, only the initial step in the judicial process of inquiry and deliberation. One might imagine the justices in conference discussing the specific implications of this rights orientation. Since we are imagining, we can even assume that they are in agreement on the general question of rights and its relationship to constitutional aspiration. Still, unless we choose the wildest of fantasies, there will at this point be considerable disagreement. Thus, some judges will argue that in late twentieth century America the notion of what constitutes security, as well as what constitutes minimum conditions for the pursuit of happiness, requires an expansion of constitutionally guaranteed rights. Others will respond by pointing out that it is not the Court's responsibility to facilitate the practice of rights; that the

Constitution enables other institutions, as matters of policy, to address the socioeconomic preconditions of rights enjoyment.

An impasse? Maybe. But at least an intellectual context has been established within which further discussion might yield useful distinctions and standards for adjudication. Each side of the debate will have a common philosophical and historical tradition to anchor its arguments; to the extent that a genuine commitment to constitutional aspiration exists among all participants, there is a reasonable chance that the quality of judicial decisions will be enhanced, or at least that the caliber of discourse in judicial opinions will command more respectful attention. By seeking to justify specific interpretations by their compatibility with certain basic principles of liberal constitutionalism, the judges will be sensitized, in a way that is potentially more productive than formal incantations of such doctrines as judicial restraint and judicial activism, to the philosophic underpinnings of judicial review. They will be drawn to the principles that animated the founders, and will elaborate and deploy them to sharpen their understanding of contemporary constitutional issues. In some instances this will result in a broad exercise of judicial power; in others, a passive role in relation to alternative governmental actors. Constitutional aspiration, rather than formalistic prescriptions of functional roles, should indicate the appropriate scope of judicial authority.

Perhaps, then, it would be helpful to conclude this study by specifying a couple of general interpretive principles that are suggested by our examination and contrast of founding and modern perspectives in constitutional theory.

Sources

For the purpose of determining constitutional meaning, an obvious question is: To which extra-textual sources is it legitimate for judges to appeal? Even the narrowist interpretivist will accept the propriety of consulting the debates at the Constitutional Convention, and in most cases the *Federalist Papers* will pass the test for acceptability. These sources, as well as some of the debates in the ratifying conventions, bear directly on the issue of founding intent. After this, consensus disintegrates. If, however, the Constitution incorporates principles of natural right within such clauses as due process and obligations of contracts as well as within the general framework of constitutional structure and design, then it is appropriate to elucidate meaning with sources—for example, *The Second Treatise of Government* and *An Essay Concerning Human Understanding* by John Locke—that speak to the substance of the relevant principles. A different way of putting this is to say that a judge engaged in constitutional interpretation should be able to demonstrate that the extra-textual sources that he or she contemplates using are unambiguously illuminating of the principled commitments of the authors of the document.

Justice Holmes was correct in reminding us that the Constitution does not incorporate the socioeconomic principles of Herbert Spencer's *Social Statics*;[8] as is John Hart Ely in observing that the Constitution's meaning should not follow the prevailing orthodoxy of the *New York Review of Books*.[9] They are mistaken, however, if their larger point is to cast doubt upon the legitimacy of all judicial appeals to extra-textual articulations of political philosophy. Again, one should not imagine that the answers to complex constitutional problems will come dropping off the pages of this or that seminal text. On the other hand, it is worth contemplating how much of the Court's doctrinal gymnastics in such areas as free speech or free exercise might have been avoided had its responses to these issues been more systematically organized in accordance with the premises of appropriately selected external sources.[10]

Change

In addition, there are of course extra-textual sources of a nontextual character. Roscoe Pound was instrumental in causing judges to look beyond the printed page to appreciate the interpretive significance of social facts. But his assault upon the excesses of mechanical jurisprudence engendered its own excesses, in particular the facile notion developed later of the "living Constitution," the idea that the meaning of the Constitution changes with evolving socioeconomic conditions. A more subtle formulation of this transparently problematic position, exemplified in the work of Ronald Dworkin, emphasizes the continuity of fundamental constitutional principles through the use of an appealing concepts/conceptions distinction. This distinction, however, as we have seen, achieves by indirection what is not concealed in the sociological school, the adaptation of constitutional meanings to significant changes in the American social condition.

The question of adaptation is a vexing one in constitutional theory. Clearly, as Marshall put it in *McCulloch* v. *Maryland*, the Constitution was intended "to be adapted to the various *crises* of human affairs."[11] Yet, for Marshall, as has been often pointed out, this meant that the Constitution provided Congress with great flexibility in responding to changing circumstances, not that the Supreme Court had authority to alter the meaning of the document to accommodate the needs of the times. Yet Marshall's commitment to a Constitution embodying principles of natural right requires us to give further thought to the Supreme Court's role in connection with social facts.

Here again it is useful to distinguish between constitutional and political or social aspirations. The adaptation referred to in *McCulloch* enables the legislature to seek the realization of aspirations that are consistent with constitutional, that is, "legitimate"—ends. Indeed, it is consistency with "the letter and spirit of the Constitution" that Marshall insists upon. The ends do not undergo change; however, they are sufficiently flexible (without ultimately being open-ended) to permit the political system to respond in a variety of ways to the emergence of new social realities.

Marshall and Hamilton both wrote of the "spirit of the Constitution," a reference to the animating, vital principles immanent within the document: its aspirations. While subsumed in its specific clauses, these aspirations transcended any particular language. Thus, for example, the Fourth Amendment's protection against unreasonable searches and seizures embodies a principle that is similar to what we have seen in the Fourteenth Amendment, takes precedence over the *specific* intent of its framers—if, that is, it can be demonstrated that this principle will be preserved only through an assertion of such a priority. The history and language of the Fourth Amendment might suggest that the guarantee applies to actual physical intrusion into one's home. Developments in electronic surveillance, however, might reasonably be cited by a judge wishing to honor the broader constitutional aspiration toward security in one's person, even if doing so means, in the case of a particular "bug," going beyond the specific intent of the framers.

In such a case, the judge does *not* alter principles in response to social facts in order to accommodate change. Thus, a new empirical reality cannot be the occasion for judicial reassessment of fundamental principle, despite what might appear to some to be the desirability of a major substitution of aspirational commitment. In short, arguments over the interpretive significance of social facts should take place within the context of agreement over the immutability (at least as far as judges are concerned) of constitutional aspirations. (Remember James Wilson: "The law of nature, though immutable in its principles, will be progressive in its operations and effects.") Perhaps such an initial agreement will serve as well to stimulate a more concerted scholarly effort to reach greater agreement on the substance of these aspirations.

Let us conclude, as we began, with Frederick Douglass. There is a way, he maintained, to enforce the "external principles" of the Constitution, if the document is "interpreted as it *ought* to be interpreted." This from an ex-slave whose people were being oppressed with the sanction of specific clauses in the Constitution.

Douglass denied that the Constitution contained "a single proslavery clause,"[12] but, of course, he knew of the fateful compromises the framers had made that led to a continuation of the traffic and profit in slaves. In his "Fourth of July Oration" he chose not to dwell on specific clauses (referring his listeners to the legal analyses of several well-known lawyers). Instead, he focused on constitutional purpose, as evinced, for example, by the language of the Preamble. Judges do not have that luxury, and yet they would do well to consider Douglass's example. They need, in other words, to address themselves to both specific meanings and to the purposive dimensions of constitutional law, to interpret the particular in light of the whole.

But only, we should add, if this is accompanied by "a disposition to be detached and withdrawn." Otherwise the "tendency to reach results agreeable to desire" will empty purpose of its intended meaning, filling its now hollow shell with the "feelings and fluctuations of the transient." This is not the detachment of indifference, as in Stephen Douglas's neutrality position on slavery. It is the detachment of discipline, necessary to nurture the most demanding of judicial commitments—to what is permanent in our fundamental law, to constitutional aspiration.

Notes

Chapter 1

1. Frederick Douglass, "Fourth of July Oration," 32.
2. Ibid., 36.
3. Ibid., 31.
4. Ibid., 29.
5. Ibid., 30.
6. *The Collected Works of Abraham Lincoln*, vol. 2, ed. Roy Basler, 401.
7. Martin Luther King, "I have a Dream," speech delivered in Washington, D.C., Aug. 28, 1963.
8. Douglass, "Fourth of July Oration," 37, 30.
9. Ibid., 37.
10. Leo Strauss, *Natural Right and History*, 2.
11. *McCulloch* v. *Maryland*, 4 Wheat. 316 (1819), at 415.
12. Roscoe Pound, "Mechanical Jurisprudence," 609.

Chapter 2

1. Oliver Wendell Holmes, Jr., "Law in Science and Science in Law," 462.
2. Earl Warren, "Science and the Law: Change and the Constitution," 4.
3. Ibid., 3.
4. Garry Wills, *Inventing America: Jefferson's Declaration of Independence*, 93.
5. J. H. Randall, "The Newtonian World Machine," 161.
6. A number of studies consider the connection between Locke and Newton. Among the best are Ernst Cassirer, *The Philosophy of the Enlightenment*, and Charles C. Gillespie, *The Edge of Objectivity*.
7. *The Works of James Wilson*, vol. 1, ed. Robert G. McCloskey, 183. For a dissenting voice regarding the importance of Newton in guiding thinkers in the development of moral laws of nature, see Morton White, *The Philosophy of the American Revolution*, 157–60. White, contrary to scholars such as Edward S. Corwin and Carl Becker, argues that Locke himself distinguished epistemologically between moral laws of nature and a law of nature such as the law of gravitation. Even if true, however (White provides very little supporting evidence), Newton's depiction of an ordered, harmonious universe could still be viewed as a model for thinkers determined to show the necessity of certain principles of moral science.
8. McCloskey, ed., *The Works of James Wilson*, vol. 1, 97.
9. A good discussion of Mather's Newtonianism may be found in George H. Daniels, *Science in American Society*.

147

10. John Dewey, *The Quest for Certainty: A Study of the Relation of Knowledge and Action*, 110.
11. As Dewey's contemporary, the physicist Werner Heisenberg wrote, "It is to be expected that the present changes in the scientific concept of the universe will exert their influence upon the wider fields of the world of ideas" (*Philosophic Problems of Nuclear Science*, 21).
12. William Bennett Munro, "Physics and Politics—An Old Analogy Revised," 3, 5.
13. In some cases the references were inapposite: for example, the use of relativity theory to support ethical relativism. See, for example, an article by the important realist legal philosopher Walter W. Cook, "Scientific Method and Law." In some cases a rather sophisticated application of both scientific and epistemological nuances of the complex new physical theories is evident.
14. McCloskey, ed., *The Works of James Wilson*, vol. 1, 147.
15. Roscoe Pound, *Interpretations of Legal History*, 149.
16. Roscoe Pound, *The Spirit of the Common Law* (hereafter cited as *SCL*), 7.
17. Ibid.
18. Most notably in *Lochner* v. *New York*, 198 U.S. 45 (1905).
19. Because they had much in common it is easy to overlook the fundamental differences between Pound and Charles Beard, the period's foremost proponent of the economic interpretation of constitutional origins and development.
20. Pound, *The Formative Era of American Law*, 82. "The outstanding phenomenon is the extent to which a taught tradition, in the hands of judges drawn from any class one will, and chosen as one will, so they have been trained in the tradition, has stood out against all manner of economically or politically powerful interests" (p. 83).
21. Pound, *SCL*, 37.
22. Ibid., 13.
23. Quoted in ibid., 53.
24. Ibid., xii.
25. Blackstone's influence in America is an interesting and oft-told story. See, in particular, Dennis R. Nolan, "Sir William Blackstone and the New American Republic: A Study of Intellectual Impact." One should note that Blackstone's ideas were not met with universal acclaim in America. James Wilson and Thomas Jefferson, for example, expressed major disagreement on a number of key issues.
26. Pound, *SCL*, 15
27. Ibid., 20.
28. Ibid., 68.
29. Ibid., 30.
30. The most notable denial may be found in Raoul Berger's book *Government by Judiciary: The Transformation of the Fourteenth Amendment*.
31. Thus, in his plea for a scientific jurisprudence, the philosopher Felix Cohen argued that "intuitive or common sense ethics recognizes no dependence upon positive science" (*Ethical Systems and Legal Ideals*, 46). In so doing, Cohen accurately stated a commonly accepted tenet of

modern science, but one that would have stirred up considerable controversy had it been uttered in the presence of a group of eighteenth century philosophers of science.

32. Pound, *SCL*, 89.
33. Pound, *An Introduction to the Philosophy of Law*, 1.
34. See, especially, Field's opinion in *Butcher's Union Slaughter-House and Live-Stock Landing Company* v. *Crescent City Live-Stock and Slaughter-House Company*, 111 U.S. 746 (1884), at 766–67. As an earlier example of the judicial practice of "laying out philosophical and political and legal charts by which men were guided for all time," Pound cites Chief Justice Marshall's opinion in *Fletcher* v. *Peck* in Pound, *SCL*, 97.
35. Pound, *SCL*, 204.
36. White, *The Philosophy of The American Revolution*, 238–39.
37. Ibid., 239.
38. Arnold Brecht, *Political Theory: The Foundations of Twentieth Century Political Thought*, 159.
39. Hamilton was perhaps the most Lockean of all the founding fathers, but James Wilson—probably the least Lockean—affirmed a similar view. "Morality, like mathematics, has its intuitive truths, without which we cannot make a single step in our reasonings upon the subject" (McCloskey, ed., *The Works of James Wilson*, vol. 1, 133). He, too, spoke of "the science of morals," based on self-evident principles, and suggested that "all sound reasoning must rest ultimately on the principles of common sense" (ibid., 133, 213). Unlike Hamilton, whose Lockean epistemology was grounded in rational intuition, for Wilson these principles were not demonstrable or provable through reason. Nevertheless, they both addressed principles of scientific knowledge in the language of self-evidence, an important underlying assumption of which is that subsequent empirical investigation will not yield refutation of truths derived through the faculties of common sense.
40. *The Federalist*, ed. Jacob E. Cooke, no. 31, 193. It should be noted here that modern scholarship lacks a consensus regarding the epistemology of the self-evident propositions referred to by the founders. One school of thought, best represented in the work of Carl Becker (for example, *The Declaration of Independence*), maintains that Locke's rational intuitionism is the key to this epistemology; another, reflected in the work of Garry Wills (*Inventing America: Jefferson's Declaration of Independence*), argues for the decisive influence of the "moral sense" understanding of the Scottish Enlightenment. Of course, it is quite possible that disagreement also characterized the founders' thinking on these matters.
41. McCloskey, ed. *The Works of James Wilson*, vol. 2, 505. This position is quite consistent with the thought of the principal seventeenth-century theorists of scientific method—Bacon, Doyle, Descartes, Locke, Newton—who believed in instant, infallible scientific theories. None of the founders was known to question the underlying philosophic assumption of Newtonian physics, that the diverse phenomena of the physical world were ultimately knowable through the operation of an absolute and final set of purely quantitative laws.

42. "[W]hen it comes to the question whether human beings are 'essentially' equal, and whether all ought to be treated equally, science cannot claim authority to give a direct answer" (Brecht, 312). Brecht also notes that "scientific literature has . . . withdrawn from references to the 'self-evidence' of human equality" (ibid., 307).
43. Pound, *SCL*, 197.
44. White, *The Philosophy of the American Revolution*, 249.
45. Ibid., 251.
46. In recent years the notion of affirmative constitutional obligations has received growing attention. See, in particular, Arthur Selwyn Miller, "Toward a Concept of Constitutional Duty."
47. Pound, *SCL*, 102.
48. Ibid., 135.
49. *The Federalist*, no. 10, 58.
50. 12 Wheat. 419 (1827).
51. Sir William Blackstone, *Commentaries on the Laws of England*, vol.1, 125.
52. Pound, *SCL*, 151.
53. Letter to John Cartwright, June 5, 1824, in *The Political Writings of Thomas Jefferson*, ed. Edward Dumbauld, 126.
54. Pound, *SCL*, 181.
55. Ibid., 171.
56. Ibid., 172.
57. Quoted in Benjamin F. Wright, *American Interpretations of Natural Law: A Study in the History of Political Thought*, 125.
58. *The Federalist*, no. 81, 543, and no. 78, 523. This should be contrasted with Pound's declaration that "We should abandon to some extent the hard and fast line between the judicial and the administrative involved in our legal tradition" (Pound, *SCL*, 215).
59. *The Federalist*, no. 78, 523.
60. *Osborn* v. *Bank of the United States*, 22 U.S. 738, 866 (1824).
61. Morton J. Horwitz, "The Emergence of an Instrumental Conception of American Law, 1780–1820," 295.
62. Pound, *SCL*, 193.
63. Ibid., 183. This is a view that was shared by Benjamin N. Cardozo, with whom Pound has much in common. See, for example, Cardozo, *The Nature of the Judicial Process*, 116.
64. For an extended discussion of Pound's relationship to the pragmatic movement in American philosophy, see Gary J. Jacobsohn, *Pragmatism, Statesmanship, and the Supreme Court*.
65. Pound, *SCL*, 195.
66. See, for example, Alexander M. Bickel, *The Supreme Court and the Idea of Progress*.
67. Pound, *SCL*, 84.
68. Ibid., 93. See also his discussion of a new natural law ("with a changing or growing content") in his *Interpretations of Legal History*, 149.
69. William James, "The Moral Philosopher and the Moral Life," 201, 205. This essay had a profound impact upon Pound, who remarked that

"this seems to me a statement of the problem of the legal order" (Pound, *Interpretations of Legal History*, 157).

70. Pound, *Introduction to the Philosophy of Law*, 47.
71. Pound, *SCL*, 196.
72. Ibid., 199.
73. Bickel, *The Supreme Court and the Idea of Progress*, 103.
74. I have discussed the limitations of this theory elsewhere. See Jacobsohn, *Pragmatism, Statesmanship, and the Supreme Court*, 76–78.
75. Martin Diamond, "Ethics and Politics: The American Way," 47.
76. *The Federalist*, no. 10, 57.
77. Pound, *SCL*, 190.
78. *The Federalist*, no. 78, 529.
79. Ibid., 527.
80. Pound, "Law in Books and Law in Action," 18.
81. Pound, *Introduction to the Philosophy of Law*, 66.
82. Ibid., 68.
83. See, for example, William Kunstler, "Jury Nullification in Conscience Cases"; Joseph L. Sax, "Conscience and Anarchy: The Prosecution of War Resisters"; and Jan Van Dyke, "The Jury as a Political Institution."
84. *Sparf and Hansen v. United States*, 156 U.S. 51, 106 (1895).
85. Statements of Jefferson, Adams, and many others in support of the practice appear in *Sparf and Hansen v. United States*. See also *The Works of John Adams*, vol. 2, ed. Charles Francis Adams, 253; and *The Writings of Thomas Jefferson*, vol. 3, ed. H.A. Washington (letter to M. L. Abbe Arnold, July 19, 1789, 81).
86. The best historical accounts may be found in Mark DeWolfe Howe, "Juries as Judges of Criminal Law"; Note, "The Changing Role of the Jury in the Nineteenth Century"; and Pound, *Criminal Justice in America*.
87. Nelson Polsby, "The Institutionalization of the U.S. House of Representatives."
88. Carl J. Friedrich, *The Philosophy of Law in Historical Perspective*, 91.
89. Ibid., 90.
90. See *The Adams Papers: Legal Papers of John Adams*, vol. 1, ed. L. Kinvin Wroth and Hiller B. Zobel, 229.
91. Ibid., 230.
92. Pound, *Criminal Justice in America*, 116.
93. Lysander Spooner, *An Essay on the Trial by Jury*, 15.
94. Ibid., 138. Interesting discussions of jury nullification in the context of the slavery issue (the issue that concerned Spooner) may be found in Stanley W. Campbell, *The Slave Catchers: Enforcement of the Fugitive Slave Law 1850–1860*; and Robert Cover, *Justice Accused: Antislavery and the Judicial Process*.
95. For a succinct summary of this rise, see Edgar Bodenheimer, *Jurisprudence: The Philosophy and Method of the Law*, 90–95. The separation of law from morality did not mean that moral standards could (and should) not be used to evaluate the law. It did mean that such standards were not relevant in establishing the validity of law.

96. Lawrence M. Friedman, *A History of American Law*, 254.
97. Pound, "Law in Books and Law in Action," 23.
98. Pound, *Criminal Justice in America*, 115–30.
99. Ibid., 130.
100. Ibid.
101. Holmes, "Law in Science and Science in Law," 460.
102. Holmes, *The Common Law*, 36.
103. On this point see Jacobsohn, *Pragmatism, Statesmanship, and the Supreme Court*, chap. 4.
104. Carleton Kemp Allen, *Law in the Making*, 422. See also Huntington Cairns, *Legal Philosophy from Plato to Hegel*, chaps. 2 and 3.
105. Benjamin N. Cardozo, *The Nature of the Judicial Process*, 173.
106. McCloskey, ed., *The Works of James Wilson*, vol. 1, 130.
107. Ibid., 296.
108. Thomas Hobbes, *The Leviathan*, 23.
109. Ibid., 41.
110. *The Federalist*, no. 9, 51.

CHAPTER 3

1. Ronald Dworkin, *Taking Rights Seriously* (hereafter cited as *TRS*), 149.
2. Ibid., vii.
3. Ibid., 132–33.
4. *The Federalist*, no. 84, 581.
5. Dworkin, *TRS*, 142.
6. Michael Walzer, "Philosophy and Democracy," 393.
7. Dworkin, *TRS*, 133.
8. Ibid., 190.
9. Ibid., 87.
10. For a thoughtful critique of Dworkin's analysis of judicial discretion, see Noel B. Reynolds, "Dworkin as Quixote." Reynolds argues that Dworkin's notion of discretion does not describe the term as it has been applied in the American legal tradition. A good example of the latter is John Marshall's comment at the trial of Aaron Burr. "This is said to be a motion to the *discretion* of the court. . . . But a motion to its *discretion* is a motion not to its *inclination,* but to its judgment; and its judgment is to be guided by sound legal principles" (quoted in Robert K. Faulkner, *The Jurisprudence of John Marshall*, 67).
11. Dworkin, *TRS*, xi, 339.
12. Ibid., 313.
13. Ibid., 136.
14. Ibid., xi.
15. Ibid., 22.
16. John Rawls, *A Theory of Justice*, 135.
17. Dworkin, *TRS*, 85.
18. David A. J. Richards finds the principle/policy distinction ultimately unpersuasive as a way of distinguishing the appropriate tasks of judicial

and legislative bodies, arguing that "both principle and policy may underlie both legislation and adjudication." See "Taking *Taking Rights Seriously* Seriously: Reflections on Dworkin and the American Revival of Natural Law," 1312.

19. Dworkin, *TRS*, 269.
20. David A. J. Richards, "Human Rights and the Unwritten Constitution: The Problem of Change and Stability in Constitutional Interpretation," 299.
21. See, for example, Charles E. Lindblom, "The Science of 'Muddling Through.'"
22. Quoted in Faulkner, *The Jurisprudence of John Marshall*, 79.
23. Dworkin, *TRS*, 143.
24. *The Federalist*, no. 10, 57.
25. Ibid., 61.
26. Ibid., 64.
27. Dworkin, *TRS*, 143.
28. *The Federalist*, no. 10, 59.
29. Ibid., 59.
30. *United States* v. *Carolene Products Company*, 304 U.S. 144 (1938).
31. On this point, see Steven G. Calabresi, "A Madisonian Interpretation of the Equal Protection Doctrine." Madisonian theory is employed here to call for a less stringent equal protection approach at the federal level.
32. Richard Funston, "The Supreme Court and Critical Elections," 809. See also Ralph K. Winter, Jr., "The Growth of Judicial Power." Winter argues that "Where national sentiment is supportive . . . the track record of the judiciary simply does not support the view that it is a dependable barrier to majority abuse" (p. 62). For a different perspective on this question see Jesse H. Choper, *Judicial Review and the National Political Process: A Functional Reconsideration of the Role of the Supreme Court*, 79–122.
33. *Barron* v. *Baltimore*, 32 U.S. 243 (1833).
34. See, in this regard, Ralph Lerner, "The Supreme Court as Republican Schoolmaster."
35. Dworkin, *TRS*, 147.
36. Richards, *The Moral Criticism of Law*, 51.
37. *McCulloch* v. *Maryland*, 4 Wheat. 316 (1819), at 407.
38. Dworkin, *TRS*, 135.
39. Ibid., 137.
40. Charles A. Beard, *An Economic Interpretation of the Constitution*, 324. See also Edward S. Greenberg, "Class Rule Under the Constitution"; and Michael Parenti, "The Constitution as an Elitist Document."
41. *Lochner* v. *New York*, 198 U.S. 45 (1905).
42. *The Federalist*, no. 10, 58.
43. *Wilkinson* v. *Leland*, 2 Pet. 627, 658 (1829).
44. See, for example, Sanford Levinson, "Taking Law Seriously: Reflections on 'Thinking Like a Lawyer'"; and Thomas Pangle, "Rediscovering Rights."
45. Dworkin, *TRS*, 278.
46. Ibid., 276.

47. Ibid., 277.
48. Notice, for example, how Richard Parker, who with Richards and Michelman is the most explicitly Rawlsian of the liberal constitutional theorists, discusses the constitutional implications of Rawls's Second Principle of Justice (the Difference Principle regulating the distribution of wealth). He indicates initially that the Constitution "clearly does not require the Difference Principle, [a point that Rawls himself acknowledges] [which] is a problem." (See Richard Parker, "The Jurisprudential Uses of John Rawls," 274.) But then he points out that "to the degree that the Difference Principle can be defended as a necessary consequence of the theory unifying so much else of what American lawyers believe about the Constitution, it may in time be accepted that the Constitution requires realization of the Difference Principle" (pp. 274–75).
49. *Ogden* v. *Saunders*, 25 U.S. 213 (1827), at 347.
50. Dworkin, "The Forum of Principle," 470.
51. Ibid., 494.
52. Ibid., 478.
53. See, for example, Paul Brest, "The Misconceived Quest for the Original Understanding."
54. Dworkin, "The Forum of Principle," 477.
55. Other theorists avow similar understandings: Paul Brest, for example, advocates "nonoriginalist adjudication" and candidly dismisses constitutional text and surrounding history as necessarily authoritative (Brest, "The Misconceived Quest," 228). Similarly, Parker indicates that the views of the framers "are not dispositive"; rather the Constitution should be interpreted to "give expression to our own best vision . . . of what is just" (Rawls's book being the "best available formulation of that vision") (Parker, "The Jurisprudential Uses of John Rawls," 275). And from Frank Michelman: "being a Constitution—being thus cast in generalities, in the language of generations of the past, and in terms fitting to their circumstances and their imaginations—its application to the case at hand sooner or later turns out to be fairly debatable in ways for which evidence of original intent supplies no answer. At that moment the judge must start to rationalize—to 'perfect' the text—according to principles not strictly derivable from it" (Frank Michelman, "Constancy to an Ideal Object," 413).
56. See, for example, John Griffiths, "Legal Reasoning from the External and Internal Perspectives." There is an interesting discussion of this in Richards, "Taking *Taking Rights Seriously* Seriously," 1276—79.
57. Dworkin, *TRS*, 208.
58. *Ogden* v. *Saunders*, at 332.
59. Parker, "The Jurisprudential Uses of John Rawls," 275.
60. Joseph Story, *Commentaries on the Constitution of the United States*, vol. 1, 329.
61. Ibid., 396.
62. Ibid., 410.
63. Story, *Commentaries on the Constitution*, vol. 3, 717–18.
64. Ibid., 473.

65. Story, *Commentaries on the Constitution*, vol. 1, 300.
66. Ibid., 388.
67. Ibid., 387.
68. Charles L. Black, Jr., *Structure and Relationship in Constitutional Law*. See also, in this regard, Winter, "The Growth of Judicial Power."
69. Winter, "The Growth of Judicial Power," 40.
70. Michael J. Perry, *The Constitution, the Courts, and Human Rights*, 66–69.
71. Winter, "The Growth of Judicial Power," 41.
72. Note, in this regard, the view of Chief Justice Marshall: "It is more than possible that the preservation of rights of this description was not particularly in view of the framers of the Constitution, when the clause under consideration was introduced into that instrument . . . But although a particular and rare case may not, in itself, be of sufficient magnitude to induce a rule, yet it must be governed by the rule, when established, unless some plain and strong reason for excluding it can be given. It is not enough to say that this particular case was not in the mind of the convention when the articles were framed, nor of the American people when it was adopted. The case, being within the words of the rule, must be within its operation likewise." (*Dartmouth College* v. *Woodward*, 4 Wheat. 518 [1819], at 645.) It is also worth noting what Alexander M. Bickel had to say in his noted article on the *Brown* decision. "One inquiry should be directed at the congressional understanding of the immediate effect of the enactment [of the Fourteenth Amendment] on conditions then present. Another should aim to discover what if any thought was given to the long-range effect, under future circumstances, of provisions necessarily intended for permanence" (Bickel, "The Original Understanding and the Segregation Decision," 59).
73. Bickel, "The Original Understanding and the Segregation Decision," 62. Bickel also notes that the debate over the amendment "was often accompanied on the Republican side by generalities about the self-evident demands of justice and the natural rights of man" (p. 61).
74. Dworkin, "Liberalism," 143.
75. Dworkin, *TRS*, 181.
76. "Government must not only treat people with concern and respect. It must not distribute goods or opportunities unequally on the ground that some citizens are entitled to more because they are worthy of more concern" (Dworkin, *TRS*, 272–73).
77. Dworkin, "The Forum of Principle," 516.
78. Dworkin, "Liberalism," 137. See also note 76, above.
79. Ibid., 138.
80. Rawls, *A Theory of Justice*, 15.
81. As an example of a significantly different point of view reflected in *The Federalist*, notice should be taken of Hamilton's position in no. 36: "There are strong minds in every walk of life that will rise superior to the disadvantages of situation, and will command the tribute due to their merit, not only from the classes to which they particularly belong, but from the society in general. The door ought to be equally open for all" (p. 223). In this regard, Paul Eidelberg has commented that the attribution

of success to accident "is to minimize the significance of unequal faculties which Madison speaks of in *Federalist* 10, the very faculties from which the rights and unequal distribution of property originate" (Paul Eidelberg, *A Discourse on Statesmanship: The Design and Transformation of the American Polity*, 337).

82. See, for example, Charles G. Haines, *The Revival of Natural Law Concepts.*
83. Morton White, *The Philosophy of the American Revolution*, 250.

CHAPTER 4

1. Robert H. Bork, *Tradition and Morality in Constitutional Law*, 2.
2. Ibid., 5.
3. Ibid.
4. Ibid., 2.
5. Ibid., 8.
6. Raoul Berger, *Government by Judiciary: The Transformation of the Fourteenth Amendment.*
7. Ibid., 290.
8. Ibid., 250.
9. Ibid., 285–86.
10. Ibid., 289.
11. Ibid., 262.
12. Ibid., 316.
13. Ibid., 291.
14. *Adamson* v. *California*, 332 U.S. 46 (1947).
15. Berger, *Government by Judiciary*, 275.
16. Ibid., 257.
17. Ibid., 252.
18. John Austin, *The Province of Jurisprudence Determined*, 184.
19. *The Federalist*, no. 78, 523.
20. Quoted in Berger, *Government by Judiciary*, 296. Among the best examples of legal realism in the field of constitutional jurisprudence are Fred Rodell, *Nine Men*, and Arthur S. Miller and Ronald F. Howell, "The Myth of Neutrality in Constitutional Adjudication," 661–95.
21. *The Federalist*, no. 81, 546.
22. Berger, *Government by Judiciary*, 295.
23. Ibid., 396.
24. Robert Cover, *Justice Accused: Antislavery and the Judicial Process*, 29. Cover's characterization is basically correct; however, in the case of at least one very important positivist, John Chipman Gray (*The Nature and Sources of the Law*), a qualification is necessary in order to accept a view of the courts as the source of the state's law-making power.
25. Morton J. Horwitz, "The Emergence of an Instrumental Conception of American Law, 1780–1820," 287.
26. Ibid., 288.
27. Ibid., 295.

28. Ibid., 296. The quoted material comes from Josiah Quincy's argument for the defense in *Rex* v. *Wemms* (1770).
29. Ibid., 326.
30. It is, of course, quite possible to question these assumptions. A fundamental ambiguity about the nature of law existed during the revolutionary period, and this ambiguity still exists with regard to scholarly treatments of American adaptions of the common law. See, for example, Gordon S. Wood, *The Creation of the American Republic, 1776–1787*, 291–305. See also A. E. Dick Howard, *The Road from Runnymeade: Magna Carta and Constitutionalism in America*, 274–76. For a treatment of the common law as an expression of principles of natural justice or reason, see Charles Haines, *The Revival of Natural Law Concepts*. Ultimately, alternative interpretations on this question are all traceable to Blackstone, whose reflections on the nature of law are characterized, as many commentators have pointed out, by contradiction and ambivalence. See, especially, Dennis R. Nolan, "Sir William Blackstone and the New England American Republic: A Study of Intellectual Impact," 731–68.
31. *Osborn* v. *Bank of the United States*, 22 U.S. 738, 866 (1824).
32. See, for example, Miller and Howell, "The Myth of Neutrality in Constitutional Ajudication," 675.
33. Faulkner, *The Jurisprudence of John Marshall*, 194.
34. Berger, *Government by Judiciary*, 253.
35. Ibid. The quotation is from Felix Frankfurter, "John Marshall and the Judicial Function," 225. For a discussion of Frankfurter's thoughts on Marshall, see Gary J. Jacobsohn, *Pragmatism, Statesmanship, and the Supreme Court*, 124–30.
36. On the subject of this continuity, see Samuel J. Konefsky, *John Marshall and Alexander Hamilton: Architects of the American Constitution*.
37. *Ogden* v. *Saunders*, 12 Wheat. 213, 332. In fact, Berger does quote approvingly from part of this statement (Berger, *Government by Judiciary*, 378).
38. *Ogden* v. *Saunders*, at. 353–54.
39. Ibid., at 346.
40. Ibid., at 345.
41. See, for example, his opinion in *Fletcher* v. *Peck*, 6 Cranch 87 (1810).
42. Berger, 294. The reference is to Justice Douglas's opinion in *Griswold* v. *Connecticut*, 381 U.S. 479, 484 (1965).
43. Berger, *Government by Judiciary*, 294.
44. Ibid.
45. Ibid., 257. The question is from *Hepburn* v. *Griswold*, 75 U.S. 603, 638 (1869).
46. Berger, *Government by Judiciary*, 258.
47. Ibid., 306.
48. *The Federalist*, no. 81, 543.
49. Ibid., 542.
50. Clinton Rossiter, *Alexander Hamilton and the Constitution*, 123. The best treatment of Hamilton's political philosophy is Gerald Stourzh, *Alexander*

Hamilton and the Idea of Republican Government. See, in particular, pp. 9–37 for an analysis of Hamilton's commitment to principles of natural right.

51. *The Papers of Alexander Hamilton,* vol. 1, ed. Harold C. Syrett (New York, 1961), 122.
52. Ibid., 137.
53. Ibid., vol. 3, 548.
54. *Cohens* v. *Virginia,* 19 U.S. (6 Wheat.) 264, 383 (1821).
55. Ibid., at 384.
56. *Dartmouth College* v. *Woodward,* 17 U.S. (4 Wheat.) 518, 645 (1819).
57. *McCulloch* v. *Maryland,* 17 U.S. (4 Wheat.) 316, 421 (1819).
58. Syrett, ed., *The Papers of Alexander Hamilton,* vol. 1, 88.
59. Berger, *Government by Judiciary,* 388.
60. Quoted in Benjamin F. Wright, *American Interpretations of Natural Law,* 127.
61. Henry Steele Commager, "Constitutional History and the Higher Law," 228. Among the more recent works that accept the natural rights basis of the Constitution are Archibald Cox, *The Role of the Supreme Court in American Government*; Paul G. Kauper, "The Higher Law and the Rights of Man in a Revolutionary Society"; and Walter F. Murphy, "Constitutional Interpretation: The Art of the Historian, Magician, or Statesman?", 1752–71. Some judges were explicit in invoking natural rights, as noted by Murphy, who writes of a "judicial reading of natural rights into 'the spirit' of the Constitution" ("The Art of Constitutional Interpretation: A Preliminary Showing," 141).
62. Quoted in Wright, *American Interpretations of Natural Law,* 123.
63. Ibid., 138. Wright points out that Fisher Ames was the only Federalist who questioned the validity of the natural law concept.
64. *The Federalist,* no. 84, 581.
65. Ibid., no. 31, 193–94. The subject under consideration was the power of taxation. Morton White cites Hamilton's argument as an example of how Americans "invoked the epistemology of self-evident truth in support of concrete political views." (See Morton White, *The Philosophy of the American Revolution,* 91.)
66. *The Federalist,* no. 31, 194. Recently there has been a resurgence of interest in the application of Enlightenment ideas in America. See, in particular, Commager, *The Empire of Reason*; Garry Wills, *Inventing America: Jefferson's Declaration of Independence*; and (by far the best treatment) White, *The Philosophy of the American Revolution.*
67. *The Federalist,* no. 31, 195.
68. Ibid.
69. *The Federalist,* no. 78, 527.
70. Ibid., 526.
71. Bork, "Neutral Principles and Some First Amendment Problems," 30.
72. Ibid., 18.
73. Ibid.
74. Ibid., 10. Ronald Dworkin is also quite critical of Bork's moral skepticism and his unwillingness to make objective discriminations among gratifica-

tions. See Ronald Dworkin, "Reagan's Justice," 30. Of course, Dworkin, as we have seen in the previous chapter, would make such discriminations on the basis of contemporary liberal moral philosophy.

CHAPTER 5

1. Michael J. Perry, *The Constitution, the Courts, and Human Rights*, 6.
2. Thomas C. Grey, "Do We Have an Unwritten Constitution?", 703.
3. Grey, "Origins of the Unwritten Constitution: Fundamental Law in American Revolutionary Thought," 843.
4. Ibid.
5. Ibid., 881.
6. McCloskey, ed., *The Works of James Wilson*, vol. 1, 2.
7. Grey, "Origins of the Unwritten Constitution," 887.
8. Alfons Beitzinger, "The Philosophy of Law of Four American Founding Fathers," 17.
9. McCloskey, ed., *The Works of James Wilson*, vol. 1, 145.
10. Winton Solberg, ed., *The Federal Convention and the Formation of the Union*, 235.
11. Ibid., 236.
12. Ibid., 237.
13. Ibid., 238–39.
14. Wilson notes the contradiction by quoting Blackstone to the effect that "on the two foundations of the law of nature, and the law of revelation, all human laws depend; that is to say, no human laws should be suffered to contradict these." Wilson summarizes his reference here to the earlier use of Blackstone by exclaiming: "Surely these positions are inconsistent and irreconcilable" (McCloskey, ed., *The Works of James Wilson*, vol. 1, 328).
15. Ibid., 327.
16. Ibid., 328.
17. Ibid., 330.
18. Ibid., 77.
19. Ibid., 333.
20. Ibid.
21. This distinction is nicely elaborated upon by Walter Berns, "Judicial Review and the Rights and Laws of Nature." See also his essay "The Constitution as Bill of Rights."
22. McCloskey, ed., *The Works of James Wilson*, vol. 1, 299.
23. See, for example, *Polish National Alliance* v. *NLRB*, 322 U.S. 643, 650 (1944); *West Virginia State Board of Education* v. *Barnette*, 319 U.S. 624, 646-50 (1942) (dissenting opinion); and *Osborn* v. *Ozlin*, 310, U.S. 53, 62 (1940). And off the Court, see Frankfurter, *The Public and Its Government*, 79.
24. Quoted in Grey, "Origins of the Unwritten Constitution," 869.
25. Ibid.

26. Ibid., 868. See also Andrew C. McLaughlin, *Foundations of American Constitutionalism*, 120.
27. Edward S. Corwin, *The "Higher Law" Background of American Constitutional Law*, 77–78; McLaughlin, *Foundations of American Constitutionalism*, 120; Bernard Bailyn, ed., *Pamphlets of the American Revolution: 1750–1776*, 411–13; Gordon S. Wood, *The Creation of the American Republic, 1776, 1787*, 9.
28. Bailyn, *Pamphlets of the American Revolution*, 417.
29. J. W. Gough, *Fundamental Law in English Constitutional History*, 206.
30. Ibid.
31. Grey does not assert categorically that this was Otis's intent. His qualified judgment seems to be this. "Otis may have seen the courts as possessing an initial power to invalidate unconstitutional statutes, while believing that if Parliament persisted in supporting a statute declared unconstitutional, it should have the last word" (Grey, "Origins of the Unwritten Constitution," 873).
32. Ibid., 893.
33. Grey, "Judicial Review and the Unwritten Constitution." In this paper, however, Grey argues that our early constitutional history evinces no disinclination by judges to appeal to the unwritten constitution in much the same way that earlier judges had done.
34. Grey, "Origins of the Unwritten Constitution," 867.
35. Ibid., 864.
36. Corwin, *The "Higher Law" Background of American Constitutional Law*, 89.
37. Sylvia Snowiss, "From Fundamental Law to the Supreme Law of the Land: A Reinterpretation of the Origin of Judicial Review in the United States."
38. Ibid., 4.
39. Quoted in ibid., 21.
40. Paul Leicester Ford, ed., *Pamphlets on the Constitution of the United States*, 181.
41. The special responsibility was severely criticized in Judge Gibson's famous opinion in *Eakin v. Raub*, 12 Sergeant and Rawle (Pennsylvania Supreme Court) 330 (1825).
42. *The Federalist*, no. 84, 581.
43. Herbert J. Storing, "The Constitution and the Bill of Rights," 46.
44. Ibid.
45. Bailyn, *Pamphlets of the American Revolution*, 428.
46. Spooner, *The Unconstitutionality of Slavery*, 138.
47. For an interesting discussion of the implications of this minimalism, see Wilson Carey McWilliams, "Democracy and the Citizen: Community, Dignity, and the Crisis of Contemporary Politics in America." See also Diamond, "Ethics and Politics: The American Way."
48. Ford, *Pamphlets on the Constitution*, 181. The effort of most of those currently engaged in constitutional theorizing seems directed to showing how a good constitution produces a good society. See, most recently, Perry, *The Constitution, the Courts, and Human Rights*.

49. Solberg, *The Federal Convention and the Union*, 288.
50. Ibid.
51. Ibid., 289.
52. Grey, "Judicial Review and the Unwritten Constitution," 9.
53. See, for example, Haines, *The Revival of Natural Law Concepts*, 86–88; Wright, *American Interpretations of Natural Law*, 294; and John Hart Ely, *Democracy and Distrust: A Theory of Judicial Review*, 210–11. The latter treatment is in essential agreement with the interpretation provided here, although Ely's assessment of Chase's opinion as "fiercely positivistic" goes beyond the claim of my argument. The most recent treatment of *Calder* v. *Bull* is in David Currie, "The Constitution in the Supreme Court: 1789–1801."
54. *Calder* v. *Bull*, 3 Dall. 386 (1798), at 387.
55. Ibid., at 388.
56. Ibid., at 391.
57. Ibid.
58. Justice Paterson's opinion is also consistent with this observation. "I had an ardent desire to have extended the provision in the Constitution to retrospective laws in general. There is neither policy nor safety in such laws; and, therefore, I have always had a strong aversion against them. It may, in general, be truly observed of retrospective laws of every discipline, that they neither accord with sound legislation, nor the fundamental principles of the social compact. But on full consideration, I am convinced, that *ex post facto* laws must be limited in the manner already expressed; they must be taken in their technical, which is also the common and general, acceptation, and are not to be understood in their literal sense" (ibid., at 397).
59. Ibid., at 398.
60. Ibid., at 399.
61. Berger, *Government by Judiciary*, 252.
62. *Wilkinson* v. *Leland*, 2 Peters 627 (829), at 657.
63. Ibid., at 656.
64. Ibid., at 632.
65. Ibid., at 646.
66. Ibid., at 661.
67. *Fletcher* v. *Peck*, 6 Cranch 57 (1810), at 143.
68. Ibid., at 139.
69. See, for example, Currie, "The Constitution in the Supreme Court: State and Congressional Power, 1801–1835," 889–99.
70. *Ogden* v. *Saunders*, 12 Wheat. 213 (1827), at 353.
71. *Terret* v. *Taylor*, 9 Cranch, 43 (1815), at 52.
72. Currie, "The Constitution in the Supreme Court: State and Congressional Power, 1801–1835," 902.
73. *Vanhorne's Lessee* v. *Dorrance*, 2 Dall. 304 (1795), at 308.
74. Ibid., at 307.
75. Ibid., at 308.
76. Ibid., at 310.

77. Thus, he connects his noninterpretivist approach to many of the social reforms facilitated by the work of the modern Court (Grey, "Do We Have an Unwritten Constitution?", 710–14).

78. The literature on this development can also be described as increasingly expansive. Several noteworthy accounts are Archibald Cox, *The Role of the Supreme Court in American Government*; Nathan Glazer, "Toward an Imperial Judiciary?"; Donald L. Horowitz, *The Courts and Social Policy*; A. S. Miller, "Toward a Concept of Constitutional Duty"; and Stuart A. Scheingold, *The Politics of Rights: Lawyers, Public Policy, and Political Change*.

79. See, especially, in this regard, *San Antonio v. Rodriguez*, 411 U.S. 1 (1973), and *Shapiro* v. *Thompson*, 394 U.S. 618 (1969). And note Grey, "Do We Have an Unwritten Constitution?", 712: "All of the 'fundamental interests' that trigger 'strict scrutiny' under the equal protection clause would have to be discarded, if the interpretive model were to control constitutional adjudication."

80. Grey, "Do We Have an Unwritten Constitution?", 718.

81. Ibid., 706.

82. *The Federalist*, no. 49, 341.

83. Ralph Lerner, "The Supreme Court as Republican Schoolmaster."

84. Perry, *The Constitution, the Courts, and Human Rights*, 101.

85. Ibid., 106. Sotirios A. Barber argues in similar fashion that the Court should concern itself with "the moral aspirations of the American people, or moral growth simply" (*On What the Constitution Means*, 11). His "aspirational approach to constitutional meaning" (ibid., 10) sounds very much like the argument we have been making about the founders; however, in the latter case aspirations are not tied to "moral growth." Or again, in Perry, the object of constitutional interpretation is that of "*aspiring* to give, in any generation, right answers to the fundamental political-moral problems that exercise that generation" (Perry, *The Constitution, the Courts, and Human Rights*, 115).

86. *Van Horne's Lessee* v. *Dorrance*, at 309.

CHAPTER 6

1. See John Hart Ely, *Democracy and Distrust: A Theory of Judicial Review*.

2. Roy Basler, ed., *The Collected Works of Abraham Lincoln*, vol. 3, 130.

3. Sotirios A. Barber, *On What the Constitution Means*, 48.

4. Ibid., 56.

5. The charge comes from Steven A. Douglas in the course of his fifth debate with Abraham Lincoln, Oct. 7, 1858. (Basler, ed., *Collected Works*, vol. 3, 242.)

6. Jesse H. Choper, *Judicial Review and the National Political Process: A Functional Reconsideration of the Role of the Supreme Court*, 157.

7. Ibid.

8. Basler, ed., *Collected Works*, vol. 3, 242.

9. Ibid., vol. 1, 112.

10. Ibid.
11. Dworkin, *TRS*, 211.
12. Ibid., 214.
13. Basler, ed., *Collected Works*, vol. 2, 400–401.
14. Ibid., vol. 4, 268.
15. Don E. Fehrenbacher, "Lincoln and Judicial Supremacy: A Note on the Galena Speech of July 23, 1856," 201. Fehrenbacher builds a convincing case that the Galena speech, wherein Lincoln reportedly had reflected on the subject and had come to the opposite conclusion from what he declared after *Dred Scott*, is of doubtful authenticity. The report of the Galena speech included these words: "I grant you that an unconstitutional act is not a law; but I do not ask, and will not take your construction of the Constitution. The Supreme Court of the United States is the tribunal to decide such questions, and we will submit to its decisions" (Basler, ed., *Collected Works*, vol. 2, 355). For a different view of the Galena speech, which sees it as reflecting Lincoln's clear belief that the *Dred Scott* case was going to be decided along the lines of the eventual dissenting opinion, see Wallace Mendelson, "Dred Scott's Case—Reconsidered."
16. Basler, ed., *Collected Works*, vol. 2, 495.
17. Douglas in ibid., vol. 3, 243.
18. On this point see John Agresto, "The Limits of Judicial Supremacy: A Proposal for 'Checked Activism,'" 471–95. In pointing out the differences here, Agresto, however, rightly recognizes the continuity of the three statesmen on the basic issue of judicial supremacy.
19. Fehrenbacher, *The Dred Scott Case*, 442. John Agresto has astutely observed that "our popular contemporary ideas of judicial review are always spoken by Douglas and never by Lincoln" ("The Limits of Judical Supremacy," 471). (The reference is to Douglas's sentiment, expressed in the third debate, that "it is the fundamental principle of the judiciary that its decisions are final.") One should note here that in opting to confront the doctrine of judicial supremacy directly, Lincoln abjured the strategy adopted by some of his Republican colleagues of regarding much of the language in *Dred Scott* as *obiter dictum*, thus depriving the decision of the ordinary force of law. For discussion of this choice see the Fehrenbacher book and also Edward S. Corwin, "The Dred Scott Decision in the Light of Contemporary Legal Doctrines," 52–69; and David M. Potter, *The Impending Crisis 1848–1861*.
20. Basler, ed., *Collected Works*, vol. 4, 268.
21. Fehrenbacher, *Dred Scott Case*, 442.
22. Basler, ed., *Collected Works*, vol. 1, 170–71.
23. Ibid., vol. 2, 401.
24. Ibid.
25. Ibid., vol. 3, 131.
26. Ibid. See also vol. 3, 531, for further elaboration on this view.
27. Ibid., vol. 2, 401.
28. Ely, *Democracy and Distrust*, 226.
29. Ibid., vii.

30. Basler, ed., *Collected Works*, vol. 3, 534–35.
31. Ibid., 535.
32. Ely, *Democracy and Distrust*, 1.
33. Ibid., 87. The concern of this chapter is not with Ely's goal of maximizing the process and procedural opportunities in the Constitution. For a critique of this effort, see Mark Tushnet, "Darkness on the Edge of Town: The Contributions of John Hart Ely to Constitutional Theory," 1037–62. Tushnet argues that Ely overstates the value-free character of his process orientation, as well as exaggerating the prominence of participation as a value embodied in the Constitution.
34. Ely, *Democracy and Distrust*, 88.
35. Ibid., 50.
36. Ibid., 51.
37. Ibid., 39. On this point Ely relies in particular on the work of Robert Cover, whose *Justice Accused: Antislavery and the Judicial Process* is also, as we have seen, an important scholarly source for Raoul Berger. Berger, despite other significant differences, shares Ely's views regarding the role of natural law in the founders' plans. See also Edwin Viera, Jr., "Rights and the United States Constitution: The Declension from Natural Law to Legal Positivism," 1447–1500.
38. Ely, *Democracy and Distrust*, 49. On page 89 Ely writes: "The theme that justice and happiness are best assured not by trying to define them for all time carried over into our critical constitutional documents" (including the Declaration of Independence). According to Ely, the reason that the Constitution, unlike the Declaration, omits all references to natural law is that the political necessity for doing so no longer existed.
39. Although it is fair to say that Ely's views on natural law are quite contemporary in this basic agreement with the preponderance of modern opinion in this area, one can nevertheless find noted scholarly agreement with the contrary judgment expressed by Justice Jackson: "These truths of natural law to that age [the founding period] stood as the ultimate sanction of liberty and justice, equality and toleration" (Robert H. Jackson, *The Supreme Court in the American System of Government*, 3). A good example with a similar title is Archibald Cox, *The Role of the Supreme Court in American Government*. See also his review of Ely's book in *Harvard Law Review* 94, no. 3 (1981).
40. Basler, ed., *Collected Works*, vol. 4, 240. It is recorded that this comment was greeted with great cheering.
41. Ibid.
42. Ibid., vol. 2, 406.
43. Ibid., vol. 4, 169.
44. Ibid.
45. Ely, *Democracy and Distrust*, 74. Ely does not view the work of the Court in this respect as an endorsement of particular substantive values it had determined were fundamental. For a different view, see Alexander M. Bickel, *The Supreme Court and the Idea of Progress*.
46. Lon L. Fuller, *The Morality of Law*, 186. Unlike Ely, however, Fuller is

prepared to recognize the natural law basis of the internal morality of law. Indeed, he uses the term "substantive natural law" to describe the procedural guarantees that make up the internal morality of law. In this regard, too, see Walter F. Murphy, "The Art of Constitutional Interpretation: A Preliminary Showing." Says Murphy: "process is the hand-maiden, not the mistress, of substantive rights" (p. 156).

47. Ely, *Democracy and Distrust*, 77. This is also a major theme in Choper's *Judicial Review and the National Political Process*: "although judicial review is incompatible with a fundamental precept of American democracy—majority rule—the Court must exercise this power in order to protect individual rights, which are not adequately represented in the political processes" (p. 2).

48. Murphy, "The Art of Constitutional Interpretation," 155.

49. Harry V. Jaffa is most eloquent on this point. "Free government, according to Lincoln, was not the mere *process* of arriving at decisions without coercion by any formula embodying the principle of majority rule . . . It was government of, by, and for a people dedicated to a certain proposition" (*Crisis of the House Divided: An Interpretation of the Issues in the Lincoln-Douglas Debates*, 348).

50. Basler, ed., *Collected Works*, vol. 3, 16. For some critical views of the constitutional priorities established by the preferred freedoms doctrine of footnote number 4, see Robert G. McCloskey, "Economic Due Process and the Supreme Court: An Exhumation and Reburial"; and Richard Funston, "The Double Standard of Constitutional Protection in the Era of the Welfare State," 261–287.

51. Ely, *Democracy and Distrust*, 93, 98.

52. Ibid., 93.

53. In his Cooper Institute Address, Lincoln mentioned that "this mode of alluding to slaves and slavery, instead of speaking of them, was employed on purpose to exclude from the Constitution the idea that there could be property in man" (Basler, ed., *Collected Works*, vol. 3, 545).

54. Ely, *Democracy and Distrust*, 102–3.

55. *Abrams* v. *United States*, 250 U.S. 616, 630 (1919). Dissenting opinion.

56. Ibid., 630.

57. Ely, *Democracy and Distrust*, 112.

58. Ibid., 111.

59. Basler, ed., *Collected Works*, vol. 3, 222–23.

60. For a modern formulation of this First Amendment theory, see Walter Berns, *The First Amendment and the Future of American Democracy*.

61. Even under the pressures of his presidency, Lincoln was, despite what his enemies said about him, remarkably tolerant in matters of free expression. See James G. Randall, *Constitutional Problems Under Lincoln*.

62. Basler, ed., *Collected Works*, vol. 3, 549. This same theme appears quite early in Lincoln's political career. Thus, in his 1838 Lyceum Address, Lincoln says: "There is no grievance that is a fit object of redress by mob law. In any case that arises, as for instance, the promulgation of abolition-ism, one of two positions is necessarily true; that is, the thing is right

within itself, and therefore deserves the protection of all law and all good citizens; or, it is wrong, and therefore proper to be prohibited by legal enactments. (See vol. 1, 113.)

63. Ibid., vol. 2, 449.
64. Ibid., 459.
65. Ibid., vol. 1, 488.
66. "I wish to stand erect before the country as well as Judge Douglas, on this question of judicial authority" (Basler, ed., *Collected Works*, vol. 2, 516).
67. Bertrand Russell, *Unpopular Essays*, 8.
68. I have employed this distinction elsewhere to describe the legal philosophy of Jefferson (Lincoln's favorite founding father) and to contrast it with contemporary legal realists. See Jacobsohn, *Pragmatism, Statesmanship, and the Supreme Court*, 171–81.
69. Basler, ed., *Collected Works*, vol. 2, 406.
70. Agresto, "The Limits of Judical Supremacy," 476.
71. Cox, *Role of the Supreme Court*, 117–18.
72. Basler, ed., *Collected Works*, vol. 3, 281.
73. Ibid., vol. 2, 553.
74. Ibid., 552–53.
75. Corwin, "The Natural Law and Constitutional Law," 21.
76. Cox, *Role of the Supreme Court*, 117.
77. The term "deviant institution" was first used by Alexander M. Bickel in *The Least Dangerous Branch: The Supreme Court at the Bar of Politics*.
78. Berns, "The Constitution as Bill of Rights."

CHAPTER 7

1. *The Federalist*, no. 1, 4.
2. Harry Wellington, "The Nature of Judicial Review," 487.
3. *Cooper* v. *Aaron*, 358 U.S. 1 (1958), at 18.
4. *The Federalist*, no. 22, 144.
5. *Brown* v. *Allan*, 344 U.S. 443 (1953), at 540.
6. Quoted in William M. Meigs, *The Relation of the Judiciary to the Constitution*, 227.
7. Ibid.
8. Donald G. Morgan, *Congress and the Constitution: A Study of Responsibility*, 6.
9. Roscoe Pound, *Interpretations of Legal History*, 157.
10. Jacobsohn, *Pragmatism, Statesmanship, and the Supreme Court*, 72. For James, see "The Moral Philosopher and the Moral Life," 184.
11. Wellington, "The Nature of Judical Review," 514.
12. Ibid., 508.
13. Ibid., 516.
14. Ibid., 508.
15. Ibid., 514.
16. Ibid., 519.
17. Ibid., 516.

18. *Akron v. Akron Center for Reproductive Health, Inc.*, 103 S. Ct. 2481 (1983).
19. For a perceptive analysis of Bickel's philosophy, including his under-standing of the role of aspirational ideals in constitutional law, see Anthony T. Kronman, "Alexander Bickel's Philosophy of Prudence."
20. Alexander M. Bickel, *The Least Dangerous Branch: The Supreme Court at the Bar of Politics*, 261.
21. Alexander M. Bickel, *The Supreme Court and the Idea of Progress*, 181.
22. See Chapter 3, 41
23. Senate Committee on the Judiciary, *Hearings before the Subcommittee on Separation of Powers on S. 158, the "Human Life Bill"* (hereinafter cited as *"Human Life Bill" Hearings*), 942.
24. Raoul Berger, *Congress v. The Supreme Court*, 81.
25. Quoted in Edward S. Corwin, *Court Over Constitution: A Study of Judicial Review as an Instrument of Popular Government*, 48.
26. Ibid., 50.
27. Berger, *Congress v. The Supreme Court*, 148.
28. See Chapter 6, 107
29. Henry M. Hart, Jr., "Professor Crosskey and Judicial Review," 1458.
30. Corwin, *Court Over Constitution*, 80.
31. Berger, *Congress v. The Supreme Court*, 339.
32. Ibid., 340.
33. Morgan, *Congress and the Constitution*, 54.
34. For a good discussion of Jefferson's departmental view, see Agresto, *The Supreme Court and Constitutional Democracy*, 78–84.
35. *The Federalist*, no. 84, 545.
36. Berger, *Congress v. The Supreme Court*, 95.
37. Quoted in Corwin, *Court Over Constitution*, 68.
38. *The Federalist*, no. 51, 352.
39. Grey, "Do We Have an Unwritten Constitution?" 716.
40. Michael J. Perry, *The Constitution, the Courts, and Human Rights*, 135.
41. John Hart Ely, *Democracy and Distrust*, 54.
42. Ibid., 103.
43. Jesse H. Choper, *Judicial Review and the National Political Process*, 167.
44. A note of clarification is in order. For functional reasons Choper calls for judicial withdrawal from some areas of judicial review, areas relating to separation of powers and federalism issues. In a sense, then, in these non-rights-related fields, Choper would prefer nonjudicial institutional involvement in matters of constitutional interpretation. But this perspective does not fully address the question of judicial findings as we have been discussing it.
45. *Webster's Seventh New Collegiate Dictionary* (Springfield, Mass., 1970), 312.
46. *"Human Life Bill" Hearings*, vol. 1, 1122.
47. Ibid., 158.
48. Ibid., 15. *"Human Life Bill"—S. 158, Reports together with Additional and Minority Views to the Committee on the Judiciary, United States Senate, made by its Subcommittee on Separation of Powers*, 97th Cong., 1st sess., 37–38.
49. Ibid., 329.
50. Senate Committee on the Judiciary, *Reports together with Additional and*

Minority Views of the Subcommittee on Separation of Powers regarding S. 158, the "Human Life Bill" (hereinafter cited as *"Human Life Bill" Reports*), 37.

51. *"Human Life Bill" Hearings*, vol. 1, 252.
52. *"Human Life Bill" Reports*, 21.
53. Ibid., 6–7.
54. Stuart A. Scheingold, *The Politics of Rights: Lawyers, Public Policy, and Political Change*, 131.
55. Ibid., 84.
56. *"Human Life Bill" Hearings*, vol. 2, 950. The letter was addressed to Senator Baucus, who eventually concluded in his minority report that "the theory behind the legislation runs counter to principles of judicial independence and the separation of powers that lie at the very heart of our constitutional system." Subcommittee Report, 43.
57. Ibid., vol. 2, 250. For a good discussion of the practical and theoretical difficulties of using the amendment process to respond to a judicial decision, see Agresto, *The Supreme Court and Constitutional Democracy*, 107–116.
58. *The Federalist*, no. 78, 525.
59. Ibid., 524.
60. Ibid., 525.
61. Ibid., 526.
62. See Chapter 2, 36
63. Samuel Huntington, *American Politics: The Promise of Disharmony*, 30.
64. Ibid., 24.
65. Ibid., 30.
66. Ibid., 16.
67. Bickel, *The Least Dangerous Branch*, 24.

CHAPTER 8

1. Felix Frankfurter, *Of Law and Life and Other Things That Matter*, 94.
2. Ibid., 95.
3. Ibid.
4. Ibid.
5. Paul J. Mishkin, "Modest Reforms and Grandiose Visions," *The New York Times Book Review*, Aug. 18, 1985, 7.
6. Ibid.
7. Nathan Tarcov, "American Constitutionalism and Individual Rights," in *How Does the Constitution Secure Rights?* ed. Robert A. Goldwin and William A. Schambra (Washington, 1985), 118.
8. *Lochner v. New York*, 198 U.S. 45 (1905), at 75.
9. John Hart Ely, *Democracy and Distrust*, 58.
10. One recent study that seeks to do this is Rogers Smith, *Liberalism and American Constitutional Law*.
11. *McCulloch v. Maryland*, 4 Wheat. 316 (1819), at 415.
12. Frederick Douglass, "Fourth of July Oration," 38.

Bibliography

Adams, John. *The Adams Papers: Legal Papers of John Adams*, ed. L. Kinvin Wroth and Hiller B. Zobel. New York: Atheneum, 1968.

Agresto, John. "The Limits of Judicial Supremacy: A Proposal for a 'Checked Activism.'" *Georgia Law Review* 14, no. 3 (1980): 471–95.

———. *The Supreme Court and Constitutional Democracy*. Ithaca, Cornell University Press, 1984.

Allen, Carleton Kemp. *Law in the Making*. Oxford: Oxford University Press, 1964.

Austin, John. *The Province of Jurisprudence Determined*. New York: Weidenfeld and Nicolson, 1954.

Bailyn, Bernard, ed. *Pamphlets of the American Revolution: 1750–1776*, vol. 1. Cambridge: Harvard University Press, 1965.

Barber, Sotirios A. *On What the Constitution Means*. Baltimore: Johns Hopkins University Press, 1984.

Beard, Charles A. *An Economic Interpretation of the Constitution*. New York: The Free Press, 1941.

Becker, Carl. *The Declaration of Independence: A Study in the History of Political Ideas*. New York: Vintage—Random House, 1958.

Beitzinger, Alfons. "The Philosophy of Law of Four American Founding Fathers." *The American Journal of Jurisprudence* 21 (1976): 1–19.

Berger, Raoul. *Congress v. the Supreme Court*. Cambridge: Harvard University Press, 1969.

———. *Government by Judiciary: The Transformation of the Fourteenth Amendment*. Cambridge: Harvard University Press, 1977.

Berns, Walter M. *The First Amendment and the Future of American Democracy*. New York: Basic Books, 1976.

———. "Judicial Review and the Rights and Laws of Nature." In *Supreme Court Review*, ed. Phillip B. Kurland. Chicago: University of Chicago Press, 1982.

———. "The Constitution as Bill of Rights." In *How Does the Constitution Secure Rights?*, ed. Robert A. Goldwin and William A. Schambra. Washington, D.C.: American Enterprise Institute, 1985.

Bickel, Alexander M. "The Original Understanding and the Segregation Decision." *Harvard Law Review* 69, no. 1 (1955): 1–65.

———. *The Least Dangerous Branch: The Supreme Court at the Bar of Politics*. Indianapolis: Bobbs-Merrill, 1962.

———. *The Supreme Court and the Idea of Progress*. New York: Harper & Row, 1970.

Black, Charles L., Jr. *Structure and Relationship in Constitutional Law*. Baton Rouge: Louisiana State University Press, 1969.

Blackstone, Sir William. *Commentaries on the Laws of England*, ed. Charles M. Haar. New York: Beacon Press, 1962.

Bodenheimer, Edgar. *Jurisprudence: The Philosophy and Method of the Law*. Cambridge: Harvard University Press, 1962.

Bork, Robert H. "Neutral Principles and Some First Amendment Problems." *Indiana Law Journal* 47, no. 1 (1971): 1–35.

———. *Tradition and Morality in Constitutional Law*. Washington, D.C.: American Enterprise Institute, 1984.

Brecht, Arnold. *Political Theory: The Foundations of Twentieth-Century Political Thought*. Princeton: Princeton University Press, 1959.

Brest, Paul. "The Misconceived Quest for the Original Understanding." *Boston University Law Review* 60, no. 1 (1980): 204–38.

Cairns, Huntington. *Legal Philosophy from Plato to Hegel*. Baltimore: The Johns Hopkins University Press, 1949.

Calabresi, Steven G. "A Madisonian Interpretation of the Equal Protection Doctrine." *Yale Law Journal* 91, no. 7 (1982): 1403–29.

Campbell, Stanley W. *The Slave Catchers: Enforcement of the Fugitive Slave Law 1850–1860*. Chapel Hill: University of North Carolina Press, 1970.

Cardozo, Benjamin N. *The Nature of the Judicial Process*. New Haven: Yale University Press, 1921.

Cassirer, Ernst. *The Philosophy of the Enlightenment*. Princeton: Princeton University Press, 1951.

"The Changing Role of the Jury in the Nineteenth Century." *Yale Law Journal* 74, no. 1 (1964): 170–92.

Choper, Jesse H. *Judicial Review and the National Political Process: A Functional Reconsideration of the Role of the Supreme Court*. Chicago: University of Chicago Press, 1980.

Cohen, Felix S. *Ethical Systems and Legal Ideals*. New York: Falcon Press, 1933.

Commager, Henry Steele. "Constitutional History and the Higher Law." In *The Constitution Reconsidered*, ed. Conyers Read. New York: Columbia University Press, 1938.

———. *The Empire of Reason*. Garden City, N.Y.: Anchor Press, 1978.

Cook, Walter W. "Scientific Method and Law." *American Bar Association Journal* 13, no. 5 (1927): 303–9.

Cooke, Jacob E., ed. *The Federalist*. Middletown, Conn.: Wesleyan University Press, 1961.

Corwin, Edward S. "The Dred Scott Decision in the Light of Contemporary Legal Doctrines." *American Historical Review* 17, no. 1 (1911): 52–69.

———. *Court Over Constitution: A Study of Judicial Review as an Instrument of Popular Government*. Gloucester, Mass.: Peter Smith, 1957.

———. *The "Higher Law" Background of American Constitutional Law*. Ithaca: Cornell University Press, 1963.

———. "The Natural Law and Constitutional Law." In *Presidential Powers and the Constitution: Essays of Edward S. Corwin*, ed. Richard Loss. Ithaca: Cornell University Press, 1976.

Cover, Robert. *Justice Accused: Antislavery and the Judicial Process*. New Haven: Yale University Press, 1975.

Cox, Archibald. *The Role of the Supreme Court in American Government*. New York: Oxford University Press, 1976.

Currie, David P. "The Constitution in the Supreme Court: 1789–1801." *University of Chicago Law Review* 48, no. 4 (1981): 819–85.

———. "The Constitution in the Supreme Court: State and Congressional Power, 1801–1835." *University of Chicago Law Review* 49, no. 4 (1982): 889–99.

Daniels, George H. *Science in American Society*. New York: Alfred A. Knopf, 1971.

Dewey, John. *The Quest for Certainty: A Study of the Relation of Knowledge and Action*. New York: Minton, Balch, 1929.

Diamond, Martin. "Ethics and Politics: The American Way." In *The Moral Foundations of the American Republic*, ed. Robert A. Horwitz. Charlottesville: University of Virginia Press, 1977.

Douglass, Frederick. "Fourth of July Oration." In *What Country Have I? Political Writings by Black Americans*, ed. Herbert J. Storing. New York: St. Martin's Press, 1970.

Dworkin, Ronald. *Taking Rights Seriously*. Cambridge: Harvard University Press, 1977.

———. "Liberalism." In *Public and Private Morality*, ed. Stuart Hampshire. Cambridge: Cambridge University Press, 1978.

———. "The Forum of Principle." *New York University Law Review* 56, no. 2–3 (1981): 469–518.

———. "Reagan's Justice." *New York Review of Books* 31, no. 17 (1984): 27–31.

Eidelberg, Paul. *A Discourse on Statesmanship: The Design and Transformation of the American Polity*. Chicago: University of Illinois Press, 1974.

Ely, John Hart. *Democracy and Distrust: A Theory of Judicial Review*. Cambridge: Harvard University Press, 1981.

Faulkner, Robert K. *The Jurisprudence of John Marshall*. Princeton: Princeton University Press, 1968.

Fehrenbacher, Don E. "Lincoln and Judicial Supremacy: A Note on the Galena Speech of July 23, 1856." *Civil War History* 16 (1970): 197–204.

———. *The Dred Scott Case: Its Significance in American Law and Politics*. New York: Oxford University Press, 1978.

Ford, Paul Leicester, ed. *Pamphlets on the Constitution of the United States*. New York: Da Capo Press, 1968.

Frankfurter, Felix. "John Marshall and the Judicial Function." *Harvard Law Review* 69, no. 2 (1955): 217–238.

———. *The Public and Its Government*. Boston: Beacon Press, 1964.

———. *Of Law and Life and Other Things That Matter*. New York: Atheneum, 1966.

Friedman, Lawrence M. *A History of American Law*. New York: Simon & Schuster, 1973.

Friedrich, Carl J. *The Philosophy of Law in Historical Perspective*. Chicago: University of Chicago Press, 1969.

Fuller, Lon L. *The Morality of Law*. New Haven: Yale University Press, 1964.

Funston, Richard. "The Supreme Court and Critical Elections." *American Political Science Review* 69, no. 3 (1975): 795–811.

———. "The Double Standard of Constitutional Protection in the Era of the Welfare State." *Political Science Quarterly* 90, no. 2 (1975): 261–87.

Gillespie, Charles C. *The Edge of Objectivity.* Princeton: Princeton University Press, 1960.

Glazer, Nathan. "Toward an Imperial Judiciary?" *The Public Interest* 41 (1975): 104–23.

Gough, J. W. *Fundamental Law in English Constitutional History.* Oxford: Oxford University Press, 1955.

Gray, John Chipman. *The Nature and Sources of the Law.* New York: Beacon Press, 1909.

Grey, Thomas C. "Do We Have an Unwritten Constitution?" *Stanford Law Review* 27, no. 2 (1975): 703–18.

———. "Origins of the Unwritten Constitution: Fundamental Law in American Revolutionary Thought." *Stanford Law Review* 30, no. 5 (1978): 843–93.

———. "Judicial Review and the Unwritten Constitution." Annual Meeting of the American Political Science Association, 1977. Unpublished.

Greenberg, Edward S. "Class Rule Under the Constitution." In *How Capitalistic Is the Constitution?* ed. Robert A. Goldwin and William A. Schambra. Washington, D.C.: American Enterprise Institute, 1982.

Griffiths, John. "Legal Reasoning from the External and Internal Perspectives." *New York University Law Review* 53, no. 5 (1978): 1124–49.

Haines, Charles Grove. *The Revival of Natural Law Concepts.* Cambridge: Harvard University Press, 1930.

Hart, Henry M., Jr. "Professor Crosskey and Judicial Review." *Harvard Law Review* 67, no. 8 (1954): 1439–86.

Heisenberg, Werner. *Philosophic Problems of Nuclear Science.* London: Faber & Faber, 1952.

Hobbes, Thomas. *The Leviathan*, ed. Herbert W. Schneider. Indianapolis: Bobbs-Merrill, 1958.

Holmes, Oliver Wendell, Jr. "Law in Science and Science in Law." *Harvard Law Review* 12, no. 7 (1899): 443–63.

———. *The Common Law.* Boston: Little, Brown, 1963.

Horowitz, Donald L. *The Courts and Social Policy.* Washington, D.C.: The Brookings Institution, 1977.

Horwitz, Morton J. "The Emergence of an Instrumental Conception of American Law, 1780–1820." In *Perspectives in American History*, vol. 5, ed. Donald Fleming and Bernard Bailyn. Cambridge, Mass.: Charles Warren Center of Studies in American History, 1971.

Howard, A. E. Dick. *The Road from Runnymeade: Magna Carta and Constitutionalism in America.* Charlottesville: University of Virginia Press, 1968.

Howe, Mark DeWolfe. "Juries as Judges of Criminal Law." *Harvard Law Review* 52, no. 4 (1939): 582–616.

Huntington, Samuel P. *American Politics: The Promise of Disharmony.* Cambridge: Harvard University Press, 1981.

Jackson, Robert H. *The Supreme Court in the American System of Government.* Cambridge: Harvard University Press, 1955.

Jacobsohn, Gary J. *Pragmatism, Statesmanship, and the Supreme Court.* Ithaca: Cornell University Press, 1977.

Jaffa, Harry V. *Crisis of the House Divided: An Interpretation of the Issues in the Lincoln-Douglas Debates.* Garden City, N.Y.: Doubleday, 1959.

James, William. "The Moral Philosopher and the Moral Life." In *The Will to Believe and Other Essays in Popular Philosophy.* New York: Longmans, Green, 1915.

Jefferson, Thomas. *The Political Writings of Thomas Jefferson,* ed. Edward Dumbauld. Indianapolis: Bobbs-Merrill, 1955.

Kauper, Paul G. "The Higher Law and the Rights of Man in a Revolutionary Society." In *America's Continuing Revolution,* ed. Stephen J. Tonsor. Washington, D.C., 1975.

Konefsky, Samuel J. *John Marshall and Alexander Hamilton: Architects of the American Constitution.* New York: Macmillan, 1964.

Kronman, Anthony T. "Alexander Bickel's Philosophy of Prudence." *Yale Law Journal* 94, no. 7 (1985): 1567–1616.

Kunstler, William. "Jury Nullification in Conscience Cases." *Virginia Journal of International Law* 10, no. 1 (1969).

Lerner, Ralph. "The Supreme Court as Republican Schoolmaster." In *Supreme Court Review,* ed. Phillip B. Kurland. Chicago: University of Chicago Press, 1967.

Levinson, Sanford. "Taking Law Seriously: Reflections on 'Thinking Like a Lawyer.'" *Stanford Law Review* 30, no. 5 (1978): 1266–1340.

Lincoln, Abraham. *The Collected Works of Abraham Lincoln,* ed. Roy Basler. New Brunswick, N.J., Rutgers University Press, 1953.

Lindblom, Charles E. "The Science of Muddling Through." *Public Administration Review* 19, no. 2 (1959): 78–88.

McCloskey, Robert G. "Economic Due Process and the Supreme Court: An Exhumation and Reburial." In *American Constitutional Law: Historical Essays,* ed. Leonard Levy. New York: Harper & Row, 1966.

McLaughlin, Andrew C. *Foundations of American Constitutionalism.* New York: Fawcett Publications, 1961.

McWilliams, Wilson Carey. "Democracy and the Citizen: Community, Dignity, and the Crisis of Contemporary Politics in America." In *How Democratic Is the Constitution?* ed. Robert A. Goldwin and William A. Schambra. Washington, D.C.: American Enterprises Institute, 1981.

Meigs, William M. *The Relation of the Judiciary to the Constitution.* New York: Da Capo Press, 1971.

Mendelson, Wallace. "Dred Scott's Case—Reconsidered" *Minnesota Law Review* 38, no. 1 (1953): 16–28.

Michelman, Frank I. "Constancy to an Ideal Object." *New York University Law Review* 56, no. 2–3 (1981): 406–15.

Miller, Arthur Selwyn. "Toward a Concept of Constitutional Duty." In *The Supreme Court Review,* ed. Phillip B. Kurland. Chicago: University of Chicago Press, 1968.

Miller, Arthur Selwyn, and Ronald F. Howell. "The Myth of Neutrality in Constitutional Adjudication." *University of Chicago Law Review* 27, no. 4 (1960): 661–95.

Monaghan, Henry P. "Our Perfect Constitution." *New York University Law Review* 56, no. 2–3 (1981): 353–96.

Morgan, Donald. *Congress and the Constitution: A Study of Responsibility.* Cambridge: Harvard University Press, 1966.

Munro, William Bennett. "Physics and Politics—An Old Analogy Revised." *American Political Science Review* 22, no. 1 (1928): 1–11.

Murphy, Walter F. "The Art of Constitutional Interpretation: A Preliminary Showing." In *Essays on the Constitution of the United States*, ed. M. Judd Harmon. Port Washington, N.Y.: Kennikat Press, 1978.

———. "Constitutional Interpretation: The Art of Historian, Magician, or Statesman?" *Yale Law Review* 87, no. 8 (1978): 1752–73.

Nolan, Dennis R. "Sir William Blackstone and the New American Republic: A Study of Intellectual Impact." *New York University Law Review.* 51, no. 5 (1976): 731–68.

Pangle, Thomas. "Rediscovering Rights." *The Public Interest* 50 (1978): 157–60.

Parenti, Michael. "The Constitution as an Elitist Document." In *How Democratic Is the Constitution?* ed. Robert A. Goldwin and William A. Schambra. Washington, D.C.: American Enterprise Institute, 1981.

Parker, Richard B. "The Jurisprudential Uses of John Rawls." In *Constitutionalism: Nomos XX*, ed. J. Roland Pennock and John W. Chapman. New York: New York University Press, 1979.

Perry, Michael J. *The Constitution, the Courts, and Human Rights.* New Haven: Yale University Press, 1982.

Polsby, Nelson. "The Institutionalization of the U.S. House of Representatives." *American Political Science Review* 62, no. 1 (1968): 144–68.

Potter, David M. *The Impending Crisis 1848–1861.* New York: Harper & Row, 1976.

Pound, Roscoe. "Mechanical Jurisprudence." *Columbia Law Review* 8, no. 8 (1908): 605–23.

———. "Law in Books and Law in Action." *American Law Review* 44, no. 1 (1910).

———. *The Spirit of the Common Law.* Boston: Marshall Jones, 1921.

———. *An Introduction to the Philosophy of Law.* New Haven: Yale University Press, 1922.

———. *Interpretations of Legal History.* New York: Macmillan, 1923.

———. *Criminal Justice in America.* New York: Da Capo Press, 1930.

———. *The Formative Era of American Law.* Gloucester, Mass.: Peter Smith, 1960.

Randall, James G. *Constitutional Problems Under Lincoln.* Urbana: University of Illinois Press, 1964.

Randall, J. H. "The Newtonian World Machine." In *Science and Ideas*, ed. A. B. Arons and A. M. Bork. Englewood Cliffs, N.J.: Prentice-Hall, 1964.

Rawls, John. *A Theory of Justice.* Cambridge: Harvard University Press, 1971.

Reynolds, Noel B. "Dworkin as Quixote." *University of Pennsylvania Law Review* 123, no. 3 (1975): 574–608.

Richards, David A. J. *The Moral Criticism of Law.* Encino, Calif.: Dickenson, 1977.

———. "Taking *Taking Rights Seriously* Seriously: Reflections on Dworkin and the American Revival of Natural Law." *New York University Law Review* 52, no. 6 (1977): 1265–1340.

———. "Human Rights and the Unwritten Constitution: The Problem of Change and Stability in Constitutional Interpretation." *University of Dayton Law Review* 4 (1979): 295–324.

Rodell, Fred. *Nine Men*. New York: Random House, 1955.

Rossiter, Clinton. *Alexander Hamilton and the Constitution*. New York: Harcourt, Brace & World, 1964.

Russell, Bertrand. *Unpopular Essays*. New York: Simon & Schuster, 1951.

Sax, Joseph L. "Conscience and Anarchy: The Prosecution of War Resisters." *Yale Review* 57, no. 4 (1968): 481–94.

Scheingold, Stuart A. *The Politics of Rights: Lawyers, Public Policy, and Political Change*. New Haven: Yale University Press, 1974.

Senate Committee on the Judiciary. *Hearings before the Subcommittee on Separation of Powers on S. 158, the "Human Life Bill."* 97th Cong., 1st sess., vol. 2.

———. *Reports Together with Additional and Minority Views of the Subcommittee on Separation of Powers regarding S. 158, the "Human Life Bill."* 97th Cong., 1st sess.

Smith, Rogers. *Liberalism and American Constitutional Law*. Cambridge: Harvard University Press, 1985.

Snowiss, Sylvia. "From Fundamental Law to the Supreme Law of the Land: A Reinterpretation of the Origin of Judicial Review in the United States." Annual Meeting of the American Political Science Association, 1981. Unpublished.

Solberg, Winton, ed. *The Federal Convention and the Formation of the Union*. Indianapolis: Bobbs-Merrill, 1958.

Spooner, Lysander. *The Unconstitutionality of Slavery*. Boston: B. Marsh, 1860.

———. *Essay on the Trial by Jury*. New York: Da Capo Press, 1971.

Storing, Herbert J. "The Constitution and the Bill of Rights." In *Essays on the Constitution of the United States*, ed. M. Judd Harmon. Port Washington, N.Y.: Kennikat Press, 1978.

Story, Joseph. *Commentaries on the Constitution of the United States*. Boston: Hilliard, Gray, and Company, 1833.

Stourzh, Gerald. *Alexander Hamilton and the Idea of Republican Government*. Stanford: Stanford University Press, 1970.

Strauss, Leo. *Natural Right and History*. Chicago: University of Chicago Press, 1953.

Tushnet, Mark. "Darkness on the Edge of Town: The Contributions of John Hart Ely to Constitutional Theory." *Yale Law Journal* 89, no. 6 (1980): 1037–62.

Van Dyke, Jan. "The Jury as a Political Institution." *The Center Magazine* 3, no. 2 (1970): 17–26.

Viera, Edwin, Jr. "Rights and the United States Constitution: The Declension from Natural Law to Legal Positivism." *Georgia Law Review* 13 (1979): 1447–1500.

Walzer, Michael. "Philosophy and Democracy." *Political Theory* 9, no. 3 (1981): 379–99.

Warren, Earl. "Science and the Law: Change and the Constitution." *Journal of Public Law* 12, no. 1 (1963): 3–8.

Wellington, Harry. "The Nature of Judicial Review." *Yale Law Journal* 91, no. 3 (1982): 486–520.

White, Morton. *The Philosophy of the American Revolution*. New York: Oxford University Press, 1978.

Wills, Garry. *Inventing America: Jefferson's Declaration of Independence*. Garden City, N.Y.: Doubleday, 1978.

Wilson, James. *The Works of James Wilson*. ed. Robert G. McCloskey. Cambridge: Harvard University Press, 1967.

Winter, Ralph K., Jr. "The Growth of Judicial Power." In *The Judiciary in a Democratic Society*, ed. Leonard Theberge. Lexington, Mass.: Lexington Books, 1979.

Wood, Gordon S. *The Creation of the American Republic, 1776–1787*. Chapel Hill: University of North Carolina Press, 1969.

Wright, Benjamin F. *American Interpretations of Natural Law: A Study in the History of Political Thought*. Cambridge: Harvard University Press, 1931.

Index